COLOR LINES, COUNTRY LINES

COLOR LINES, COUNTRY LINES
RACE, IMMIGRATION, AND WEALTH
STRATIFICATION IN AMERICA

LINGXIN HAO

Russell Sage Foundation · New York

The Russell Sage Foundation

The Russell Sage Foundation, one of the oldest of America's general purpose foundations, was established in 1907 by Mrs. Margaret Olivia Sage for "the improvement of social and living conditions in the United States." The Foundation seeks to fulfill this mandate by fostering the development and dissemination of knowledge about the country's political, social, and economic problems. While the Foundation endeavors to assure the accuracy and objectivity of each book it publishes, the conclusions and interpretations in Russell Sage Foundation publications are those of the authors and not of the Foundation, its Trustees, or its staff. Publication by Russell Sage, therefore, does not imply Foundation endorsement.

Library of Congress Cataloging-in-Publication Data

Hao, Lingxin
    Color lines, country lines : race, immigration, and wealth stratification in America / Lingxin Hao.
        p. cm.
    Includes bibliographical references and index.
    ISBN 978-0-87154-338-7
    1. United States—Emigration and immigration—Social aspects. 2. Social stratification—United States. 3. United States—Race relations. I. Title.
    JV6475.H35 2007
    339.2'208900973—dc22   2006038672

Text design by Suzanne Nichols.

RUSSELL SAGE FOUNDATION
112 East 64th Street, New York, New York 10021
10 9 8 7 6 5 4 3 2 1

= Contents =

═ About the Author ═

Lingxin Hao is professor of sociology at Johns Hopkins University.

= Acknowledgments =

I would like to thank the people and organizations whose help made a significant contribution to this book. The idea for this book came to me near the end of my year as a visiting scholar at the Russell Sage Foundation and I would like to thank the Foundation for encouraging me to write. In addition, this work was partially supported by grant SES-0518870 from the National Science Foundation. Two anonymous reviewers of my manuscript raised challenging questions and provided constructive suggestions that help shape the final version. Several colleagues provided me with important guidance from their fields of expertise. Bernard Yeung and Giovanni Arrighi helped me think through the development of the typology of wealth regime to categorize immigrant sending countries. Suet-ling Pong provided advice on developing the theoretical framework. I gained a deeper understanding of wealth stratification from insight and suggestions of Seymour Spilerman, Dalton Conley, and colleagues at my seminars at The Center for the Study of Wealth and Inequality at Columbia University and at the Center for Advanced Social Science Research at New York University. My colleagues in the Sociology Department at Johns Hopkins University provided constructive critique on my work on wealth. In addition, the graduate students in my seminar on immigration provided helpful comments on the integrated framework. Regarding the actual development and writing of the book, I would like extend my deep thanks to Sahan Savas Karatasli for his unique contribution to the construction of the typology of wealth regime and his diligent research assistance with data work and graphs. My sincere thanks go to Caitlin Cross-Barnet for her professional editing with substantive sociological suggestions, Michael Cross-Barnet for his creative title suggestion, and Julie Kim for her careful grammatical and stylistic editing and assistance with the bibliography. My husband, Allen Ruby, has been an integral part of the study and a source of critical thinking, wide knowledge, and indispensable support along a long and often difficult road.

═ Chapter 1 ═

Introduction

This book is about the impact of immigration on wealth stratification in America and the wealth assimilation of immigrants. The term immigrant refers to anyone who has crossed the U.S. border and settled in the United States for a substantial period, regardless of legal status. The era that followed the 1965 immigration law was characterized by a spike in immigration, mostly from Latin America and Asia. The volume, continuity, overwhelming racial and ethnic diversity, and high proportion of low skilled individuals have raised renewed concerns about the adaptability and assimilation of immigrants. Less attention, however, is paid to the impact of immigration on American society. My central argument is that to understand assimilation we must consider the impact immigration has on society and that to make a valid assessment of this impact we must consider assimilation.

Why would immigration affect the host society? If immigrants were similar to the native-born population in all aspects—such as race, education level, skill composition, and culture and lifestyle—and if resources and opportunities were abundant, the impact of immigration would be minimal. Contemporary immigration to the United States, however, does not follow this pattern. Scholars have emphasized how contemporary immigration has transformed the American population. It has been noted, for example, that immigration counts for 60 percent of U.S. population growth; one in nine are foreign born and one in five children have a foreign-born parent; about half of Hispanics and Asians are foreign born; many cities now have predominantly minority populations; and whites are projected to account for less than half of the population within a few decades. Such a large-scale, ongoing population change can profoundly interfere with the social structure and social processes of a society, most notably in the stratification system. Stratification distributes a country's population across the spectrum of well-being. Scholarly attention to immigrants does not for the most part reference the larger picture of immigration-induced social change. This book is devoted to bridging the gap.

1

Why is assimilation so important? Beyond humanitarian and nationalist concerns, the future of the United States depends, to a great degree, on the assimilation of generations of immigrants. The classical literature on assimilation was established in the mid-1940s during a period of historically low immigration, which had followed a peak around the turn of the century. Without a large immigrant generation, studies focused on the assimilation of second and higher generations. Recent literature has focused on the changing demographics of contemporary immigration and continued to study second and higher generations. Both classical and contemporary assimilation literatures thus deemphasize the assimilation of the immigrant generation. The assimilation of higher generations, however, hinges on it. The heredity of social class and the intergenerational transfer of resources and of status all point to the linkages between generations. Thus, to understand the assimilation of second and higher generations, one must first understand the assimilation of the immigrant generation. This book is about the assimilation of the first generation.

Wealth is a promising vehicle for answering this book's questions about the impact of immigration on American society and about assimilation under immigration-induced social change. Unlike wages, income, employment, and occupation, wealth is a multifaceted concept that absorbs the consequences of many economic activities. As a concept, it encompasses assets and debts. In turn, assets and debts manifest earning, saving, consuming, and portfolio allocating behaviors. These embody cultural values and lifestyles that govern people's expectations for their children, their plans for asset building and future consumption, and their preparations for old age. The balance between assets (homes, stocks, mutual funds, and retirement accounts) and debts (mortgages and credit card debts) constitute wealth. In addition, wealth is accumulated over time. The level of wealth at any given time reflects all previous behaviors and cultural practices. Thus, by providing people with strong economic security and creating future opportunities, sufficient wealth acts as a marker of middle-class status.

These unique features of wealth make the wealth stratification system an ideal tool for studying the impact of immigration on American society. The black-white wealth disparity is much more severe than the black-white income disparity. Less is known about the wealth of Hispanics and Asians. Human capital differences and behavioral differences in saving and consumption can differ among racial groups. Given the racial and ethnic diversity, the high proportion of the low-skilled, and the cultural diversity of post–1965 immigration, wealth stratification is more promising than income stratification as a way to illustrate the impact of immigration.

The unique features of wealth also make attainment of it an ideal tool for studying assimilation. Because its dimensions are multifaceted, wealth measures socioeconomic assimilation better than income. Given any income level, differences between natives and immigrants in consumption behavior and expectation for children will result in different levels of wealth. Thus, evidence of assimilation will be missed if only income is used. Moreover, because it is cumulative, wealth captures the unfolding stages of the assimilation process without losing sight of continuity. Sufficient wealth holding determines the middle-class status toward which immigrants assimilate, so wealth can accurately pinpoint the distance from middle-class status and the time such status is achieved.

In one common framework, this book unites insights from immigrant selection, immigrant assimilation, social stratification, and wealth accumulation theories to assess and understand immigration's impact on wealth stratification and immigrants' wealth assimilation. To address the impact of immigration, the conceptual framework introduces nativity as a factor into the racial-ethnic stratification system and suggests a rethinking of multifactor stratification systems generally. It also proposes that distinguishing between primary and secondary stratification factors is essential. Rationales are provided as to why race is primary and nativity is secondary in a two-tiered system. Under this system, race stratifies wealth. Within racial groups, nativity stratifies wealth. Long-term consequences of this two-tiered system are the weakening of the racial hierarchy, the transcendence of color lines, and the assimilation of certain immigrant groups.

This two-tiered approach hinges on the nativity differentiation process, which is developed via addressing two challenges from the literature. In the post–1965 immigration era, some immigrant nationality groups have surpassed their native-born ethnic counterparts despite the fact that they have not received inheritances. This fact challenges existing wisdom about the pivotal role of intergenerational transfers in the black-white wealth gap. Why does the lack of inheritances severely damage African Americans' prospects of wealth, but does not seem to prevent all immigrant racial-ethnic minority groups from achieving upward mobility? This book uses characteristics of the sending country and of the binational migration system to understand the self-selection of immigrants to take on the first challenge.

Self-selection by immigrants is only one part of the story of nativity's differentiation process. By virtue of migration, immigrants are not burdened by the intergenerational consequences of slavery, Jim Crow laws, redlining, and overt personal and institutional discrimination, all of which still resonate for natives. Consequently, immigrants handle racial relations differently and employers treat immigrants differently. In addition, immigrant settlement patterns have been changing the landscape of racial residential segregation while simultaneously exposing immigrants to racial segregation, a spatial form of discrimination. The lack of resources and opportunities available in minority neighborhoods affect everyone living there.

The post–1965 immigration era poses a second challenge to immigration research: a rising trend of transnational activities, a phenomenon in which immigrants work in the United States but invest in their home country. What makes the geographic separation between labor market activities and credit-capital market activities emerge and deepen? This book develops a typology of wealth regime to consider the likelihood of cross-border investment in various home countries. The typology helps correct the underestimation of immigrants' wealth attainment when cross-border activities are increasing but the related data are not available.

The empirical heart of this book compares immigrant nationality groups with their native-born racial-ethnic counterparts and with native whites. Comparisons also take into account other important socioeconomic and demographic factors of wealth, including human capital, marital status and number of children, life cycle stage, and year. The observed nativity-nationality patterns of net worth, components of assets, and conditions of liabilities are described at the national as well as the within racial-ethnic group level. The corresponding analytic patterns are revealed in multivariate analyses that take into account household factors and contextual factors.

Immigration, Race-Ethnicity, and Wealth

Immigration has an increasingly important impact on the American population. The U.S. Census Bureau (2003) estimates the nation's foreign-born population at 32.5 million, or 11.5 percent of the total. Immigration has become the most important factor in the growth of the American population. Newcomers and children born to immigrant parents constitute about 60 percent of total growth (U.S. Census Bureau 2003). Moreover, the ethnic and racial composition of immigrants has profoundly changed. Once primarily from Europe, immigrants today arrive from developing countries in Asia (26 percent) and Latin America (52 percent). From 1990 to 2000, the foreign-born Hispanic population increased by 58 percent and the foreign-born Asian population by 52 percent, compared with an increase of only 9 percent in the entire native population.

Immigration changes the landscape of racial residential segregation. On the one hand, the rapid growth of Hispanic and Asian subpopulations increases racial-ethnic diversity, which decreases black-white racial residential segregation (Frey and Farley 1996; Krivo and Kaufman 1999; Iceland 2004). On the other hand, the expansion of the Hispanic and

Asian subpopulations places more immigrant minorities in racially seg-regated communities and subjects them to the potentially negative con-sequences of racial segregation.

The possible economic impact of immigration up to the mid 1990s was systematically studied by the National Research Council of the National Academy of Sciences (Smith and Edmonston 1997). According to James Smith and Barry Edmonston's microeconomic model, if low-skilled im-migrants are substitutes for low-skilled native and earlier immigrant workers, an influx of low-skilled immigrants will increase the supply of low-skilled labor and drive down wages. Because newcomers are usu-ally willing to take jobs with below-market wages, they may displace low-skilled native-born workers. However, if immigrants take jobs that low-skilled native and earlier immigrant workers reject, immigration will have no impact on the labor market.

Many Americans are concerned about immigration issues. Over the past four decades, the Gallup poll has asked respondents the same ques-tion: whether they think that in the United States "immigration should be decreased." On average, 50 percent of the respondents have said that immigration should be kept at its present level or increased (Gallup 2007). This percentage has fluctuated with the economic cycle. At the same time, the share of respondents who thought that immigration should be decreased has remained substantial and stable at about 30 per-cent. One concern of those who wish to limit immigration is that immi-grants and natives will lack a unified sociocultural identity. Ultimately, this worry is linked to the success or failure of assimilation for immi-grants and their successive generations.

The last great immigration peaked around the turn of the twentieth century and then ebbed. Assimilation was assessed using the outcomes of second or higher generations. Now, with new immigrants arriving every year, the successful adaptation and assimilation of the first gener-ation eases public concerns, whereas slow adaptation reinforces them. Public concern provides a strong motive for immigration policy changes. Studying immigrants' wealth provides a new and reliable benchmark for assessing the adaptation and assimilation of the first immigrant genera-tion rather than subsequent ones. Because middle-class households have similar living standards, immigrants' attainment of middle-class wealth may indicate that they have moved closer to a unified sociocultural iden-tity.

Immigrants' wealth rather than income may better capture motiva-tion for upward mobility and economic attainment. First, economic mo-tives underscore why many immigrants come to the United States. Im-migration is a life-changing experience with high real costs but also high expected benefits, assuming that the immigrant also expects to make great efforts. Risk and uncertainty factors select individuals whose motivation for upward mobility and willingness to work hard is especially strong (Jasso, Rosenzweig, and Smith 2000). Thus, income-generating behavior among immigrants can be different from that of natives. Immigrants may be willing to work multiple shifts, combine formal and informal jobs, and be self-employed (including unpaid work by children and elderly family members). While immigrants are in the process of adaptation, their consumption behaviors may differ from natives. In the early stages of wealth accumulation in the United States, immigrants from developing countries may tailor their consumption to their home country's lower living standards. Lower consumption increases savings rates. Motivation to help their children achieve social mobility and optimism about their children's achievements (Portes and Rumbaut 2006; Kao and Tienda 1995) may promote savings earmarked for college education and other such investments. Among those with the same level of income, differences in motivation, consumption, and saving may contribute to immigrants having a higher level of wealth than natives do.

Income alone is therefore not enough to gauge immigrants' economic attainment and structural assimilation. Conclusions based only on income can be tentative or even misleading. Wealth, however, provides a means to assess both and thus to make predications on the assimilation of future generations.

The Approach

This book's approach to wealth in the era of immigration applies stratification, immigration, assimilation and wealth theories. Chapter 2 formulates the structure of multifactor stratification systems with three conceptual scenarios and develops arguments that support a two-tier dominance-differentiation system. To address a paradox in the role of inheritance in blacks versus immigrants' upward mobility, issues about the self-selection of immigrants are highlighted. To address a theoretical deficiency in explaining immigrants' transnational, non–labor market activities, this book addresses the importance of the characteristics of sending countries and of the economic, financial, and political structures of sending and destination countries. It also develops the typology of wealth regime that illuminates why some immigrants invest in their homeland, helping correct bias in observed patterns of wealth holding based on survey data. This model has implications for empirical investigations into how immigration helps transform the U.S. stratification system and extends assimilation theory to wealth attainment to capture socioeconomic assimilation and cultural assimilation.

In a two-tiered stratification system, the primary factor of race-ethnicity (color lines) dominates the secondary factor of nativity-nationality of immigrants (country lines) which further differentiates within racial-groups. Within the social stratification perspective, institutionalized rules, laws, and practices are powerful social forces and significant causes of wealth stratification. Color lines have long segregated ethnic-racial minorities and impeded assimilation. Multiple forms of discrimination against ethnic and racial minorities—from the dual labor market and ethnic queues in the job market to dual housing and lending markets—contribute to persistent wealth inequality. Growing homeownership and stock and mutual fund ownership across the population can actually be a source of rising wealth inequality because the growth amplifies discrimination in housing and financial markets. Wealth inequality is further exacerbated by intergenerational transfers of wealth, which drastically differentiate the initial wealth levels of successive generations. In the patterns of these institutional effects, history matters. Once established, racial-ethnic stratification tends to be long lasting. Structural factors give rise to the rationale for race-ethnicity as the primary driving force of social stratification of wealth.

The stratification literature generally has not considered nativity and immigrant characteristics. Nativity and immigrant characteristics, however, further differentiate members within racial-ethnic groups and are secondary stratification factors. Within racial-ethnic groups, three mechanisms lead to stratification by nativity and immigrant characteristics. First, although all contemporary institutional settings and mechanisms apply to immigrant racial-ethnic minorities, these immigrants do not bear the burdens of the intergenerational transmission of historical discrimination.

Second, specific institutional rules and practices particularly address naturalized immigrants, nonnaturalized legal immigrants, and illegal immigrants. As newcomers, immigrants as a whole may be blamed for economic problems such as recessions and for low incomes and unemployment among native-born unskilled workers (Smith and Edmonston 1997; Borjas 1999). In 2002, the estimated number of illegal immigrants was more than 10 million, about one third of the foreign-born population. Illegal status imposes institutional barriers to important opportunities. Undocumented immigrants are denied permission to work legally and thus work in the shadow market. Because they are not protected by labor laws, they are subject to poor working conditions and earning less than the minimum wage. Their jobs do not offer medical insurance, retirement plans, or any claims on the welfare state, such as unemployment compensation, the earned income tax credit, or social security. Without a valid social security number and driver's license, illegal immigrants have little access to property rights because these documents are required to secure the title of a car, the deed of a house, a bank account, or a small business license. Legal immigrants do not of course face these institutional barriers. Immigrants can also be classified by naturalization status. About half of all foreign-born residents are naturalized. Naturalization transforms immigrants from ethnic aliens to American citizens. Naturalized immigrants enjoy full constitutional rights. Nonnaturalized immigrants do not.

Third, immigrant-native differences in language, cultural practices, work ethic, and attitudes toward race relations serve to differentiate subgroups. Within a racial-ethnic group, immigrants may be subject to additional discrimination because of their accents and foreign cultural and religious practices (Portes and Rumbaut 2006). On the other hand, employers may prefer to hire foreign-born rather than native-born workers because employers believe that immigrants have a stronger work ethic and are less likely to make race relations a work issue (Waldinger 1996; Waters 1999).

This dominance-differentiation system of stratification posits that race-ethnicity is the primary factor governing the entire population. At the same time, the dominance-differentiation system addresses the significant role of immigrant status, which is nested within racial-ethnic stratification. Institutional forces behind differentiation within racial-ethnic groups have a profound impact on racial-ethnic inequality. It is possible that greater within-group differences will reduce the saliency and degree of differences between racial ethnic groups, thereby reducing racial-ethnic inequality.

Advances in institutional analysis incorporate the theoretical traditions of both structure and agency. In this study, the structural focus is on primary racial-ethnic stratification and secondary nativity-nationality stratification, and the agency focus is on economic theories of wealth accumulation. Individuals act according to their cultural beliefs, but their rational decisions about generating income, consumption, saving, and portfolio allocation are bounded by institutional constraints and opportunities. In the face of discrimination, households may respond with different strategies, which then lead to different wealth outcomes. In this book, neither the role of households nor the role of institutions is ignored. The agency approach allows a full examination of behavioral differences between immigrants and natives, whereas the structural approach explains the limits of the effects of behavioral differences on wealth accumulation.

Education is another significant factor in the distribution of wealth. A higher level of education provides opportunities for a well-paying, stable job, an occupation with a mobility ladder, and thus high and steady streams of income over the life cycle (Becker 1964). Since 1980, education has been increasingly important in income stratification. Wage rates have been on the rise for college graduates, but have stagnated for high school graduates and have declined for high school dropouts (Bernhardt et al. 2001). Those with different levels of education also have different access to financial institutions, affecting their ability to accumulate wealth.

Other factors influencing wealth accumulation include marital status and the presence of children. Marriage not only opens the possibility for two household incomes but also enhances incentives for and access to asset building, particularly when children are present (Smith 1995b). In contrast, female-headed households do not have a father's income and thus earn less due to gender discrimination, factors that constrain wealth accumulation (Hao 1996). The delay of marriage has increased single-person households, whereas delayed nest-leaving and adult children returning to their parents' homes have decreased the number of unmarried households (Goldscheider and Waite 1991; Goldscheider and Da Vanzo 1989). Households headed by a married couple have higher amounts and more sources of income than households that are not.

Immigrants' assimilation can be studied through the effects of structural factors and individual behaviors on wealth. Middle-class status is the norm for non-Hispanic whites and Asians. Structural factors facilitate assimilation of immigrants belonging to these groups to middle-class status relatively easily. However, working-class status is the norm for other racial-ethnic groups, such as non-Hispanic blacks and Hispanics. Immigrants belonging to these groups have a longer way to go to reach middle-class status. Where a racial group falls within the overall distribution of wealth is one of this book's guiding principles in investigating immigrants' assimilation.

This book's theoretical framework leads to a better understanding of how immigration may transform the U.S. wealth stratification system and how some immigrants achieve upward mobility. Immigrants can differ from natives in variations in economic circumstances, cultural backgrounds, and migration and adaptation experiences. Intergenerational transfers, human capital levels, and consumption, saving and portfolio allocation behaviors vary between immigrants and natives. When these factors play into the family life cycle of wealth accumulation, nativity differences in age structure, marriage, fertility, and other demographic characteristics also become important considerations. Moreover, labor, housing, and lending market discrimination and residential segregation resulting from the U.S. racial-ethnic hierarchy are major structural constraints on wealth generally. The effects of these micro and macro factors may differ by nativity and immigrant nationality because immigrants are treated differently by the government and the labor market and may respond differently to these treatments.

To describe the wealth stratification by race and nativity and test hypotheses derived from the theoretical framework, this book analyzes data from a national survey—the Survey of Income and Program Participation (SIPP)—conducted from 1984 to 2003. The design incorporates a continuous series of twelve national panels with sample sizes ranging from approximately 11,000 to 35,000 interviewed households for each panel. This book uses data from core questions on labor force participation and income and uses data from three topical modules: migration history, assets and liabilities, and education history. The assets and liabilities module is included in ten of the twelve SIPP panels, which together provide eighteen cross-sections of data for fourteen years (some panel years overlap). The analytic sample for the book varies for different analyses. Chapters 3, 7, and 8 use eighteen cross-sections covering 1984 to 2003 and chapters 4 through 6 use seven cross-sections covering 1996 to 2003. The total study sample is 216,246 (see details in appendix).

Organization of the Book

Chapter 3 depicts an overall portrait of race-nativity patterns of wealth using data on 216,246 households from 1984 to 2003, a high tide of immigration. The chapter extends the concept of asset poverty (Haveman and Wolff 2004; Shapiro 2004) to a five-category wealth holding status that identifies sufficient and insufficient statuses for those above the asset poverty line and asset poor, net-debtor and paycheck-to-paycheck statuses for those under the asset poverty line. This refined categorization facilitates the analysis of upward versus downward mobility. The chapter also examines the group-specific percentile distribution of net worth, assets and debts. Life cycle patterns for different racial-ethnic groups and different immigrant arrival cohorts are examined. The eighteen pooled cross-sections of the SIPP data over the twenty years from 1984 to 2003 make it possible to identify the effects of age, period, birth cohort, and arrival cohort.

To reveal nativity differentiation, examining patterns within racial-ethnic groups is carried out in chapters 4 through 6. In these chapters, all comparisons take native non-Hispanic whites as the basic benchmark, using native whites as a proxy for the core of the American mainstream. Within each racial ethnic group, the native born is a benchmark for that particular group. Immigrants are grouped by country of origin in order to capture immigrants' self-selection and cultural roots. To provide the economic, political, social, and education condition of the origin country and the history of the binational migration system between the origin country and the United States, each chapter provides a brief sketch of the sending countries. Recent data from the SIPP, which cover seven years from 1996 to 1999 and 2001 to 2003, identify more countries of birth, allowing the analyses of more countries of origin in chapters 4 through 6.

Chapter 4 studies immigrants from six Latin American sending countries: Colombia, El Salvador, Guatemala, Mexico, Cuba, and the Dominican Republic. The sample sizes range from 4,362 for Mexican immigrants to 177 for Guatemalan. Chapter 5 examines immigrants from seven Asian countries and regions: Hong Kong and Taiwan, China, the Philippines, Japan, India, Korea, and Vietnam. The largest group is Filipino immigrants (659) and the smallest group is Japanese (168). Chapter 6 addresses black immigrants from Haiti (204), Jamaica (247), and sub-Saharan Africa (184). These chapters provide detailed analyses of wealth holding status; the percentile distribution of net worth, assets, and debts; portfolio composition; and single components of assets and debts, including homeownership, home equity, number and conditions of mortgages, liquid financial assets, retirement accounts, life insurance, credit card debts, and business equity.

In chapters 7 and 8, multivariate analyses are performed based on the full sample of more than 200,000 households. Wealth attainment has two aspects, the probability of having positive net worth and the amount of positive net worth, and is defined as the total value of assets being greater than the total value of debts. Chapter 7 tests whether race-ethnicity is a primary factor and nativity a secondary factor of wealth stratification. Five empirical models are estimated, progressing from a pooled analysis of the entire population to separate analyses for each racial-ethnic group. Chapter 7 also examines the effects of household characteristics, which capture behavioral differences. For example, marriage and the presence of children capture saving motivations, age at arrival captures the number of productive adult years in the United States, and naturalization captures an assimilation milestone.

Chapter 8 turns to the local context in which households accumulate wealth. Black-white residential segregation reflects both contemporary and historical institutional discrimination, which benefits native whites but harms African Americans and other native minority groups. The chapter examines how black-white segregation affects racial minority immigrants, whether Hispanic-white segregation produces harmful consequences, and whether a large presence of immigrants reduces opportunities for particular groups. Other contextual factors besides racial residential segregation facilitate or constrain households' wealth attainment. Local unemployment rates largely define the economic environment in which households accumulate wealth. Using the metropolitan subsample (134,845) of the whole sample, the analysis merges racial residential segregation measures and immigrant share of the metropolitan population with the metropolitan identification of survey individual's residence. The chapter offers new findings regarding the spillover effects of racial residential segregation.

Chapter 9 concludes the book by returning to the central questions about immigration's impact on American society and immigrants' assimilation based on wealth analyses. Evidence from the analyses of wealth conducted in the book supports the proposed dominance-differentiation stratification system. In addition, wealth, a better measure of assimilation than conventional measures such as income, facilitates the evaluation of contemporary immigrants' assimilation under the dominance-differentiation stratification system.

This volume provides useful information, a conceptual framework, and a variety of analytical methods for a wide range of readers, including those studying immigration, social stratification, social inequality, or racial ethnic relations; policy makers concerned with issues of immigration; and anyone else with interests or concerns regarding immigration.

═ Chapter 2 ═

A Theoretical Model for Wealth
in an Era of Immigration

Existing wealth theory no longer seems adequate to explain immigrants' wealth when we consider that, without an inheritance, some immigrants can achieve wealth attainment within a generation yet African Americans cannot. Can a simple addition of wealth theory and immigration theory lend insight to wealth stratification in an era of immigration? Although the second approach improves on the first one, the addition suffers two limitations. For one, immigration theory, which explains the decision to migrate and subsequent adaptation in the host society, largely ignores immigrants' activities outside the labor market in credit or capital markets in either their host or their home country. The second limitation stems from the fact that the contemporary immigration is a large-scale population movement of self-selected individuals from countries with very different economic, political, and cultural characteristics that have varying historical and contemporary geopolitical relationships with the United States. Immigration can impact wealth stratification and thus wealth outcomes for both immigrants and natives. This chapter takes on these theoretical challenges and develops an integrated framework that sheds light on the phenomenon of wealth stratification in the post-1965 immigration era.

Immigrant wealth can differ from native wealth for a number of reasons. The sheer proportion of non-white immigrants, particularly Hispanics, brings the wealth level of immigrants as a whole down because of the racial-ethnic hierarchy inherent to the wealth distribution. In addition, the economic, social, political, and cultural conditions of origin countries and the migration process select different types of immigrants—such as professional versus labor, legal versus undocumented, economic versus refugee—each with different motivations. The combination of background, motivation, and reception lead to various assimilation processes. Finally, differences in economic behaviors between immigrants and natives can result in different strategies and outcomes in

13

wealth accumulation. To help us better understand the rationales behind these complex processes, in this chapter I systematically review three relevant theories and develop an integrated framework to guide the analyses that follow.

The first relevant theory is about the racial-ethnic stratification of wealth. The second is about international migration and assimilation. The third is about economic behaviors in wealth accumulation. Racial-ethnic stratification theory addresses the macro structural forces in the racial-ethnic hierarchy and residential racial segregation that shape the wealth distribution. International migration theories provide rationales for potential migrants' engaging in cost-benefit calculations, minimizing risks facing their households, drawing on network resources to reduce migration costs, and making migration decisions under the bi-national migration system of the origin and destination countries. Whereas international migration theories deal with decisions and actions taken during the migration process, assimilation theories deal with immigrants' lives after arrival in the United States. This discussion will address classical assimilation, transnationalism, segmented assimilation, and the new assimilation. Economic theories of wealth accumulation focus on micro-level factors generating households' life cycle income, consumption, saving, and portfolio allocation behaviors. Together, the three theories constitute a useful basis for an integrated framework in which to understand race, immigration, and wealth stratification. This framework is featured by the conceptual treatment of the structure of a multifactor stratification system, from which immigration's impact on wealth stratification can be predicted; the development of a typology of wealth regime, which extends wealth theory; and use of the notion of wealth attainment, which extends assimilation theory.

Theories on International Migration

Douglas Massey and his colleagues (1993) provide a comprehensive survey of multidisciplinary theories on international migration, including neoclassical economics, new economics, world systems theory, segmented labor market theory, and cumulative causation of migration theory. George Borjas's (1987) relative inequality theory postulates that relative inequality between the sending and receiving countries determines positive versus negative self-selection of immigrants.

Neoclassical Economics of Migration

According to the neoclassical economic theory of migration, geographic differences in the supply and demand for labor are the driving force behind international migration (Ranis and Fei 1961). Countries with abundant capital but limited labor are generally characterized by high wages, and countries with limited capital but abundant labor by low wages. This imbalance generates the current of labor flows from low-wage to high-wage countries. At the micro level, potential migrants calculate the relative benefits and costs of migration. Benefits are generally the higher wages expected in the host country. The costs include traveling, moving, settling, higher costs of living in the destination country, the difficulty of learning a new language and adapting to a new labor market, and the psychological burden of cutting off old social and cultural ties and forging new ones (Todaro and Maruszko 1987). A potential migrant making a rational decision will decide to migrate if the benefits are substantially greater than the costs. This rational approach has great power to explain why people migrate and stay in the new country.

This theory, however, addresses only labor-market activities. It also isolates individuals and ignores families and households. We often see temporary, circular, or return migration, which are hard to explain using neoclassical economics. New economics of labor migration theory was developed to address neoclassical economics' limitations.

New Economics of Labor Migration

New economics of labor migration theory (Stark and Bloom 1985) focuses on collective strategies households use to diversify risks of material well-being. In more developed countries, the welfare state, public assistance programs, and private insurance provide a safety net that protects households from the consequences of unemployment, economic recession, sickness, natural disasters, and other problems. Well-developed credit markets allow households to borrow to maintain their standard of living in the face of hardship. In poor countries, safety nets and credit markets are underdeveloped. The government may not sponsor public assistance programs; the market may not insure farms, businesses, or households; and the credit market may be weak. Households in less developed countries may be motivated to send a household member to a more developed country to diversify risks. If the home country conditions deteriorate, households can rely on the migrant member's remittances. This theory has great power in explaining temporary, circular, and return migration, particularly when this migration is unauthorized. Although the new economic theory pays attention to credit and capital markets in the home country as pushing forces, it does not consider that the home country may gradually become an attractive place for emigrants to invest.

Both neoclassical and new economic theory suggest that individuals and households make migration decisions regardless of variations in structural constraints. The social positions of individuals, households, communities, and countries generate powerful forces influencing both individual and household decision making. To address the limitations of economic theories, structural theories have been developed. These include world systems theory, which explains structural push forces, and segmented labor market theory, which explains structural pull forces.

World Systems Theory of Migration

World systems theory considers the changing scope and structure of global markets as the origin of international migration (Portes and Walton 1981; Sassen 1991). When markets expand into peripheral, nonmarket, or pre-market societies, the expansion creates out-migration in these societies. Large companies and firms in developed countries actively search for land, raw materials, labor, and markets in countries on the periphery of the world economy. Modern agriculture strips farmers of their land; new industries in raw material extraction and assembly plans offering paid jobs alter traditional productive relations and social organizations. These expansions and penetrations disrupt traditional social and economic relations and generate a mobile labor force in poor countries, one that is uprooted economically and socially and therefore prone to migration. Global movements of capital, technology, equipment, information, communication, and commodities from developed to poor countries reduce the costs of transportation and communication infrastructures, facilitating labor flows from poor to developed countries. World systems theory provides a structural explanation as to why the labor force in poor countries is prone to migration, adding to neoclassical economics' explanation of wage differentials. World systems theory of migration suggests that because the United States is the power with global economic hegemony, it is the destination of migrants from many poor countries.

Although the global structure plays an important role in pushing emigration, world systems theory ignores developments in the home country that may make it a better place for investment for emigrants. The destination country's labor market structure plays an equally important role in determining international migration. Segmented labor market theory applies this structural view to international migration.

Segmented Labor Market Theory of Migration

In a developed country, the primary labor market consists of stable, well-paying jobs with occupational ladders, and the secondary labor market offers temporary, low-paying work with little prospect of upward mobility. This dichotomy creates a segmented labor market. Building on institutional economics, segmented labor market theory (Piore 1979) posits that international migration is a response to a demand for unskilled labor from the segmented labor market in the destination country. The reasons labor markets are segmented and unskilled workers are in permanent demand include structural inflation, problems employers have in motivating domestic workers, and the relationship between capital and labor.

Structural inflation arises from the institutionalized rigid relationship between wages and social status, not the invisible hand of supply and demand. Labor unions, civil service rules, bureaucratic regulations, and human resource classifications reinforce the correspondence of wages to the hierarchy of social status. Unskilled labor is at the bottom of the occupational hierarchy and thus is the lowest paid. When unskilled labor is in short supply, employers cannot simply raise wages for the jobs at the bottom because that would upset the rigid wage-status relationship. If job wages at the lowest level increased, strong institutional and social pressure would make them increase proportionally for everyone at every level, creating structural inflation. Employers thus have incentives to distinguish the lowest level jobs from others. At the same time, the low status of those jobs creates strong social motivations for those in the domestic labor force to avoid or refuse to accept them. This further supports the segmentation of the labor market and the demand for unskilled labor.

The relationship between capital and labor is another reason labor markets are segmented and unskilled labor is in demand. Because it is expensive to replace skilled workers, employers have incentives to create distinctions so that when a business has little work, the employer bears the costs of maintaining skilled workers and dismissing unskilled workers, allowing the latter to bear the costs of their own unemployment. This further contributes to segmentation of the labor market and creates a relatively permanent demand for unskilled workers.

In industrial societies, women, teenagers, and domestic rural-to-urban migrants are the usual secondary labor market supply. In advanced industrial societies such as the United States, however, this supply has drastically shrunk because of high levels of urbanization, increased career opportunities for women, and prolonged formal education for youth. Importing unskilled labor is a viable solution because immigrants want to earn money and have different standards than native workers. At least at the earlier stages of their stay in the United States, immigrants generally compare their status to that of their counterparts at home rather than to domestic workers. The relatively permanent demand for unskilled labor creates strong structural pull for international migration and explains both labor immigration and illegal immigration.

The structural push forces postulated by world systems theory and the structural pull forces postulated by segmented labor market theory identify country-specific structural factors. Still, the relative structural conditions of a source country and a destination country can generate forces that drive international migration, as the relative inequality theory suggests.

Relative Inequality Theory of Migration

Borjas (1987) distinguishes between positively and negatively selected immigrants. Depending on the relative inequality of the sending and receiving countries, some immigrants are more skilled or motivated than both non-immigrants and U.S. natives (positively selected), whereas others are less skilled or less motivated (negatively selected). Rather than being driven by small wage differentials, positively selected immigrants from developed countries may be attracted by the prospect of higher status in the United States. They may believe that they will attain higher positions in the occupational and status hierarchy in the United States, which has high inequality relative to most developed countries. In other words, those from developed countries who have both high observed education and experience and unobserved skill attributes expect to reach a higher social position by migration. Regarding negative self-selection, economic inequality in Mexico is higher than in the United States; those at the bottom of the Mexican distribution will therefore certainly gain a great deal if they move to the United States, whereas those at the top are not certain to do so. Those with lower skills than the Mexican average, in terms of both observed educational level and unobserved ability, belong to this negatively selected group.

The relative inequality theory bases its premise on a comparison of within-country inequality and ignores between-country inequality. High wage differentials and strong structural push and pull forces indicate high between-country inequality. Under these conditions, relative within-country inequality becomes less important. The relative inequality theory best explains why emigrants from developed European countries and Canada go to the United States. It also explains emigration from Latin American countries that have a relatively high development level and a relatively high inequality such as Mexico. It does not have the same predictive accuracy for Asian immigrants and Latino immigrants from poor countries. Guillermina Jasso and Mark Rosenzweig (1990) argue that immigration costs for immigrants from developing countries are strongly related to positive selection because only the highly skilled or highly motivated can meet these costs. They also suggest that Asian immigrants, because they must travel far from home and live in a new country with a very different culture, are more likely to be positively selected.

Considering structural push and pull forces and relative inequality, individuals decide to migrate to achieve a net gain or to diffuse household risks. However, immigration seems to continue regardless of these motivations. This leads us to consider the role of immigrant networks.

Cumulative Causation of Migration

Cumulative causation of migration theory states that social capital accumulates over time and perpetuates international migration (Massey et al. 1993). According to social capital theory, resources from network relationships—social capital—facilitate actions (Coleman 1988). Whereas the first migrant bears the full costs of migration, information and sponsorship provided by this person subsequently reduce costs of migration for relatives and friends. Each new migrant expands the networks through social ties to the destination area. Potential migrants draw on the obligations of kinship and friendship to gain access to assistance and employment in the United States, which leads to chain migration. The causation of migration becomes cumulative, increasing the likelihood of additional movement. Once the networks grow large, the number of potential migrants becomes small, and the rate of migration declines. This theory does much to explain the dynamics of chain migration, which has only a weak association with the full costs of migration, risk diversification, structural push and pull forces, and relative inequality.

Each of the reviewed theories of international migration—neoclassical economics, new economics, world systems, segmented labor market, relative inequality, and cumulative causation—provides logical rationales for part of the immigrant self-selection process or applies to part of the immigrant population. Combined, these theories provide a comprehensive view of the entire process and the entire population. When we investigate nativity differences in wealth, we must consider the different ways immigrants are self-selected. Empirically, country of origin is a good anchor. We must consider the degree to which wage differentials, migration costs, household risks, structural push forces, structural pull forces, relative inequality, and immigrant communities determine attributes of immigrants.

Theories of international migration assist us in understanding immigrants' self-selection at the point of migration. What governs immigrants' adaptation and incorporation processes after arrival? To answer this, we turn to assimilation theories.

Assimilation Theories

Classical assimilation theory (Gordon 1964) has been the guiding principle for studying generations of early massive immigration from European countries. Post-1965 immigration, primarily from Asia and Latin

America, has posed a serious challenge to it, however. Alternative theories such as transnationalism or cultural pluralism (Schiller, Basch, and Blanc-Szanton 1995) and segmented assimilation (Portes and Zhou 1993) were developed to address the uniqueness of post–1965 immigration. Richard Alba and Victor Nee (2003) propose a new theory that adapts the vital core from Milton Gordon's assimilation to the ethnically diverse and dynamic American population and revives the continuity of assimilation as one of the important processes of immigrants' incorporation into American society.

Classical Assimilation Theory

Classical assimilation theory, first delineated in William Warner and Leo Scrole (1945) and later synthesized in Gordon (1964), is characterized by four features: inevitability, full incorporation, ethnocentrism, and lack of a positive ethnic group role. In this tradition, assimilation to the Anglo-Saxon majority is the natural end point of the full and successful process of immigrants' incorporation into American society. The most objectionable aspect of this view is its ethnocentrism, which makes middle-class white Anglo-Saxon Protestants (WASPs) the normative standard for all other groups. This leads to ranking the assimilation of ethnic groups by the closeness of their ethnic culture to the normative culture. For example, among the early waves of immigrants, western European cultures were the closest to WASPs, southern European cultures were the next, and eastern European cultures were a distant third. Western Europeans were thus judged to assimilate most quickly, and eastern Europeans thought to assimilate slowly if at all. Ethnocentrism means that other ethnic cultures are valueless and that immigrants must give up their cultures if they are to assimilate.

Despite these limitations, classical assimilation theory dominated studies of early mass immigration. For example, Barry Chiswick (1978) found that early immigrants caught up to and even surpassed natives in one to two decades, even in the face of initial lower socioeconomic status. However, this theory has become increasingly inadequate since the United States entered a new era of non-European immigration. Alternative theories have been developed to address the new phenomenon.

Transnationalism

One form of transnationalism, also called cultural pluralism (Schiller, Basch, and Blanc-Szanton 1995), was developed to fit the new context of globalization and non-European immigration. This perspective defies the premise of classical assimilation theory, which assumes that only assimilating to the WASP mainstream affords advantages. Instead, trans-nationalists maintain that a pluralistic ethnic social and cultural environment affords greater advantages. Facilitated by advances in information technology, market integration, and mass air transportation, generations of immigrants maintain significant relationships with their home countries and achieve benefits, such as bilingualism, ethnic economies, and ethnic employment and occupational niches. Transnationalism also recognizes the long-standing image of the American melting pot, which implies that ethnic cultures exist in tandem with WASP culture. The utility of bilingualism, ethnic economies, ethnic employment and occupational niches is a reason to promote transnationalism, which expands cultural, social, and economic ties to origin countries.

Portes and colleagues document that transnational entrepreneurship is common among immigrant entrepreneurs, particularly the better-off, elite immigrant entrepreneurs (Portes, Guarnizo, and Haller 2002). Entrepreneurship involves income generating, capital accumulating, and asset building activities. Whereas the anthropological and cultural studies literature uses transnational entrepreneurship as an alternative to assimilation, Portes et al. suggest that transnational businesses may accelerate rather than retard the long-term integration of contemporary immigrants.

Transnationalism envisions opportunities provided by every ethnic culture. In contrast, segmented assimilation theory distinguishes between upward assimilation and downward assimilation.

Segmented Assimilation

Alejandro Portes and Min Zhou (1993) postulate that assimilation is segmented by the race and class locations of immigrants. In particular, the theory calls attention both to the potential problem of downward assimilation and to the potential protection from downward assimilation that a resilient ethnic culture can provide. Constrained by class and nonwhite status, low-income immigrants from Central America, the Caribbean basin, and Asia are likely to settle in proximity to inner-city neighborhoods populated by native-born blacks and Latinos. In these locations of racial and class segregation, first-generation immigrants often face chronic unemployment and joblessness, blocking their upward mobility. Consistent with John Ogbu's (1978) oppositional culture, children of these immigrants perceive that they are likely to remain at the bottom of the occupational hierarchy and are thus tempted to drop out of school and join the inner-city underclass. The experiences of Haitian immigrants and their descendants provide an example of downward assimilation. In contrast, a Vietnamese immigrant community in New Orleans overcame the adversity of surrounding inner-city neighborhoods to provide economic and social opportunities for the first and second generations via maintaining a strong ethnic identity, providing network and community resources, and upholding upward-mobility norms (Zhou and Bankston 1998).

Although segmented assimilation theory focuses attention on the potential influence of the underclass rather than on the typical image of upward assimilation, we should not overlook that the majority of immigrants settle in diverse urban areas, areas where nonwhite minorities, such as African Americans and Latino Americans, have jobs and families and aspirations for their children. This leads us turn to Alba and Nee's (2003) new assimilation theory.

The New Assimilation Theory

Alba and Nee (2003) trace the root of the assimilation concept to the Chicago School and raise a fundamental question: What is the mainstream as the destination of assimilation? The Chicago School (Park 1930) asserts that it is a composite rather than a homogeneous WASP culture. Using this revised definition, Alba and Nee redefine assimilation as the weakening role of ethnicity in assimilated people's life chances. In essence, the mainstream is not fixed but dynamic, which can consist of multiple ethnic groups as long as ethnicity is no longer a significant factor in people's life chances. Changes in institutions are the major reason why this new assimilation is possible. Minorities have greater opportunities in occupational and educational structures because of the civil rights movement, the federal regulation of equal employment opportunities, and wider availability of college education. Whenever opportunities for immigrants are greater in the mainstream than in the ethnic economy, there is a motive for assimilation.

According to new assimilation theory, human capital and social capital play different roles. Human capital is particularly important in accelerating assimilation so that ethnicity has a weakening role among highly educated people. By contrast, social capital derived from ethnic networks and immigrant communities may be valuable in the short run but harmful in the long run, because ethnicity is at the center of this type of social capital. These arguments have important implications for immigrants' eventual incorporation into American society.

Assimilation theories address the incorporation of generations of immigrants into American society. A central issue in these theories is whether there is a mainstream, and if there is, what it is. The classical assimilation theory takes a normative approach. It sets the white Anglo-Saxon Protestant culture of the earliest settlers from Britain as the mainstream. Transnationalism, also known as cultural pluralism, however, defies the idea of a mainstream and embraces all ethnic cultures as playing a positive role in promoting upward social mobility. The segmented assimilation theory addresses the influence of the underclass on the downward mobility of certain immigrants but praises the protective function that ethnic identity and network support provide for others. The new assimilation theory takes a different view on the mainstream, saying that it can be ethnically heterogeneous as long as ethnicity is no longer significant in the social domain. The three contemporary assimilation theories (transnationalism, segmented, and new) reject the classical assimilation theory and pose conflicting ideas with different emphases. These, however, provide us with insights into different aspects of immigrants' adaptation and incorporation and thus have important implications for my study of immigrant-native differences in wealth. For example, new assimilation theory suggests that human capital plays the ultimate role in wealth accumulation; segmented assimilation theory suggests that nonwhite race-ethnicity dampens mobility opportunities because of discrimination and segregation; and both transnationalism and segmented assimilation theories claim benefits from ethnic identity, networks, and communities. These principles are useful in formulating an integrated framework. Additionally, wealth theory informs assimilation theory by presenting wealth attainment as a phenomenon where multiple dimensions of assimilation are manifested.

Theories on Racial-Ethnic Stratification of Wealth

In the literature on wealth inequality, stratification by race-ethnicity is the most important topic. The bleak picture of black-white inequality in wealth is documented in Melvin Oliver and Thomas Shapiro (1995), but we know relatively little about wealth differences among whites, Hispanics, and Asians. Structural factors are at the core of explaining racial-ethnic inequality in wealth. The structural perspective is based on theories such as dual labor market (Doeringer and Piore 1971), dual housing market (Alba and Logan 1991) and spatial segregation (Massey and Denton 1993). Institutional barriers and discrimination in the labor market can block racial-ethnic minorities from achieving high social status and a high level of wealth accumulation (Oliver and Shapiro 1995). Redlining (the practice of excluding minorities) in certain housing markets reduces minorities' homeownership and forces them into racially segregated neighborhoods with lower home values (Oliver and Shapiro 1995; Conley 1999). Lending discrimination affects the probability of acquiring wealth, the level of wealth acquired, and portfolio allocation (Keister 2000).

The uneven spatial distribution of race creates racial residential segregation, which reinforces discrimination in the labor, lending, and housing markets. The literature has widely documented the intensity and persistence of black-white segregation and its negative impacts on the social mobility of black residents (Massey and Denton 1993). Black-white segregation is unparalleled by the residential experiences of any other group. Immigration has greatly changed the landscape of racial segregation. In a given metropolitan area, the proportion of immigrants from different countries of origin varies because of different ethnic settlement patterns shaped by ethnic niche markets, refugee settlement programs, chain migration patterns, and historical recruitment efforts. Immigrants, particularly Hispanics, have steadily moved into predominantly black neighborhoods, triggering the succession of black communities. The ethnically diverse, rapidly growing Southwest, a region with relatively low black-white segregation, is home to many Latino immigrants (Fossett and Waren 2005). As Hispanic immigration has increased and spread to many other nontraditional immigrant areas, formerly predominately black neighborhoods have become black and Latino neighborhoods (Alba et al. 1995; Frey and Farley 1996). Thus, the increasing presence of immigrants, particularly Latinos, is altering the pattern of residential segregation between whites and blacks and between whites and Hispanics in contemporary America.

More deeply, immigrants' settlement changes the degree of black-white antagonism in segregated areas. The presence of other groups may alter the perception of the residential housing market among native-born blacks and whites because Latino and Asian residents serve as buffers between segregated neighborhoods (Frey and Farley 1996; Iceland 2004). As the level of antagonism goes down, the distribution of resources will be less uneven and the availability of opportunities will increase in minority neighborhoods. This argument stresses the role of immigrant settlement in reducing the formerly strong negative consequences of black-white segregation.

Even though immigrant settlement patterns contribute significantly to the dynamics of American segregation, the life chances of immigrants are profoundly shaped by racial residential segregation. An argument to address this paradox considers the negative externality of black-white segregation. By externality I mean consequences not originally intended. Here, the target of black-white segregation is blacks and the negative consequences of black-white segregation are originally intended to affect blacks. Because residents living in primarily black neighborhood face the same uneven distribution of resources and opportunities, nonblack minorities also shoulder the negative consequences of scarce resources and block of opportunities, hence negative externality. Thus, the lack of resources and opportunities generated by deep-rooted black-white segregation may have negative externality or a spillover effect on other minorities living in primarily black neighborhoods, with a close reference to new Latino immigrants. Thus even not being black, new Latino immigrants living in black-white segregated areas may face the negative externality of black-white segregation.

Economic Theories on Wealth Accumulation

Economic theories consider wealth as related to income, consumption, savings, and portfolio allocation. The difference between income and consumption results in either savings or debts. Households may have savings or debts at a given time, but over a longer period, whether the accumulation results in a surplus or deficit determines the household's wealth. Many factors influence this accumulation, including intergenerational transfers (inheritances and parental transfers), human capital (education and work experience) and earned income, consumption behaviors (essential, education, pleasurable, social network needs), saving motives (precautionary saving, human capital investment in children, old-age security, and bequests), portfolio allocation (homeownership, retirement accounts, stocks, bonds, and bank accounts), asset-generated income (rent, interests, and dividends), and attitudes toward loans and debts.

Human Capital

In general, much wealth accumulation depends primarily on earned income. Higher education and other human capital investments lead to higher earned income. To a large degree, parental investments in a child's education set the path of that child's human capital acquisition, and in turn that child's future income. Pre-college private schooling and college education are the two largest investments wealthy parents make in human capital for their children. Investment in extracurricular activities and home-learning enrichment also entail significant expenses because both involve long-term, day-to-day costs. Many well-off parents who send their children to public schools still make major investments. They may pay a premium price for housing to live in a high quality public school district or invest in out-of-school activities to facilitate their children's enrollment in magnet programs. Such investments help the children enter prestigious universities and make them more likely to pursue graduate or professional degrees because students graduating from such institutions are more likely to complete postgraduate and professional programs. Education has been increasingly important in income stratification, in part because of rapid technological advancements in the last two decades. Wage rates have been rising for college graduates, stagnating for high school graduates, and declining for high school dropouts, particularly those with fewer than nine years of schooling (Bernhardt et al. 2001), making education the most important stratification factor in labor market outcomes. Children from poor or working-class families are handicapped by their parents' limited ability to invest in their education.

Horizontal as well as vertical differentiation in educational levels contributes to the initial level of household wealth for those with bachelor's degrees. Employee shortages in mathematics, computer sciences, engineering, medical and life sciences, and health professions, for example, have especially increased earnings in these fields (Grogger and Eide 1995).

Human capital contributes not only to initial wealth levels but also to growth rates of wealth. Parental and self investment in education has life-long implications for an individual's income trajectory (Becker and Tomes 1979). Human capital theory emphasizes the importance of work experience in generating income over an individual's life cycle. However, returns to work experience are so closely tied to education levels that the age profile of earnings is much flatter for people with low education than for their highly educated counterparts (Polachek 1975).

Consumption Behavior

Household consumption includes meeting essential, pleasure, social network, and education needs, but official federal poverty thresholds lend clarity on the amount needed to meet needs essential to American living standards. Developed by Mollie Orshansky (1965), poverty thresholds were originally set at three times the cost of an economical food plan for a nutritionally adequate diet. The most recent data available at the time of Orshansky's study were from 1955, when families spent about one-third of their after-tax income on food. Since 1965, poverty thresholds have been adjusted for family size, number of children, old-age status, and farm households. Although raised in accordance with the inflation rate every year, the official poverty thresholds have become increasingly inadequate because of rising living standards and variations in costs by region. The Panel on Poverty and Family Assistance at the National Research Council (Citro and Michael 1995) proposes that the budget allowance for essential needs should include allocations for food, clothing, and shelter (including utilities), plus a small additional amount to allow for household supplies, personal care, and transportation. The level of this budget allowance is set at the thirtieth to the thirty-fifth percentile of expenditure on these items for the population. The proposed poverty thresholds are between 14 and 33 percent higher than the current poverty thresholds. The panel does not include a budget for medical care (also an essential need) because medical care needs vary widely across the population, and in any case benefits received in the form of insurance cannot be converted into cash to spend in other areas. In addition, because the panel considers only after-tax income, the proposed new poverty threshold does not budget for income and payroll taxes or Social Security and Medicare taxes (FICA). The panel does not include a number of other essential expenses, such as child care, professional clothing or other work-related expenses, and noncustodial parents' child support payments. Note that many essential expenses, particularly housing, vary across geographic areas, and that adjustments should thus be made by region. Based on these considerations, my version of essential needs includes food, clothing, housing, utilities, household supplies, personal care, transportation, medical care, child care, child support to another household, and Social Security, Medicare, federal, state, and local taxes. Many of these expenses differ geographically.

Household consumption goes beyond meeting essential needs. Nonessential consumption includes spending on pleasure purchases, social relationships, and education. Families without tight budget constraints often spend for pleasure or "value of life" purchases, such as nonessential services and entertainment. Depending on a household's lifestyle, pleasure spending may be tied to restaurant meals, fashionable clothing, luxurious housing, high-end appliances, expensive transportation, or high-end childcare or medical care. Whereas people in poverty only dream of a $250 per person dinner, a $150 show ticket, or a $3,000 cruise package, such luxuries are common for some wealthier households. The economic value of these expenses comes from enjoyment and pleasure.

Social relationships within and beyond households are a part of cohesive webs of families, kinship networks, neighborhoods, communities, and friendships. Monetary and in-kind support to ease financial difficulties of parents, siblings, relatives, and friends can also be a large part of a household's expenses. In addition, participation in these webs involves expenses for gifts for holidays, birthdays, and anniversaries. Overall, these expenses for people outside the immediate household are reinforced by social or cultural norms and the expectation of reciprocal support.

Educators, child psychologists, and sociologists have long emphasized the importance of an intellectually stimulating home environment and extracurricular activities in both children's cognitive and emotional development and their academic achievement. As children grow, parents purchase books, computers, newspaper and magazine subscriptions, and musical instruments. They enroll children in music, dance, painting, language, and sports classes, and they take children to museums, theaters, and sports events. An even larger expense for some well-off parents is the cost of private pre-college education, which many choose because of the uneven quality of public schools in some districts or status consciousness. Last is the largest expense, the college education itself. Both tuition, which rises at an annual rate of about 10 percent, and living expenses for the four years require working- and middle-class parents to save for a long time. Costs are much higher for private universities, especially Ivy League and other prestigious private universities. Often, parents or students must take educational loans.

Saving Motives

Households save for a variety of reasons. The 1983 Survey of Consumer Finances found that 43 percent of households saved for emergencies, 29 percent for future expenses for family members or for durable goods, 15 percent for retirement, and 7 percent for investment (Avery and Kennickell 1989). Data from the Panel Study of Income Dynamics also show that between 39 and 46 percent of household wealth is precautionary saving, that is, money saved to compensate for the potential of future income decline (Carroll 1997). Evidence suggests that precautionary saving is important for all households, even more so than investment in children and retirement. Household income uncertainty can result from job loss, job transitions, declining real wages, delayed promotion, or salary freezes. Although both natives and immigrants face economic uncertainty, income uncertainty can be greater for immigrants. Little education and English proficiency among immigrants lead to unstable, low-paying jobs in the secondary labor market. Day laborers gathered around street corners of wealthy neighborhoods in Los Angeles, for example, are not certain how much they can earn per day. More highly educated immigrants, handicapped by non-American communication styles and foreign degrees, may be the first to be laid off and the last to be promoted. The downturn of the computer engineering industry in 2000 led to a large number of laid off engineers, more of whom were foreign born than native born. Because greater income uncertainty leads to greater precautionary saving motives, immigrants may have a greater precautionary saving motive than natives. However, depending on whether a household has met its saving goals, it may be either *prudent* (using precautionary saving motives) or *impatient* (consuming more than current income). Prudent consumption behaviors may dominate impatient consumption behaviors for immigrants because immigrants have often come to the United States to achieve economic security.

Households also save for children's education and the financial and medical needs of extended families. In this respect, immigrant households can have much stronger motives than natives. Given diffusing household risk and improving the life chances of children as the reasons for migration, it is possible that immigrants—unlike natives—consider saving for their families more important than saving for emergencies. Empirically, we would expect that immigrants' use of savings is more uneven than natives'.

Portfolio Allocation

Income uncertainty plays an important role in determining what people believe to be their optimal portfolio allocation. Finance literature focuses on obtaining an optimal portfolio allocation by balancing risky and risk-free assets. Economic literature considers liquid versus illiquid assets. A typical household holds most of its stocks and bonds in quasi-illiquid retirement accounts, accounts that have constraints and penalties when funds are withdrawn before the holders reach retirement age. In fact, U.S. households hold the majority of their wealth in illiquid forms (Otsuka 2004). The largest component of wealth is typically home equity. Households that rent typically hold most of their savings in quasi-illiquid retirement accounts such as individual retirement accounts (IRAs) or 401(k) plans. In general, households determine their portfolio allocation according to saving goals, asset growth potential, and transaction costs of liquidation. For example, bank accounts are easy to draw on and have low transaction costs, but their interest rates are generally low as well. Although income-growth liquid assets such as stock-based mutual funds and stock are easy and quick transactions, they can be costly because their highly fluctuating profiles mean that their values may be low when the household needs funds. In addition, income-guaranteed liquid assets such as bonds and certificates of deposit impose penalties if drawn upon before maturity. Illiquid assets such as a house and other real estate often feature both high rates of return and high transaction costs if a household needs to draw funds at a particular time.

Asset-Generated Income

There is a seemingly sequential process of earning income, consuming, saving, and making portfolio allocations. In reality, however, certain assets, such as real estate, stocks, and mutual funds, generate income in forms of rents, capital income, dividends, and interest. This unearned income allows a feedback process in which households can consume, save, or further build their assets without working to earn income. Unearned income facilitates an upward-spiral of wealth accumulation for the advantaged, whereas lack of unearned income leads to stagnant wealth accumulation for the disadvantaged; thus those with a high initial wealth level have a high wealth growth rate. For example, households in the top 1 percent of the wealth distribution earn about 10 percent of wages and salaries but receive 50 percent of capital income, dividends, and interest. Undoubtedly, this high rate of unearned income contributes to the high growth rate of households in the top 1 percent of the wealth distribution, generating greater inequality in wealth than in income.

Attitudes toward Loans and Debts

Asset building often involves loans. Property can serve as collateral for a loan, in which case the loan is called a secured debt. If the loan is based on future income, it is an unsecured debt. Examples of secured debts include home mortgages and car loans. Households purchase a car or a home with a combination of a down payment and a loan. The loan uses the car or the home as the collateral in case of default. Lenders make unsecured loans, such as credit cards, based on the probability that the borrower will earn enough in the future to repay them. Unsecured debts also arise from receiving costly medical care that is not paid for promptly.

Life Cycle Hypothesis

Based on mechanisms of income, consumption, saving, and portfolio allocation, the life cycle hypothesis posits that an individual accumulates wealth until retirement and then consumes the accumulated wealth (Modigliani 1986). The major empirical finding based on this hypothesis is that if the elderly use their accumulated wealth, they do so at a lower rate and at a later age (see Keister and Moller 2000). The notion of a family life cycle offers a better conceptual tool than an individual age-based life cycle because considering family as a whole is a more accurate way to assess wealth. Family sociologists describe the family life cycle as running through several stages—formation, school-age children, college-age children, early empty nest, and older empty nest. Along the cycle, three characteristics change. The first, age, parallels family life cycle stages. A second, marriage, is intertwined with each stage. Before family formation, most people are not married, and after, marital status may change. A family is formed either by a marriage or by an unmarried childbirth. Marriage is a wealth-enhancing institution that fosters saving to guard against future financial risks (Lupton and Smith 2003), whereas female-headed families have fewer resources and therefore usually little in savings (Hao 1996). A third characteristic, the presence of children, increases parents' incentive to save during earlier stages and to pay for their children's education later. These three characteristics interact and determine the level of wealth along the family life cycle.

Wealth is accumulated along these life cycle stages. The formation stage is the first. Typically, families formed by marriage acquire a bank account, a car, and a house. Forming a family through unwed motherhood immediately disadvantages the family and hinders future wealth accumulation. After children are born, married parents are better able to save for their children's education and inheritance than their unmarried counterparts. When their children are attending college, parents use their accumulated wealth to pay for tuition and other costs. When children begin to form their own families, empty-nester parents often transfer money to their children, which further decreases their own wealth. When a household reaches the older empty nest stage and no longer brings in earnings, it uses its accumulated wealth for the increasing demands of health care and old-age care. Most research examines the entire life cycle. This volume focuses instead on the period between ages twenty-five and sixty-four—beginning with family formation and continuing through the school-age, college-age, and early empty-nest stages.

An Integrated Framework for Wealth in an Era of Immigration

Under the broader context of economic structure and racial-ethnic hierarchy, the existing theoretical model for wealth accumulation considers earning, spending, saving, and investment behaviors along a household's life cycle. Recent attention to the role of intergenerational transfers in wealth accumulation suggests that the significant black-white wealth gap is an intergenerational phenomenon (Oliver and Shapiro 1995; Conley 1999; Spilerman 2000). In the post–1965 immigration era, the within racial-ethnic group wealth distribution has become more dispersed. Some immigrant nationality groups surpass their native-born ethnic counterparts despite the fact that many immigrants neither benefit from inheritances nor begin the wealth accumulation process as early as natives (Hao 2004). This fact challenges existing wisdom about the pivotal role of intergenerational transfers. Why does the lack of inheritances severely damage African Americans' prospects of wealth, and hence their life chances, but not seem to affect those of immigrant racial-ethnic minority groups? Recognizing the heterogeneity among immigrants, I use the sending countries' characteristics, the characteristics of the migration system, and the consequential self-selection of immigrants to take on the challenge of this question.

In light of the diverse wealth patterns among ethnic and origin-country groups, the post-1965 immigration era has posed a second challenge: a rising trend of transnational activities, a phenomenon where immigrants work in the United States but invest in their home country. International migration theory largely ignores this phenomenon. Neoclassical economic theory oversimplifies economic behavior by focusing on only wage differentials and labor market activities. New economic theory takes note when credit-capital markets in the home country are poorer than the host country, but ignores the increasing attractiveness of the home-country credit-capital markets while developing its economy and capital-credit markets. In explaining international migration, world systems theory similarly emphasizes the penetration of markets in pre-market countries that pushes the uprooted peasant population to out-migrate but does not consider that the subsequent development of the home-country market economy may attract emigrants' investment. What makes the geographic separation between the generation of income (labor market activities) and the investment of savings (credit-capital market activities) emerge and deepen? Building on assimilation theory, international financial economics, and explanations for economic globalization, I develop a typology of wealth regime that classifies countries according to their development level and growth, investment environment, and the in-country purchasing capacity of U.S. currency. Immigrants from countries with favorable conditions are more likely to invest and build some of their wealth in their home country. As this transnationalism becomes more common, an extension of the existing theory on household wealth can account for cross-national variations in development, credit-capital markets, economic institutions, and political structures, which have been taken as constants in existing wealth theory.

To face both challenges of the paradox of the role of inheritance in immigrants' wealth and the emerging cross-border investment of immigrants, existing wealth theory must integrate immigration theory that explains immigrants' self-selection, assimilation processes, and wealth accumulation behaviors. At the same time, this integration will strengthen assimilation theory, which has not yet considered wealth attainment.

Integrating Wealth Theory and Immigration Theory

International migration theory explains how migration decision is made and assimilation theory explains how immigrants adapt to the host society. Endogenous migration decisions point to the importance of immigrants' self-selection. This is still under debate, but many researchers consider that immigrants do not have the same level or kind of unobserved characteristics, traditionally conceived of as high motivation and a strong work ethic. Instead, a set of macro- and meso-level forces shape the decision to emigrate. Macro-level forces are generated from the structure of the sending and receiving countries and the binational migration system. For example, origin-country characteristics, such as economic, educational and social development levels, growth, and political regime generate push forces propelling various types of emigrants. The dual U.S. labor market and its immigration laws pull and screen the kinds of immigrants admitted. Binational forces include historical and geopolitical relationships, physical distance, and perhaps, relative inequality in the returns to individuals' skills between the sending country and the United States. In addition, meso-level factors of immigrants' networks link people between the host and the home countries as well as within the host society, reducing migration's costs and risks and perpetuating chain migration. Time dimensions further differentiate immigrants. Because the conditions of the sending and receiving countries, the binational migration system, and immigrant social networks change over time, successive entry cohorts of immigrants are exposed to changing conditions and thus likely to be selected differently from the same sending country. These theoretical accounts indicate that it is unwise to make a blanket assessment of all immigrants from different sending countries who arrive at different times. Instead, immigrant nationality groups and entry cohorts from the same sending country are intrinsically heterogeneous, and their differences are rooted in factors above the individual level, requiring careful analysis for nationality-cohort groups of immigrants. I predict that, holding constant observed skills and race, positively selected immigrants who have economic ambitions and have overcome immense barriers to migrate to and settle in the United States are likely to possess unobserved abilities that help negate the precondition of intergenerational transfer in wealth accumulation. By contrast, immigrants with low costs and risks of out-migration and initial settlement are likely to face problems similar to natives lacking an inheritance.

Wealth is accumulated over time. For most immigrants, this process starts after they enter the United States. In this sense, assimilation theory, which explains immigrants' adaptation experience, contributes to an understanding of immigrants' wealth accumulation compared to natives'. All strands of assimilation theory, however, have not considered wealth accumulation and wealth attainment. For example, new assimilation theory, with its focus on the role of human and social capital, is powerful in explaining income attainment. Segmented assimilation theory reminds us that racial-ethnic segregation can lead immigrants along dramatically different paths of income attainment. These theories need to explain wealth accumulation behaviors beyond income generation. The theory on transnational entrepreneurs explains what facilitates conducting businesses in the home country and how this transnational entrepreneurship accelerates integration into the mainstream. This theory can be extended to include immigrant households' asset building. Ultimately, the extended assimilation theory on the wealth accumulation of immigrants will help explain the whole population's wealth in an era of immigration.

Modifying Wealth Theory

How does immigration theory inform wealth theory? Immigration theory addressing migration experience, cultural roots, networks, and the treatment in the host labor, lending, credit and housing markets are used to explain the nativity differences in wealth accumulation behavior.

Self-Selection in Wealth Accumulation   Boundaries of social groups are defined according to ascribed characteristics such as race, gender, and age, and achieved characteristics such as socioeconomic status. In light of this distinction, the nationality of a country's people is an ascribed trait because it is determined by place of birth and parentage. Although emigrants from a country are a part of its population, because they were not randomly selected to emigrate, their national origin in the host society is no long ascribed. Rather, the decision to emigrate is a key to determining who does or does not cross the border. International migration theory and immigrant self-selection theory suggest that the motivation of immigrants can range from very high to very low, depending on the characteristics of the binational migration system and the scale and functioning of immigrant networks. Thus, international migration theory informs wealth theory that a simple treatment of the immigrant population as if they only bring in exogenous characteristics of national origins is bound to obscure the different wealth accumulation processes. Here the initial shock and the lasting effect of immigrants' self-selection are considered.

The initial shock to wealth accumulation is widely observed. On arrival, highly motivated immigrants take any job they can find and work more than one shift. Although they are paid less, they earn more because of higher employment probability and number of hours worked. After paying for home-country standard consumption, these immigrants start to save soon after arrival, boosting their wealth accumulation. Such an initial shock, however, is unlikely to occur among less-motivated immigrants who rely at least in part on U.S. public assistance. Using public assistance often delays asset building because asset ownership disqualifies people from receiving public assistance.

One may argue, however, that the initial shock is short-lived because wealth accumulation behaviors driven by high motivation at the beginning of the adaptation process may fade with the deepening of acculturation—for example, learning more English, getting more familiar with the American labor market and society, and adopting the American lifestyle. For the boosting effect of positive selection to last, sufficient counteracting factors must exist. One of these factors is the responsibility to bring eligible immediate and extended family members to the United States. Funds are needed to pay for the application fees, the travel costs, the settlement expenses, and the financial support for the young and the old. Another factor is the long-term migration goal among positively selected immigrants of improving the well-being of the younger generation. These immigrants are in an unusual position in that they typically receive no or little inheritance but do make large transfers to their children. Their optimism has a material basis. Parents invest heavily in their children's education by spending more on primary and secondary education and saving larger sums for college education. Both responsibilities uphold the long-lasting effects of the positive selection of immigrants.

What is the implication of immigrants' self-selection for the racial-ethnic stratification of wealth in the United States? The nativity composition within broad racial-ethnic groups, particularly Hispanics and Asians, has profoundly changed since the resurgence of large immigrant flows. Self-selection and heterogeneity may lead to further vertical differentiation within racial-ethnic groups. There may even be cases in which the within-group vertical differentiation breaks through racial-ethnic divides. For example, results from this book show that immigrants from Hong Kong and Taiwan acquire more wealth than native whites, that Cuban immigrants are comparable with Asian immigrant groups, and that Dominican immigrants fare more poorly than blacks. Does this boundary blurring suggest the equal importance of race-ethnicity and nativity? Or will an order of importance emerge as the immigration era develops into a mature stage?

When the immigrant population becomes larger and more diverse, nativity may serve as an additional social stratification factor. Most existing theories of social stratification focus on one stratification factor while holding other factors constant. Little conceptual attention has been paid to the underlying structure of a multi-factor stratification system. Figure 2.1 attempts to illustrate the major possible conceptual scenarios of multi-factor stratification systems, such as race, class, and nativity. A first distinction is between all primary factors (the left panel) and some primary factors (the right panel). If all factors are primary, a second distinction is between the independence of all factors and the interdependence of all or some factors. A hypothetical example of independence is that the class effect is not contingent on race, that is, that the effect of class is the same for all races (and vice versa—the race effect is the same for all classes). A hypothetical example of interdependence is that the class effect is stronger for blacks than for whites (and vice versa—the race effect is smaller for the higher classes than for the lower classes). I argue that the contested terrain of all primary stratification factors, which are either independent or interdependent, reinforce between-group gaps and leave little room for within-group differentiation, reproducing the existing stratification order and maintaining social inequality—a scenario of persistence.

The right panel of figure 2.1 depicts two other scenarios. The first identifies that only some, not all, stratification factors are primary and the other factors are secondary (do not stratify the entire population). For instance, the effect of nativity for the population as whole is insignificant.

Figure 2.1   Structure of a Multifactor Stratification System: Three Conceptual Scenarios

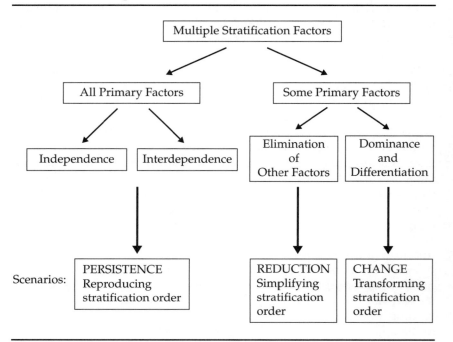

Source: Author's compilation.

Should nativity then be eliminated as a stratification factor? I propose a further distinction between elimination, in which a secondary factor (nativity) is eliminated because it does not differentiate within groups, and a two-tiered system of dominance-differentiation, in which primary factors (race and class) dominate and secondary factors (nativity) differentiate within groups. The elimination of a factor reduces the complexity of social inequality and simplifies the stratification order—a scenario of reduction. On the other hand, the dominance-differentiation system provides an opportunity for change in an unusual way. Although primary factors dominate initially, differentiation by secondary factors within primary-factor groups creates great within-group variations, ultimately leading to the weakening of the divides by the primary factors. For instance, concerning wealth, Hong Kong and Taiwan immigrants surpass native whites, Cuban immigrants within the Hispanic group are comparable with the Asian group and Dominican immigrants within the Hispanic group are comparable with the black group. These differentiations

economic, social, and political institutions between the sending country and the United States. Incentives may be derived from the relative size of the credit market, the degree of protection of private property rights, political stability, and the prospect of future returns to investment. An institutional development explanation from theories on international financial markets (Morck, Yeung, and Yu 2000) highlights the importance of the size of the domestic credit market and the protection of property right as well as the political stability of the country. Whether the country's credit market is adequate can be captured by the amount of domestic credit lent to private sectors, such that the purchase of an asset is possible. In any given country at a given time, politicians can shut down a business, evict it, or even refuse to allow it to start (Shleifer 1994; La Porta et al. 1998). Institutional means of violating property rights include illegal licensing requirements and repudiation of commitments. When property rights are not protected, asset values are predominantly affected by political connections rather than by market forces.[1] In such circumstances, political events could cause large market-wide stock price swings and generate unstable asset values. In short, there are countries where politicians and small entrenched elites preserve their sweeping control over the private sectors by using political influence to undermine the financial systems (Durnev et al. 2004). The situation in these countries discourages their emigrants from investing in their homeland. In contrast, reasonable protection of property rights and relatively stable political situations, combined with a sizable credit market, constitute a favorable investment environment and offer strong incentives for potential investors, including emigrants.

As developed countries, particularly the United States, provide much better investment environments than developing countries, it seems logical that immigrants would only invest in the United States. Two other considerations are warranted. First, developing countries with stably high growth rates (typically much higher than the growth rates of developed countries) offer a great prospect of future returns to investment. Second, the strong purchasing capacity of U.S. currency in a sending country offers a competitive advantage when buying assets in the sending country.

Concerning the future returns to investment or the appreciation of assets, financial economic theories argue for a causal relationship from the financial system to the economic growth of a country (Levine 1997). A five-year economic growth rate can be used to proxy the direction of asset markets in terms of returns to individual investments. Because economic growth instability leads to unstable market performance and influences the asset and financial market, such instability creates a disincentive for immigrants to invest.

Because immigrants work in the United States and earn U.S. wages, the purchasing capacity of U.S. currency makes investing in some sending countries more attractive than others. The purchasing capacity is the amount of goods a U.S. dollar buys in the home country after being exchanged to the home currency versus the amount of goods it can buy in the United States. A high purchasing capacity in the sending country offers a final incentive to build assets in the homeland with the U.S. savings.

Taking the previously noted theoretical accounts together leads to the following reasoning: with a certain level of savings, immigrants make decisions as to the allocation of investments between the United States and the home country. This decision is largely determined by three factors in the home country: the investment environment (how large the credit market is, how rigorous the property right protection, and how stable the political environment), the purchasing capacity of the U.S. currency, and the economic development, growth, and stability.

The simultaneous consideration of the economic, financial, and political conditions constructs a typology of wealth regime, which characterizes the structural conditions of a country for cross-border investment by individual investors (primarily emigrants). The typology of wealth regime is a theoretical tool that plays a key role in modifying wealth theory. An immediate application of this typology of wealth regime is a broader horizon for understanding immigrants' investment and wealth accumulation. With deepening economic globalization, wealth regime may provide incentives for immigrants and natives alike to allocate investments and build assets in countries or larger regions outside of the United States (for example, the Asian stock market).

Modifying Assimilation Theory

Assimilation theory distinguishes between economic assimilation and that in areas beyond the economic realm, such as American culture and values, political and civic outlooks, familial and intergenerational relationships, and relationships between citizens and the state. Income (wage) attainment, the concept used most often in the assimilation literature, taps only economic attainment and does not give adequate attention to other aspects of assimilation. On the other side, acculturation emphasizes language, customs, and cultural learning without reference to economic assimilation. Considerations of only economic or noneconomic aspects are apparently one-sided, yet a simple addition of the multiple dimensions of assimilation presents difficulties when judging the degree of assimilation. Not having a comprehensive type of attainment makes it difficult to determine which type of assimilation is more fundamental—socioeconomic or cultural. A viable alternative would be to identify a type of attainment that reflects multiple dimensions of assimilation. Wealth attainment is such a candidate.

Wealth, with its asset-debt balance and portfolio, reflects not only economic attainment but also lifestyles that manifest multiple aspects of assimilation. For instance, a relatively large amount of net worth with a relatively small amount of debt may reflect a cautious attitude toward debts and loans. An overwhelming portfolio allocation in real estate as opposed to stocks and mutual funds captures a wide difference from modern modes of investments. Less directly, greater wealth than income attainment reflects an economical style of consumption. Consumption styles may be in reference to the immigrants' home country, a testimony of their upholding their cultural heritage rather than of their acculturating. Cross-border investment signals a combination of economic attainment and maintenance of origin culture, a high probability of developing stronger connections with the home country, and the prospect of return migration, at least on retirement.

The contribution of wealth theory to the advancement of assimilation theory is much larger than simply an additional measure of economic assimilation. The most important theoretical thrust is that the concept of wealth, a realm of economic behaviors and outcomes, embodies values, attitudes, and lifestyles, overcoming the well-recognized gap between attitudes and behaviors. In addition, it unites many aspects of assimilation and encompasses many stages of the life cycle. Overall, the concept of wealth attainment brings a fresh perspective to assimilation theory by uniting various theoretical fronts and relating intragenerational mobility with intergenerational mobility. The use of the concept of wealth attainment also facilitates the identification of the ever-updated mainstream suggested by the new assimilation theory (Alba and Nee 2003). If native whites and certain immigrant groups accumulate a similar level of wealth that provides the group members with favorable life chances, the different wealth accumulation behaviors, cultures, values, and lifestyles embedded in their wealth accumulation process may indicate the formation of an updated mainstream, one that expands the boundary of the native, white middle class to incorporate successful immigrant groups.

The experiences of wealth accumulation and wealth attainment among post–1965 immigrants provide a unique opportunity for the study of wealth. The first step is to develop a theoretical framework for wealth in the contemporary immigration era. My approach is to address two limitations of the existing wealth theory—the paradox of intergenerational transfers in wealth accumulation and the rising transnational investment activities among immigrants. The key reasoning to overcome the first limitation is the initial shock and the lasting effect of self-selection along the assimilation process of immigrants. To address the second limitation, a typology of wealth regime is developed to identify incentives created by the binational structure of economic, financial, and political institutions for immigrants' cross-border investment. This way, international migration theory and assimilation theory inform wealth theory, and in return wealth theory pushes an extension of assimilation theory. Both are inseparable elements of the integrated theoretical framework developed in this section. Empirical implications derived from this framework will be examined and tested later in this volume.

Specific Implications for Immigrants' Wealth

The integrated framework developed is also useful in better understanding immigrants' wealth accumulation. Four implications are in order. First, like natives, immigrants are subject to a common set of broad structural and institutional forces in achieving economic well-being in American society. The racial-ethnic hierarchy is a good example.

Second, unlike natives, immigrants have different demographic characteristics that relate to life cycle wealth accumulation. Immigrants are more likely not to be white, to have either very low or very high education levels, to be younger, to be married, and to have more children. All these characteristics affect wealth accumulation.

Third, immigrants of different types or from different countries are treated differently by the U.S. government and labor market. Low-skilled labor immigrants, legal or illegal, are in permanent demand by the secondary labor market, but undocumented immigrants are a constant topic in immigration policy and public debates. High-skilled professional immigrants are actively recruited in science, engineering and health care industries and are granted legal status. Political refugees and asylum seekers from communist regimes such as Cuba and Vietnam have received a more enthusiastic reception from the government and society than refugees from other authoritarian regimes such as Haiti and El Salvador.

Fourth, equally important are immigrants' different migration motivations and cultural roots, which shape patterns of income generation, consumption, saving, and portfolio allocation. Sojourner immigrants, those who plan to return to their home countries, generally have an earning goal to achieve in a short time frame. They will take any jobs, minimize consumption, send remittances, invest in businesses in their home countries, and build assets in their home countries. Immigrants who plan to stay permanently and who place a cultural value on education will save for and spend on education, make investments in the United States, and accumulate wealth in the United States.

Race-Ethnicity and Nativity

Whereas newcomers to America immediately face the racial-ethnic hierarchy in its social order, nativity could emerge to be an additional social stratification factor as the immigrant population reaches a substantial level. The large presence of immigrants has been increasingly and widely felt since the late 1980s. For three reasons, however, nativity does not claim the same importance as race-ethnicity.

First, the institutional basis of racial-ethnic stratification has deep historical roots from slavery, through Jim Crow, to contemporary racial discrimination. Thus the institutional rules, laws, and practices have potent effects on social stratification. By contrast, America has been a nation of immigrants. Most Americans can trace their roots in one or more foreign countries. Color lines are thus sharper than the nativity line.

Second, the institutional rules distinguish between natives and immigrants concern rights and responsibilities derived from citizenship—for example, citizenship by birth versus citizenship by naturalization, citizen status versus alien status, and legal status versus undocumented status. Except for one limitation—that naturalized citizens are not eligible to run for president, there is virtually no difference between native-born citizens and naturalized citizens. The restrictions on legal aliens are substantial because legal aliens have no voting rights and cannot run for government and legislative offices. The 1996 welfare reform law also denies certain welfare programs to legal immigrants. However, legal aliens are protected by the same labor market laws, such as equal opportunities for employment, fair pay, working conditions, minimum wage, unemployment insurance, medical insurance, social security, retirement accounts, and other welfare state claims. Thus, for most economic immigrants, the restrictions on naturalized citizens are not major barriers to achieving economic goals. Undocumented immigrants, however, face serious institutional barriers because they are not protected by any labor laws and denied any welfare claims, having the potential of making a new bottom stratum of the society. As the proportion of undocumented immigrants has reached a third of the immigrant population and continues to grow, the barriers facing undocumented immigrants can be a significant source of stratification. Nevertheless, the demand for low-cost immigrant labor is at an all-time high and undocumented immigrants find jobs easily, a fundamental difference from the severe joblessness among African Americans.

Third, the long-established American stratification system does not spare newcomers. The pre-1965 racial-ethnic quota system itself manifested the racial-ethnic hierarchy. Although the ethnic quota system was abolished in 1965, immigrants face the racial-ethnic hierarchy when they arrive in the United States. They are placed in the stratum of their race-ethnicity in all economic and social encounters. This inescapable allocation of social position is powerful and dominates the impact of an alien or undocumented status. Racial and ethnic stratification tends to be long-lasting once established and institutionalized. This gives rise to the rationale behind why race-ethnicity is a primary driving force of social stratification of wealth and nativity a secondary one.

Within racial-ethnic groups nativity differentiates group members. The direction of differentiation, however, can differ depending on which mechanism dominates. On the one hand, immigrant status can be inferior given the restricted rights for legal immigrants and the barriers facing undocumented immigrants. On the other, immigrant status can be superior given its freedom from historical racial burden. Color lines divide people by race-ethnicity that has long historical roots specific for American society. The consequences of historical racialized state policies have been transmitted to succeeding generations via intergenerational mechanisms (Oliver and Shapiro 1995) among natives but not immigrants. Wealth is an intergenerational phenomenon and depends heavily on historical roots (Oliver and Shapiro 1995; Conley 1999; Spilerman 2000). Intergenerational transfers in the forms of inheritance, investment in children's human capital, and growing up in secure financial environment do not necessarily apply to immigrants. Immigrants are exposed to American contemporary policies only upon arrival. Like their native counterparts, the post–1965 legal immigrants live under the civil rights laws such as equal education and employment opportunities, color-blind lending market and housing market, and the contemporary welfare state. Unlike their native counterparts, they are not burdened by the intergenerational consequences of historical slavery, Jim Crow laws, redlining, and overt personal and institutional discrimination (Waters 1999). Thus there may be room for immigrant minorities to get ahead easier than native minorities because of the freedom of no historical legacies.

Mechanisms by which nativity differentiates members within racial-ethnic groups can be complicated. Society, for example, may blame non-white immigrants for economic problems, such as recession, or for the low incomes of native unskilled workers (Smith and Edmonston 1997; Borjas 1999). Non-English-speaking immigrants may be subject to further discrimination because of their accents or their cultural or religious practices (Portes and Rumbaut 1996). On the other hand, white employers may prefer to hire foreign-born over native-born minority workers because they think the former have a stronger work ethic and are less likely to make race relations a work issue (Waters 1999).

Immigrant settlement patterns provide another example for the perplexing effects of nativity for members within racial-ethnic groups. Although spatial segregation caused by redlining in housing and lending discrimination contributes to the lower level of wealth among blacks, spatial autonomy (voluntary segregation) may benefit immigrants, particularly in earlier stages of adaptation (Bean, Van Hook, and Fossett 1999). Given their inadequate English skills and limited knowledge of the mainstream labor market when they arrive, immigrants may choose to live in ethnic enclaves. These offer employment opportunities that do not require English proficiency or familiarity with the American labor market. Spatial autonomy can harm immigrants in the long run, however, as the new assimilation theory suggests. A long history of working within immigrant communities may evolve into a barrier that blocks immigrants from developing the kind of human capital the mainstream labor market demands, which can in turn eventually prevent them from entering the market. Consequently, these immigrants lack access to the greater rewards the market offers, including higher wages, greater job protection, union membership, comprehensive health insurance, and pensions. Although spatial segregation has a detrimental effect on racial-ethnic minorities among the native-born, the total effect on immigrants depends on how long they have lived in the United States. Those who do not become long-term residents generally benefit from spatial segregation, but for those who remain it becomes a liability.

Human Capital Effects

Because wealth accumulation for many depends primarily on earned income, immigrants face greater challenges than natives. Some 20 percent have fewer than nine years of schooling, versus about 5 percent of their native counterparts. The large proportion of low-educated immigrants is a significant source of lower wealth levels for immigrants than for natives.

In addition, horizontal differentiation in educational fields has both a positive and negative impact on immigrants. On one hand, the employment-based preference system, which addresses the U.S. shortage of skilled workers, allows skilled foreign workers to enter the United States and work in the U.S. labor market, which has increasingly recruited such individuals, especially those from India, China, and the Philippines. On the other hand, educated immigrants do not necessarily see uniform returns on their home-obtained education. The home country's economic development, historical, and contemporary relationships with the United States and higher education system characteristics determine, to a large degree, how big a return immigrants get. All foreign degrees are subject to poorer degree-job matches than U.S. degrees and returns to foreign degrees vary by country (Hao 2006). In this study of Taiwanese, Indian, Philippine, and Chinese degrees, for example, Taiwanese were found to be generally the most highly regarded, followed by Indian and Philippine, with Chinese at the bottom. Although the Survey of Income and Program Participation (SIPP) does not have a large enough sample to identify those with a bachelor's degree obtained in a particular country, overall, immigrants who earn a bachelor's degree or higher in their home countries average less wealth than their U.S. educated counterparts.

Human capital determines not only the initial level of wealth but also the growth rate of wealth accumulation. Immigrants with fewer than nine years of schooling can have an even flatter income profile. Immigrants with bachelor's degrees or higher are not as competitive as natives in the labor market because the country from which an immigrant earns a degree can have a long-term effect on earning potential.

Although natives are assumed to be proficient in English if they have a high school education, variations in English proficiency, vocabulary sizes, and communication skills are huge among immigrants, even for those with high education levels. Thus, English ability is a critical component in assessing immigrants' human capital. Using a native language at home disadvantages immigrants' wealth trajectory over both the short and the long term. Age at arrival in the United States and length of residence are two determining factors of English proficiency. Children arriving before age six usually master English quickly and speak without an accent, but for those older than six it takes much longer (Cummins 1981). Adults may acquire a certain degree of English, particularly related to their jobs, more rapidly than children, but their limited vocabulary and communication styles put them at a disadvantage in the labor market and other institutions. Continuous interactions with newcomers from the home country and long-term use of the native language at home impede an immigrant's acquisition of English. Zhen Zeng and Yu Xie (2004) find that speaking a language other than English at home explains a substantial portion of the variation in earnings between immigrants and natives. A more recent finding (Hao 2006) indicates that speaking English at home facilitates better degree-job matches and higher salaries among immigrant college graduates.

Consumption Behavior

The behaviors of essential and nonessential consumption can be quite different between immigrant and native households. The government's idea of essential needs is based on a very low American living standard. Many immigrants from developing countries, however, reference their home country's standards. In immigrant communities, it's not unusual to find ten related or unrelated adults living in a two-bedroom apartment, or three unrelated men who could afford their own rent sharing a basement room. When uninsured immigrants get sick, they try to get better without medical care. Immigrants are less likely to have medical insurance provided by employers or the government, and almost half of Latino immigrants have none (U.S. Census Bureau 2004).

In addition, cultural preferences determine the value of various pleasure activities. High culture (such as Broadway shows, symphony concerts, and ballets), popular culture (such as jazz bars, baseball games, and football games), and adventurous culture (such as car races, horse races, and game hunting trips) may not be equally valued by immigrants and natives in the same social class. Dining at an ethnic restaurant and attending folk affairs and ethnic holiday activities, for example, may generate far greater enjoyment and pleasure. Such entertainment may also be less expensive.

Social network needs also place greater demands on immigrant households than native ones. Once settled in the United States, immigrant households become an anchor for chain migration. They pay for or help with migration and settlement costs for their relatives and friends. They are also the number one source of support for friends and relatives who remain in the home country. Immigrants may send extra money home for emergencies, but generally do so on a regular basis as well to help their families build economic security. Our respondents repeatedly reported that they helped their siblings and cousins come to the United States by paying the coyote and by sharing housing. They sent money home to pay medical bills for their ailing parents or siblings and helped their families make investments such as buying livestock or a small shop.

Different immigrant groups often allocate money for educational expenses differently, partly because of limited economic resources and partly because of their migration motives and culture. Latino parents with low income emphasize early work experience for their children. Many Latinos come to the United States with the short-term goal of earning money and intentions of returning home. As a result, they usually do not have a long-term plan for their children's education in the United States. Their strong family values further support pooling efforts by all family members, including children, to reach earning goals. In contrast, Asian parents, including those with low incomes, emphasize formal education, which is very important in Asian culture. Many Asian immigrants intend to stay in the United States permanently and have strong expectations of greatly improved life opportunities for their children. As a result, investment in children's education becomes the most important goal among Asian immigrant households. There are many examples of Asian parents working two or three jobs and reducing consumption to a minimum to send their children to prestigious universities. Therefore, Asian immigrant households may have low levels of day-to-day consumption but make large investments in their children's education.

Overall, migration motives and cultural values instilled prior to migration largely determine immigrants' consumption patterns. Immigrants from developing countries may have a lower essential living standard and opt for pleasure activities with lower prices, making their expenses lower than those of natives. However, immigrants may also shoulder greater expenses for maintaining social networks than natives do. There may also be greater variations in educational expenses among immigrant groups than among native groups.

Saving Motives

The motive to save for both retirement and investment is strong among immigrants, yet immigrants' motives may lead to different allocations than those natives make. Low-skilled immigrants are subject to unstable, low-paying jobs, which often do not offer contributions to retirement accounts or even pay Social Security and Medicare taxes. These immigrants are alone in shouldering the burden of old-age security despite their low, unstable earnings.

Both economic circumstances and cultural traits may shape variations in saving behaviors depending on the person's country of origin. In their study of married immigrant families using the 1980 and 1990 censuses, Christopher Carroll, Byung-Kun Rhee, and Changyong Rhee (2000) find that saving rates among immigrants differ sharply from country of origin to country of origin. For example, the saving rate is higher for those from China and India and lower for those from the Philippines and Mexico.

Other Wealth Accumulation Behaviors and Attitudes

Parental wealth is a major source of wealth gap among groups. Immigrants from developing countries are disadvantaged in intergenerational transfers. Because they are from poor countries, they are less likely to receive inheritances. Even if there is an inheritance, it is likely to be small. In addition, instead of receiving money, immigrants are expected to generate income and wealth and send it to the home country. Furthermore, because the exchange rates often make an inheritance nearly worthless, immigrants from developing countries often do not cash in an inheritance in the United States. Finally, although some countries emphasize capital immigration, in which the government grants a visa to an individual who brings a large sum to invest in the new country, the United States does not. Few immigrants from developing countries therefore enter the United States with significant wealth.[2]

Such immigrants may value traditional portfolio allocation (for example, real estate) more than modern portfolio allocation (for example, stocks). If immigrants establish retirement accounts, they may be more inclined toward bond-based than stock-based allocation. When investing to generate additional income, immigrants value and trust rents from real properties more than dividends from stocks and mutual funds. They find the fluctuations in stocks and mutual funds to be stressful.

Immigrants with enough initial wealth may strengthen their upward-spiral wealth accumulation because of both their higher propensity for risk aversion and their more prudent style of consumption. In contrast, immigrants without enough initial wealth may suffer a great deal and exhibit a flat wealth profile. Together they contribute to higher inequality among immigrants than among natives.

Immigrants often differ from natives with respect to loans and debts because of their values and experiences. The lending market is much less developed in poor countries to the extent that most purchases, large or small, are handled with cash, not loans. Borrowing money to make purchases is considered behavior of the poor or extravagant; neither extreme is respectable. Once they are in the United States, these values and experiences may continue to influence immigrants' asset building and consumption. In extreme cases, an immigrant family may purchase its U.S. home with cash. Assimilation to American ways of life, the high prices of assets such as a home, and tax credits offered for homeownership induce the majority of immigrant households to take loans, but they are likely to take smaller ones than natives do. On the other hand, low English proficiency can be a barrier for immigrants in accessing and negotiating favorable loans. Thus, immigrants may either avoid taking loans or must take loans with high interest rates.

Life Cycle Hypothesis

Nativity differences in households' wealth are derived from differences in income, consumption, saving, and portfolio allocation and evidence themselves at all stages of the family life cycle. Many people migrate to escape and avoid risks in their home countries, and their precautionary saving motives should therefore be high. However, even though they minimize their own basic needs, immigrants are likely to have less wealth initially because of low intergenerational transfers and high consumption to support chain migration. Stable marriage facilitates greater saving. Immigrants from developing countries are more likely to be married and remain married over the long term. However, many married immigrants left their spouses behind and do not have the two-income advantage of their native counterparts. Immigrants from developing countries also have high fertility. Their larger numbers of children drain family resources quickly and slow wealth accumulation. When they reach middle age, immigrants may need to cover elderly parents' medical care costs, reducing the family's accumulated wealth and further slowing wealth growth. Considering all these factors, we cannot determine a priori whether immigrant households have greater wealth than comparable native households. To clarify these nuanced differences, my empirical analysis will look into general patterns of net worth, assets, and debts as well as detailed patterns of assets and debts that emerge in various family life cycle stages.

Summary

Motivated by the potential impact of immigration on the U.S. stratification system, I have in this chapter developed an integrated model of wealth in an era of immigration. I begin with immigration theory and wealth theory, integrating them by addressing two limitations in the literature: a paradox in which the lack of inheritance is a key factor for slow upward mobility among blacks but not among all immigrants, and a theoretical deficiency in explaining immigrants' transnational, non-labor market activities. The backbone of the integrated framework is the formulation of the structure of multifactor stratification systems and the typology of wealth regime. The structure delineates three conceptual scenarios whose implications will guide empirical work to determine whether immigration contributes to the evolution of the U.S. stratification system. The typology of wealth regime fills the gap in the immigration theoretical literature, highlighting the importance of the characteristics of sending countries, the economic, financial, and political structure of sending and destination countries, and global economic, political, and social systems. It also illuminates the rationale behind immigrants' transnational investment and asset building, which help correct for bias arising from wealth holding patterns based on survey data. Just as immigration theory informs wealth theory, wealth theory informs immigration theory in the realm of assimilation. Wealth attainment is a promising candidate for studying assimilation in ways that combine multiple aspects, including socioeconomic assimilation and acculturation.

The theoretical development here also leads to a better understanding of how immigrants' and natives' wealth may differ in line with variations in economic circumstances and cultural backgrounds and migration and adaptation experiences. Intergenerational transfers, human capital levels, and consumption, saving and portfolio allocation behaviors vary between immigrants and natives. When these factors play out along the family life cycle of wealth accumulation, nativity differences in age, marriage, fertility, and other demographic characteristics also become important considerations. More important, labor, housing, and lending market discrimination and residential segregation resulting from the U.S. racial-ethnic hierarchy are major structural constraints on wealth for both immigrants and natives. Because immigrants are more likely than natives to fall into minority racial-ethnic categories, immigrants as a whole face greater structural constraints than natives as a whole. The effects of these micro and macro factors may differ by nativity and immigrant nationality because immigrants receive differential treatments from the government and the labor market and their response to these treatments may differ.

The chapters that follow will use an integrated theoretical formulation to investigate race, immigration, and wealth stratification by describing the overall pattern of nativity differences in wealth, portraying wealth components of immigrants from specific countries, testing the types of structure of the multifactor stratification of wealth, and examining the relationship between local context and wealth attainment.

= Chapter 3 =

Wealth Distribution,
An Overview

Much research has examined immigrants' employment, occupations, wage rates, income, and welfare use (Smith and Edmonston 1997; Borjas 1994; Borjas and Hilton 1996; Bean, Van Hook, and Glick 1997; Fix and Passel 1994; Jasso, Rosenzweig, and Smith 2000; Hao and Kawano 2001; Massey, Durand, and Malone 2002). However, with the exception of Lingxin Hao (2004), virtually none has been conducted on immigrant wealth, which is an important indicator of economic security and social mobility and thus a vehicle to study assimilation. Wealth indicates that someone has long-term good standing in the labor market, stable consumption habits, security in the face of economic and health uncertainty, and plans for intergenerational investments and transfers. It is also a household's protection from falling into poverty or welfare dependency. In short, studying wealth offers us a better vantage point from which to address the concerns regarding recent immigrants' economic prospects than we would have by looking merely at income and other aspects of economic well-being.

Melvin Oliver and Thomas Shapiro (1995) term wealth and income the twin pillars of American middle-class status. Income accurately reflects basic economic attainment because without a decent income most households cannot accumulate wealth. Wealth, however, encompasses economic behaviors beyond simply generating income. Wealth is derived from a combination of earning income, consuming, saving, and asset building, and thus captures a much fuller picture of economic security and mobility (or lack thereof). People need to budget income to cover a variety of needs. In addition to essential needs (such as food, clothing, and housing), people must have money to cover medical expenses, to further their and their children's education, for pleasure, and to maintain social networks by providing for needy relatives and friends.

People also have motives to save—to prepare for uncertainty of future income and health, for college education costs, for retirement, and to leave inheritances for their children. When people have savings, they then need to make decisions about strategically distributing their assets (portfolio allocation). Portfolio allocations are determined by savings needs, rates of return, and transaction costs.

Typically, people build their assets by opening a bank account, buying a car and a home, buying bonds for their children's education, establishing a retirement account for old-age security, and investing in real estate, mutual funds, stocks and bonds to increase assets and generate additional income. Some asset building, such as purchasing a home, and real estate, may involve loans. Such loans are debts, but they are secured by the properties on which the loans were granted and are thus known as secured debts. Additional loans secured on the same basis—their home, other real estate, stocks, bonds, or retirement accounts—are also a possibility. In contrast, unsecured debts have no properties as backup in case of default. When a household's current income cannot maintain its level of consumption, it is forced to borrow from its future income and incurs unsecured debts, which include credit card balances, shop bills, or medical bills. Those who are self-employed usually have additional business assets and debts for operating their businesses. Others invest in businesses run by someone other than themselves. Household wealth, then, is the accumulated balance between all assets and all debts, denoted by total net worth.

The SIPP collects information on individuals' assets and debts, including those owned by more than one adult in the household. To determine a component of household wealth (for example, a home or stocks), I sum all household member holdings in that component. According to the specific features of the SIPP wealth data, total assets are the sum of the gross market values of nine elements: principal residence, vehicle, business, interest-generating accounts, non-interest-generating accounts, stocks and mutual funds, real estate, retirement accounts, and other assets. Total debts are the sum of mortgage on principal residence, business debts, other secured debts, and unsecured debts. Total net worth is total assets less total debts. All three measures of wealth are adjusted to 2001 dollars.[1]

This chapter examines a summary measure of wealth—total net worth, supplemented by the analysis of total assets, and total debts. It asks to what extent wealth is stratified by nativity as compared with the degree to which wealth is stratified by race-ethnicity and education. It also examines the immigrant-native differences in demographic conditions and educational levels. The detailed components of specific groups' assets and debts will be examined later.

Wealth Holding Status

One basic function of wealth is to provide economic security. Economically secure households are those with adequate positive net worth; that is, their total assets are greater than their total debts. If the household's main wage earner becomes unemployed or very sick or temporarily disabled, the household must liquidate its assets to sustain household consumption. How do we judge whether a household is economically secured? I use the notion of wealth holding status to classify households five ways. Before defining the categories, I address two questions—how to determine a household's consumption and what assets can be liquidated.

In standard economic theory, consumption is assumed constant and income fluctuations give rise to borrowing and saving, resulting in accumulated wealth. Sociologists understand that the consumption style is learned through family socialization and that economic attainment sustains that lifestyle. Therefore, under normal circumstances, a household's income provides the consumption need of its members. Short-term income fluctuations are not likely to alter the consumption because an entrenched lifestyle typically takes some time to change. When the expected income stream is interrupted, the household is likely to maintain its usual consumption level by using liquidated wealth.

Although conceptually clear, consumption is difficult to measure because it involves collecting reliable data on various expenses. Many large-scale nationally representative surveys do not include complete consumption data,[2] and the SIPP is unfortunately not an exception. There is no data in the SIPP that would roughly determine what is needed to maintain a household's consumption level. In this book, I use the term *trimmed income* to proxy consumption. Depending on the household's lifestyle, the total net worth needed to provide a safety-net cushion may differ. A general practice in household economics is to have enough financial assets to cover six months of expenses with no income. I use twelve months rather than six because a year window gives a more realistic latitude for an unemployed individual to find an appropriate job or a sick or injured person to fully recover. I use current annual income to proxy consumption with bottom and top trimming. For households with income below 130 percent of the official poverty line, I use that amount of 130 percent because it is a more accurate reflection of the amount essential to cover household needs (13.1 percent of all households in the data presented in this volume belong to this group). This bottom-trimmed annual income prevents us from wrongly assuming that poor households have adequate wealth. For those households with annual income greater than $100,000, I consider the $100,000 as the maximum needed to sustain current consumption because this amount is about two and a half times the average household expenditure in 1998 (Lundberg and Rose 2003). Of the households in this data, 10.3 percent belong to this group. This top-trimmed annual income prevents wrongly supposing that affluent households might not have adequate wealth.

The second question regards what kinds of assets can be liquidated. There are two reasons that only financial net worth—meaning total net worth excluding home equity—is considered to serve as security.[3] First, selling the home would jeopardize the family's shelter. Second, selling involves large transaction costs, including closing costs and time. However, total net worth including home equity can also be considered to serve as security. Misuzu Otsuka (2004) finds that precautionary saving to guard against future uncertainty actually locates assets in high-return, illiquid forms such as the home. Households do use illiquid forms of wealth to compensate for large income shocks such as unemployment. Home equity loans are frequently used by middle-class families during difficult times (Warren and Tyagi 2003). A home's worth usually exceeds the cost of rent and home equity loans can help a household get through a difficult time. One might also question whether retirement accounts are liquid. Retirement accounts can, like home equity loans, be used as collaterals against which the owner can secure loans. Illiquid forms of assets such as home and IRAs should thus be considered as security for emergences. There is also a methodological appealing of using total net worth in determining wealth holding statuses. Using total net worth simplifies analysis because it includes the home's equity value. In contrast, using financial net worth requires the additional consideration of homeownership.

The five categories of wealth holding status used here expand the concept of asset poverty (Haveman and Wolff 2004; Shapiro 2004), which is defined as the total value of liquid assets less than 25 percent of the annual poverty threshold for the household. Asset poverty is an important concept that complements income-defined poverty. I first divide households by asset poverty. Those above it can maintain minimal consumption for three months, whereas those at or below cannot. Note that the above-asset-poverty households all have positive net worth and that those at or below can have positive, zero, or negative net worth.

Asset poverty, however, does not consider the heterogeneity of either the non–asset- or the asset-poor. First, for households above asset poverty, it is imperative to indicate which have enough wealth to maintain the usual consumption style for twelve months without income (sufficient) and which do not (insufficient). Similarly, asset poverty does not distinguish three kinds of households that differ by their capability of wealth accumulation. In my schema, I define five degrees of wealth holding: sufficient, insufficient, asset-poor, net-debtor, and paycheck-to-pay-check. The term asset poor applies to a set of households with some positive net worth. The term net-debtor indicates negative or zero net worth, the value of its total debts being greater than or equal to the value of its total assets, such as when a household has large consumer debts or high interest rates on loans and their collateral assets have depreciated. Finally, zero net worth may indicate that a household has no assets and no debt, a paycheck-to-paycheck status typical at the very early stages of the life cycle or reflecting either severe credit constraints or participation in means-tested welfare programs. These households not only have no asset to liquidate, they also have little credit history for future asset building—the gloomiest financial status of all.

The distribution of wealth holding status by four basic demographic characteristics is shown in figures 3.1 through 3.4 (see the corresponding table 3.1). Among racial-ethnic groups (see figures 3.1 to 3.4), the white-Asian groups are much better off than the black-Hispanic groups. The gulf between white-Asian and blacks-Hispanics can be summarized by the percentage of the group below the asset poverty line: about 20 percent for whites and Asians and more than 40 percent for blacks and Hispanics.

Significant advantages of whites over Asians and of Hispanics over blacks is revealed by the more refined five-category wealth holding status. A larger proportion of whites (55 percent) than Asians (50 percent) have sufficient wealth. The proportion with paycheck-to-paycheck status for Asians (3.1 percent) is more than double that for whites (1.4 percent). The advantage of Hispanics over blacks can also be seen in sufficient wealth (29 percent versus 25 percent) and in paycheck-to-paycheck (10 percent versus 14 percent). The gaps between whites and Asians and between Hispanics and blacks, though much smaller than the white-Asian and Hispanic-black gulf, are not trivial.

The disparities of wealth holding status by education levels are shown in figure 3.2. The sufficient percentages increase and the paycheck-to-paycheck percentages decline as education levels increase. Note that the difference between having some college education and having a high school education is relatively small. Having a bachelor's degree is a ticket to middle-class status because those with this degree are the most likely to have income and wealth, what Oliver and Shapiro term the two pillars of middle-class status.

Will these patterns by race-ethnicity and education levels reflect nativity differences, given that many contemporary immigrants are not white and have a bimodal education distribution? Figure 3.3 shows the nativity differences. Natives as a whole are better off than immigrants. For instance, natives are 10 percentage points higher in sufficient status and 3 percentage points lower in paycheck-to-paycheck status. However, these differences are much smaller than the gaps observed among racial-ethnic

Figure 3.1   Wealth Holding Status by Race-Ethnicity

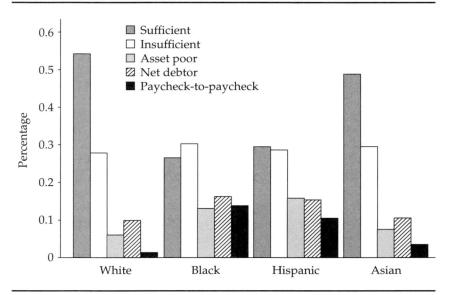

Source: Author's compilation.

Figure 3.2   Wealth Holding Status by Education Levels

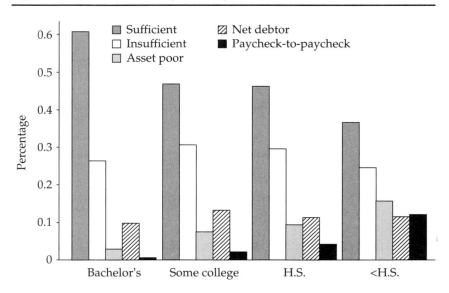

Source: Author's compilation.

Figure 3.3   Wealth Holding Status by Nativity

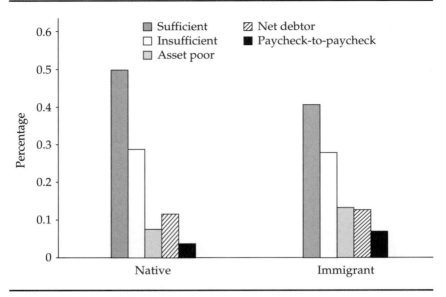

Source: Author's compilation.

Figure 3.4   Wealth Holding Status by Age Group

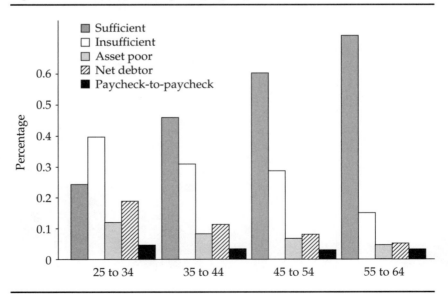

Source: Author's compilation.

Table 3.1   **Percentage Distribution of Wealth Holding Status by Nativity and Demographic Characteristics, in Percentages**

Group	Sufficient	Insufficient	Asset Poor	Net Debtor	Paycheck-to-Paycheck	% Total Households
Race-ethnicity						
White	55.2	27.2	5.9	10.2	1.4	76.3
Black	25.3	30.8	13.3	16.8	13.7	11.6
Hispanic	29.1	28.9	15.9	16.0	10.1	9.1
Asian	50.4	28.7	7.4	10.5	3.1	3.1
Education						
Bachelor's	62.6	25.0	2.6	9.2	0.5	29.1
Some college	47.0	30.4	7.2	13.4	2.1	27.8
High school	45.2	29.6	9.4	11.5	4.3	30.2
Schooling <12	33.6	24.8	16.6	12.2	12.9	12.9
Nativity						
Native	50.2	27.9	7.2	11.3	3.4	89.8
Immigrant	40.4	27.9	12.8	12.6	6.4	10.2
Age						
25–34	24.2	38.9	12.3	19.5	5.2	25.1
35–44	46.2	30.7	8.1	11.5	3.5	30.8
45–54	61.0	22.9	5.2	8.0	2.9	25.9
55–64	72.2	14.9	4.6	5.3	3.1	18.2

Source: Author's compilation.
Note: The statistics are the average for the years 1984 to 2003.
The data are based on respondents whose net worth is within the lower 99.5 percent of the original net worth distribution in the SIPP data (see appendix for details).

groups or among education groups.

Wealth is accumulated along the life cycle of a household, captured by the householder's age. Figure 3.4 shows the pattern of wealth holding status by four age groups. The life cycle pattern is clearly seen from the monotonic increase of being sufficient and decline in all other statuses.

In examining wealth holding statuses by the four basic demographic characteristics, we have learned about the stratification of wealth, which is measured qualitatively. The refined definition of wealth holding based on the asset poverty concept helps reveal the stratification by race-ethnicity, education, nativity, and age. It is essential to distinguish the best off (sufficient) and worst off (paycheck-to-paycheck) among various demographic groups. The stratification by race-ethnicity, education levels, and age groups are much wider than that by nativity. These qualitative measures, however, cannot reflect the levels and variations of wealth among demographic groups. We now turn to these issues.

Distribution of Net Worth, Assets, and Debts

Net worth, assets, and debts all vary tremendously across households. The entire household net worth distribution spreads from a large negative to a large positive value. It would be much more informative to know the entire percentile distribution for each group in addition to the nativity gap at the median or the mean so that the group gap at any position of the distribution could be determined. For example, if the tenth percentile for immigrants is lower than that for natives, we know that even if their median is similar immigrants are more disadvantaged. We focus here on the distributional differences in net worth, assets and debts by race-ethnicity and by nativity.

The distribution of net worth as a whole is remarkably uneven. Roughly speaking, the households in the top first percentile own about one-third of the household total net worth, those in the ninetieth to ninety-ninth percentile own another third, and those below the ninetieth percentile own the last third (Kennickell 2003). The wealth distribution is much wider than the income distribution and spreads more at the top than at the bottom. To reflect this highly uneven distribution and to promote a better understanding of wealth, we focus on eight different percentiles to represent the entire distribution: the fifth, tenth, twenty-fifth, fiftieth, seventy-fifth, ninetieth, ninety-fifth, and ninety-ninth percentiles.

Figure 3.5 depicts the percentile distribution of net worth by four basic demographic characteristics: race-ethnicity, education levels, nativity, and age groups. The group-specific net worth percentile distribution is a curve of the ninety-nine percentiles of net worth corresponding to the proportion of population, p, for each group. Because net worth is highly right skewed, meaning that the spread of the lower half is much narrower than that of the upper half, we see that the curve is relatively flat up to about $p = .7$ and then takes off. The group distance at $p = .5$, the median difference, is moderate; whereas that at $p = .1$ is minuscule and that at $p = .95$ is huge.

Figure 3.5 shows that the percentile distributions for whites and Asians are very similar and those for blacks and Hispanics are also similar, but the distance between these two sets of groups are vast. The white-Asian side and the black-Hispanic side start to depart at $p = .3$ and become quite far apart by $p = .8$, suggesting that the total variation does not come from the group discrepancies of the bottom 30 percent of the distribution, but instead primarily from the top 20 percent. Figure 3.6 is for the distribution by education levels. The middle two—high school graduation and some college—have a similar percentile distribution.

Figure 3.5   Net Worth Percentile Distribution by Race-Ethnicity

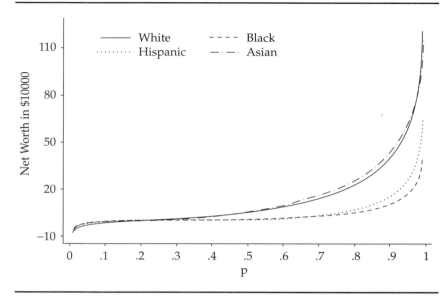

Source: Author's compilation.

Figure 3.6   Net Worth Percentile Distribution by Education Levels

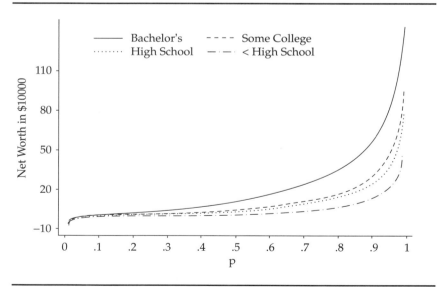

Source: Author's compilation.

Figure 3.7   Net Worth Percentile Distribution by Nativity

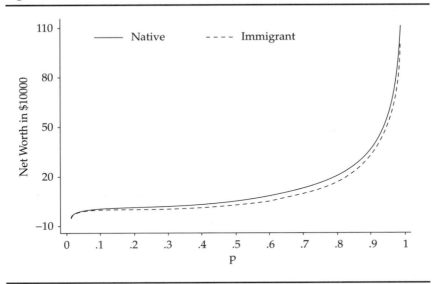

Source: Author's compilation.

Figure 3.8   Net Worth Percentile Distribution by Age Group

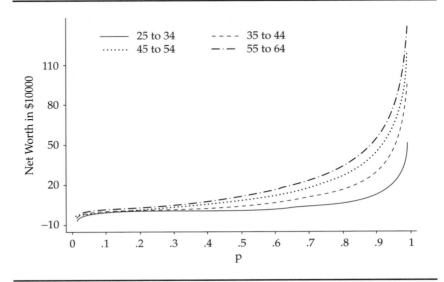

Source: Author's compilation.

The distances between the curve for high school dropout and the curve for bachelor's degree beyond $p = .8$ is wider than the largest racial gap. Figure 3.7 shows the net worth percentile distribution by nativity. The identifiable group discrepancies lie in the middle portion of the distribution from $p = .4$ to $p = .95$, with immigrants faring worse than natives. Thus, little nativity variation is found, particularly for the very poor and the very wealthy. Finally, the age patterns of net worth percentage distribution show relatively equal distances between the successive ten-year age groups, which is the pattern predicted by the life cycle hypothesis.

The graphic view of the percentile distribution conveys a clear idea about the direction and degree of wealth stratification. Detailed statistics are presented in tables 3.2 and 3.3, which show eight percentiles of net worth, total assets, and total debts by race-ethnicity and by nativity. For instance, the median net worth (fiftieth percentile) is $66,501 for white, $60,335 for Asian, $6,013 for black, and $7,510 for Hispanic (see the top panel of table 3.2). At the lower end, the fifth percentile is −$8,023 for white, −$11,130 for Asian, −$11,111 for black, and −$10,982 for Hispanic. At the upper end of the distribution, the ninety-fifth percentile is $604,642 for white, $663,984 for Asian, $168,004 for black, and $258,840 for Hispanic. These gaps provide richer information than merely mean or median differences. In addition, percentile distributions provide information on the relative within-group distribution. The ninety-fifth-to-median ratio is almost 10:1 for whites, more than 10:1 for Asian, less than 3:1 for blacks, and more than 3:1 for Hispanics. That Asians have a wider distribution than whites and that Hispanics have a wider distribution than blacks may reflect the heterogeneity among immigrant nationality groups, large proportions of Asian and Hispanic are immigrants (over 70 percent and 50 percent, respectively). Table 3.2 also shows the percentiles of assets and debts by race-ethnicity. Although the scale of assets is larger and the scale of debts is much smaller than that of net worth, the between and within race-ethnicity patterns remain similar.

Table 3.3 shows the eight selected percentiles by nativity. At each of these, nativity difference is small compared with the racial gaps observed previously. Indeed, the median difference seems more pronounced than the gaps at other locations of the distribution. For instance, the median net worth is $50,739 for natives and $22,267 for immigrants, leading to a ratio of more than 2:1; whereas the ninety-fifth percentile is $554,047 for natives and $499,130 for immigrants, leading to a ratio of 1:1.

Table 3.2 Selected Percentiles of Net Worth, Asset, and Debt by Race-Ethnicity (2001 Dollars)

Group	5th	10th	25th	50th	75th	90th	95th	99th
Net Worth								
Total	−8,850	−975	4,650	47,874	155,448	353,932	548,575	1,102,228
White	−8,023	−90	10,524	66,501	186,994	400,930	604,642	1,173,296
Black	−11,111	−3,347	0	6,013	43,620	105,756	168,004	414,617
Hispanic	−10,982	−3,125	0	7,510	54,869	154,830	258,840	654,248
Asian	−11,130	−360	6,462	60,335	204,161	440,580	663,984	1,238,326
Assets								
Total	81	2,080	16,932	113,279	248,552	478,310	704,901	1,327,954
White	1,441	5,515	35,086	138,481	283,469	528,943	769,144	1,396,391
Black	0	0	1,559	17,777	97,100	188,370	269,526	559,652
Hispanic	0	0	2,600	21,930	131,282	262,293	396,234	898,767
Asian	532	3,300	17,552	156,096	353,699	639,750	879,467	1,527,597
Debts								
Total	0	0	2,362	28,982	98,205	174,542	233,868	405,700
White	0	0	4,922	39,000	106,037	182,221	244,000	422,969
Black	0	0	0	6,046	44,116	107,236	153,248	261,865
Hispanic	0	0	0	8,167	64,374	142,399	193,936	322,156
Asian	0	0	2,716	49,222	153,371	246,633	320,000	517,622

Source: Author's compilation.
Note: The statistics are the average for the years 1984 to 2003.
Percentiles are based on respondents whose net worth is within the lower 99.5 percent of the original net worth distribution in the SIPP data.

Table 3.3   Selected Percentiles of Net Worth, Asset, and Debt: by Nativity (2001 Dollars)

Percentile	5th	10th	25th	50th	75th	90th	95th	99th
Net Worth								
Native	−8,772	−886	5,361	50,739	158,555	358,350	554,047	1,111,890
Immigrant	−9,416	−1,575	1,217	22,267	123,581	318,376	499,130	1,000,942
Assets								
Native	260	2,658	19,611	116,574	250,587	480,416	707,319	1,335,257
Immigrant	0	552	5,861	70,529	230,160	459,400	676,524	1,271,094
Debts								
Native	0	0	2,934	30,518	98,037	172,752	231,629	400,554
Immigrant	0	0	0	15,373	100,181	191,000	256,500	435,574

Source: Author's compilation using data from the SIPP 1984–2001 panels.
Note: The statistics are the average for the years 1984 to 2003.
Percentiles are based on respondents whose net worth is within the lower 99.5 percent of the original net worth distribution in the SIPP data.

Life Cycle Patterns

Life cycle patterns of wealth are a standard descriptive tool in wealth studies. Life cycle patterns are profiles of wealth accumulation over householders' ages. The two-decade coverage of the SIPP data used here better describes life cycle patterns than a single cross-section because many birth cohorts are followed for two decades. The following analysis addresses life cycle patterns by race-ethnicity and nativity within racial-ethnic groups, and examines birth cohorts of both immigrants and natives and arrival cohorts for immigrants.

Using the age group medians by racial ethnic groups, figure 3.9 presents a striking contrast in the life cycle pattern between white and Asian groups on the one side and black and Hispanic groups on the other. The age-wealth profile for whites grows with age, approaching $140,000. The profile for Asians is close to that but fluctuates after midlife because of the smaller sample size for older Asian Americans and immigrants.[4] In contrast, the profiles for blacks and Hispanics are flat, never exceeding $40,000 in median net worth over the twenty-five to sixty-four age range.

Figures 3.10 through 3.13 further depict nativity difference within racial-ethnic groups. Immigrants' age profile of wealth is not always lower or always higher than that of their native counterparts. The immigrant advantage among whites can be seen between ages thirty-five and sixty-five. The immigrant disadvantage among Hispanics and Asians can be seen across almost all the age ranges studied here. The age profile of black immigrants is similar to that of black natives. However, these nativity differences within racial ethnic groups are by no means comparable to the gap between whites-Asians and blacks-Hispanics. Figures 3.9 through 3.13 demonstrate that the effect of race-ethnicity is stronger than immigrant status.

The images emerging from figures 3.9 through 3.13 need to be further examined because different birth cohorts can have different life course experiences. In particular, immigrants who arrive at different ages can face very different opportunities over their years in the United States. At any point in time, the observed wealth of a household is determined by the age of the household head (age effect), the calendar year when the wealth is measured (period effect), and the birth cohort to which the householder belongs (cohort effect). Age effect captures the effect of number of years people have to accumulate wealth as they age. The period effect captures the effect of changes in property prices. Cohort effect captures the effect of historical events for a particular age cohort (for example, an economic recession could have affected the young age cohort's college enrollment). If the household is an immigrant household, its wealth is also determined by the number of years since the individual arrived and the calendar year of that arrival. Ideally, we would need to fol-

Figure 3.9   Age Profiles of Net Worth by Race-Ethnicity

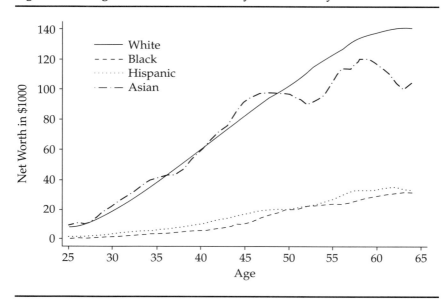

Source: Author's compilation.

Figure 3.10   Age Profiles of Net Worth, Nativity–Within White

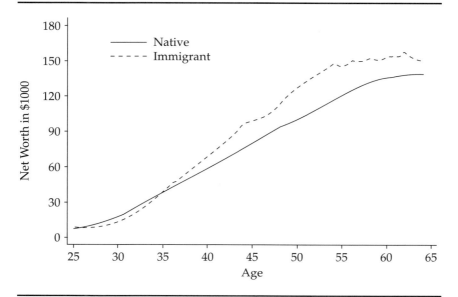

Source: Author's compilation.

Figure 3.11   Age Profiles of Net Worth, Nativity–Within Black

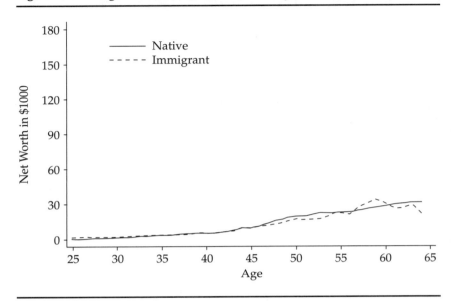

Source: Author's compilation.

Figure 3.12   Age Profiles of Net Worth, Nativity–Within Hispanic

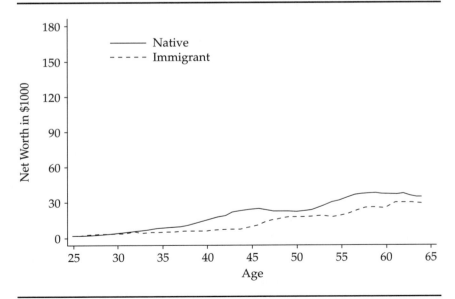

Source: Author's compilation.

Figure 3.13   Age Profiles of Net Worth, Nativity–Within Asian

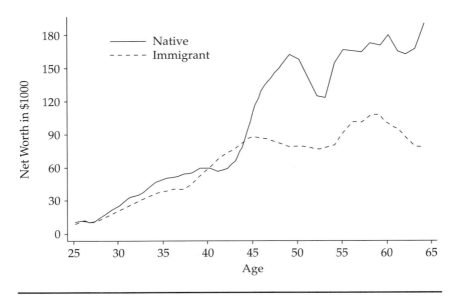

Source: Author's compilation.

low the *entire* life cycles of birth and arrival cohorts to tease out the age, period, and cohort effects. Existing data, such as censuses and surveys, do not follow households for the entire life cycle, and thus are not ideal.

Such data limitation raises a double challenge to ascertaining nativity differences in life cycle wealth patterns: a need to separate both age, period, and cohort effects for all households and the effects of length of residence and arrival cohorts for immigrant households. The first challenge comes in the perfect linear combination of age (of a householder), period (of a calendar year), and birth cohort (of a group of householders born in the same year) as age equals calendar year minus birth year, a well-known dilemma in population studies (Ryder 1964; Mason and Fienberg 1985). By the same token, the second challenge comes in the perfect linear combination of length of residence, calendar year, and arrival cohort (a group of immigrants arriving in the United States in the same year) as length of residence equals calendar year minus arrival year (Myers and Lee 1996).

When only one cross-section of data is available, researchers use a synthetic cohort, which is based on data from several age cohorts and shows hypothetical observations over time. For instance, if on average in a fixed year, twenty-five-year-olds have a net worth of $1,000, thirty-five-year-olds worth of $20,000, and forty-five-year-olds of $50,000, then we assume that the twenty-five-year-old group would have a net worth of $20,000 at age thirty-five and of $50,000 at age forty-five.

The pooled cross-sectional data of the SIPP used here cover the years from 1984 to 2003, offering a great advantage over a cross-section in ascertaining group-specific life cycle patterns. With pooled cross-sections, a birth cohort can be followed over time, relaxing the assumption of the synthetic cohort approach. Cohort analysis by pooling multiple cross-sections deals with aggregates yet retains the temporal properties of individuals (Ryder 1964). Householders born between 1920 and 1977 were twenty-five to sixty-four between the years 1984 and 2003. This age group is divided into six birth cohorts at ten-year intervals (the youngest cohort covers eight years). Wealth for each cohort was measured as the individuals aged from 1984 to 2003. For example, information is available on the cohort evolution from age twenty-five to forty-four for those born in 1959 (aged twenty-five in 1984 and forty-four in 2003).

As far as wealth is concerned, the notion of productive adult years in the United States (PAYUS) is useful. Immigrants often accumulate wealth in the United States only during their productive years there because, as mentioned, many immigrants are unlikely to bring wealth with them. However, immigrants may have fewer PAYUS than natives. Most immigrants arrive between the ages of twenty-five and forty and start to accumulate wealth only after arrival, whereas natives begin as soon as they finish school and enter the labor market, at about age twenty-five. If immigrants arrive at or before age twenty-five, their PAYUS can be considered the same as natives: from age twenty-five to the calendar year of survey. For those who arrive later, their PAYUS start from the year they arrive and end in the calendar year of survey.

Keeping PAYUS constant offers us an appropriate means to compare the life cycle pattern of wealth of natives and immigrants. Let's consider two calendar years, 1985 and 1995. Native householders aged twenty-five in 1985 (born in 1960) are thirty-five in 1995. This cohort's wealth change over the period reflects the age effect (the householder ages ten years), the birth cohort effect (societal events, such as a large flow of young immigrants, that could have affected job opportunities), and the period effect (societal events, such as a bull or bear stock market, changed between 1985 and 1995 and affected the entire population). An immigrant householder born in 1960 and arriving in 1985 would have lived in the United States for ten years in 1995. Another born the same year and arriving five years later would have lived in the United States only five years in 1995. This cohort's wealth change reflects not only the age effect, the birth cohort effect, and the period effect, but also the

PAYUS effect. A valid comparison between immigrants and natives must therefore keep constant not only birth and arrival cohort but also PAYUS.

Among those immigrants who arrived in the United States before the age of twenty-five, the question is whether having U.S. childhood experience increases their accumulation of wealth. Conventional assimilation theory suggests that a convergence of immigrants to native white mainstream takes two or more generations (Gordon 1964). The new theory suggests that assimilation is achieved if immigrants are integrated in the mainstream in which ethnicity does not play a significant role in life chances (Alba and Nee 2003). These theories imply that U.S. childhood experience increases wealth accumulation and call attention to the length of that experience. Alternatively, segmented assimilation theory (Portes and Zhou 1993) theorizes downward assimilation of immigrant children who are not white and live near or in inner-city neighborhoods. This theory implies that immigrant children of certain groups—West Indians, for example—fare worse than their first generation (Waters 1999), but that those of other groups are on the path to assimilation. Thus, among immigrants with the same PAYUS as natives, length of U.S. childhood experience could yields variations in wealth accumulation.

In sum, my method follows the evolution of birth and arrival cohorts and keeps PAYUS constant in comparing immigrants' wealth and natives' wealth. I present four incremental sets of graphs: synthetic cohorts using one cross section, synthetic cohorts using eighteen cross-sections, birth cohort evolution over two decades, and both birth and arrival cohort evolution controlling for PAYUS over two decades. Age profiles of net worth are depicted by the median net worth of households at different ages within birth-arrival cohorts. Reliable statistics require cell sizes greater than thirty households for each group at each age.

Synthetic Cohort with One Cross-Section

The native and immigrant age profiles of net worth, using the 1996 data, are presented in figure 3.14 along with three immigrant arrival cohorts. The immigrant profile starts just slightly lower than the native profile at age twenty-five, remains rather flat until age thirty-seven, and then takes off to a rate just below that of natives. From thirty-seven to sixty-four, the rate of wealth accumulation is just slightly lower for immigrants than for natives. The synthetic cohort approach suggests that the first twelve years of the life cycle mark a period of barriers that hinder immigrants, but that the period after that shows a growth rate similar to that of natives.

However, the three profiles for the arrival cohorts in figure 3.14 raise a concern. Because immigrants arrived in different years when they were relatively young, we observe a different age segment for each of the three

Figure 3.14   Age Profile of Net Worth, Synthetic Cohorts in 1996

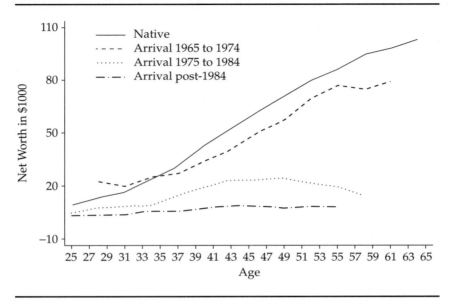

Source: Author's compilation.

arrival cohorts in 1996: later ages for the earlier and earlier ages for the later arrival cohort. Relative to natives' wealth profile, the 1965 to 1974 cohort is moderately worse off, the 1975 to 1984 cohort's wealth profile started to rise at age thirty-seven but fell at age forty-seven, and the post-1984 cohort's wealth profile is notably low and flat. That these four profiles do not connect challenges the synthetic cohort assumption that later cohorts would follow the track of earlier cohorts.

Synthetic Cohort with Pooled Cross-Sections

The major advantage of a synthetic cohort with pooled cross-sections over a synthetic cohort with one cross-section is the allowance for fuller observations of immigrant arrival cohorts (see the complete profiles for the four arrival cohorts in figure 3.15). Figure 3.15 uses eighteen cross-sections from the years from 1984 to 2003. We see that at age thirty-nine, the 1965 to 1974 arrival cohort falls below the native profile. The 1975 to 1984 cohort members' wealth stops growing after age forty-five, and the post-1984 cohort's wealth profile remains flat at all ages. Other than data improvements, the patterns shown in figure 3.15 resemble those in figure

Figure 3.15   Age Profile of Net Worth, Synthetic Cohorts 1984 to 2003

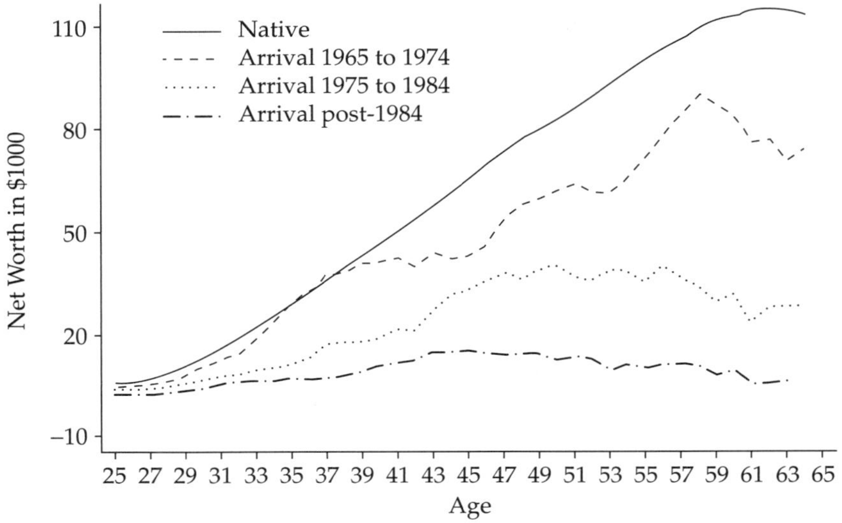

Source: Author's compilation.

3.14 and may be contaminated by the unsubstantiated assumptions of synthetic cohort approach.

Cohort Evolution

A cohort evolution approach takes advantage of the eighteen cross-sections to depict birth cohort evolution along the life cycle and to check the birth cohort assumption of the synthetic cohort approach. Here, that later birth cohorts will trace the same trajectory of earlier birth cohorts is no long assumed. Instead, separate profiles are drawn for natives and immigrants for each of the six cohorts. Because the data cover only two decades but the age range is forty years, we can follow birth cohort evolution for shorter periods for the oldest and youngest cohorts and longer periods for those in the middle. Figures 3.16 and 3.17 are for natives and immigrants, respectively. In figure 3.16, the six age profiles connect nicely to form an underlying native profile very similar to the one in figure 3.15. This suggests that the synthetic cohort assumption holds for natives. The synthetic cohort approach may therefore be appropriate for the native population. Figure 3.17, however, does not suggest the same

Figure 3.16   Age Profile of Net Worth, Evolution of Native Birth Cohorts, 1984 to 2003

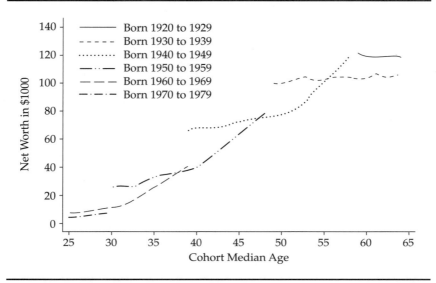

Source: Author's compilation.

Figure 3.17   Age Profile of Net Worth, Evolution of Immigrant Birth Cohorts, 1984 to 2003

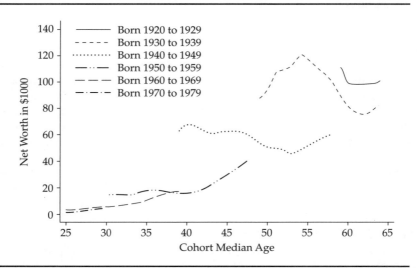

Source: Author's compilation.

for immigrants. Later cohorts do not seem to follow the track of their earlier counterparts. The two younger cohorts do line up nicely, suggesting
that the synthetic cohort approach may work for them. Immigrants born
between 1940 and 1979, who may belong to any of the four arrival cohorts, accumulate wealth from ages twenty-five to forty-seven. Comparing the native-immigrant age profiles for those born from 1950 to 1979,
we see that the wealth growth rate is higher for natives than for immigrants. By age forty-seven, natives' median net worth is about $70,000,
whereas immigrants' is about $60,000. This nativity gap is attributable to
PAYUS.

Cohort Evolution with Constant PAYUS

To better understand the nativity differences in the life cycle pattern, I
further isolate the effect of PAYUS. The next set of figures (3.18 to 3.20) focuses on birth cohorts of immigrants who have the same PAYUS as their
native-born counterparts. Effectively, this means that the comparison is
restricted to those immigrants who arrived in the United States by the
age of twenty-five. Within this group, however, individuals may differ
because some arrive in early childhood and others in late adolescence.
Such differences may have implications for wealth accumulation given
variations in U.S. childhood experience. The eighteen cross-sections offer
enough data for three sets of comparisons of wealth profiles among the
native-born and immigrants who came to the United States at or before
twenty-five, both groups thus having the same PAYUS: within the 1950
to 1959 birth cohort (figure 3.18), within the 1960 to 1969 birth cohort (figure 3.19), and within the 1970 to 1979 birth cohort (figure 3.20).

Figure 3.18 covers the thirty to forty-eight age range from within the
1950 to 1959 birth cohort with the PAYUS held constant. The native profile shows that after age thirty-eight the native born have a clear advantage. The 1975 to 1984 arrival cohort has a lower profile; the growth pattern, however, is similar to that of the native. Figure 3.19 compares
profiles from age twenty-five to thirty-nine for natives and three arrival
cohorts who were born from 1960 to 1969 while keeping PAYUS constant. Over the ages of thirty to thirty-nine, which overlaps with the early
section in figure 3.18, we can see a similar pattern for the native born and
the 1965 to 1975 and the 1975 to 1984 arrival cohorts, with a worse pattern for the post-1984 cohort. In the twenty-five to thirty age range, we
see that the most recent cohort has a lower start, which prevents them
from taking off before the age of thirty-nine, the oldest age in the data observed. Figure 3.20 shows the comparisons among the native and immigrant groups within the 1970 to 1977 birth cohort, keeping their PAYUS
constant. A short age range is observed because they are younger at the
end of the observation period. Over these six years, all immigrants start

Figure 3.18   Age Profile of Net Worth, Evolution of 1950 to 1959 Birth Cohort, 1984 to 2003

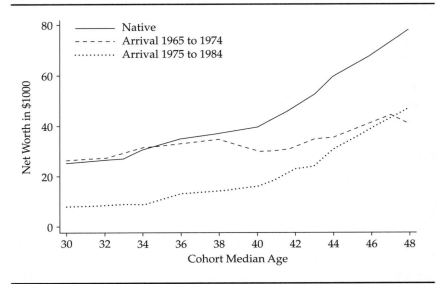

Source: Author's compilation.

Figure 3.19   Age Profile of Net Worth, Evolution of 1960 to 1969 Birth Cohort, 1984 to 2003

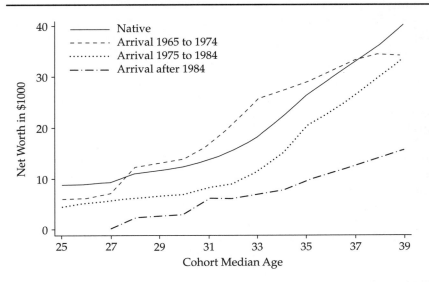

Source: Author's compilation.

Figure 3.20   Age Profile of Net Worth, Evolution of 1970 to 1979 Birth Cohort, 1984 to 2003

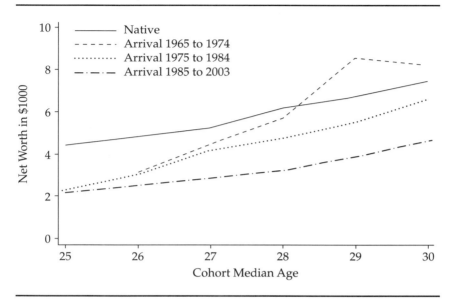

Source: Author's compilation.

at a lower point than the native born, but the two earlier arrival cohorts speed up and the most recent cohort fails to do so. Taken together, the three birth cohorts depicted in figures 3.18 through 3.20, both native and immigrant, appear to fare successively worse. For instance, at age thirty, the median net worth is lower for those born later than for those born earlier. This may reflect a period effect.

The major lesson we have learned from these examinations is that portraying life cycle patterns of wealth for immigrants requires extreme care. Although the synthetic cohort approach is appropriate for natives, it yields misleading results for immigrants. The method here, following cohort evolution and keeping PAYUS constant, provides more appropriate comparisons than the traditional synthetic cohort or cohort evolution approaches, which do not consider PAYUS.

Conclusion

The national picture of wealth disparity, then, can be described both *qualitatively* and *quantitatively*. The qualitative measure includes five categories of wealth holding status—sufficient, insufficient, and asset-poor among those with positive net worth, and net debtor and paycheck-to-paycheck among those with zero or negative net worth. The quantitative measures include both the full distribution of net worth, assets, and debts, and age profiles of net worth.

The analysis of wealth holding status shows the overwhelming importance of race-ethnicity, education, and life cycle over nativity. Nativity gaps, however, are manifested by specific demographic conditions (life cycle stages, types of households, and number of children) and educational levels. In addition, the within-immigrant variations are large, particularly when naturalization is considered.

The distributions of net worth, assets, and debts are highly dispersed and skewed. The distributional analysis seeks to identify in which region of the distribution racial-ethnic group gap manifests, and finds that it concentrates overwhelmingly in the upper tail. In contrast, little distributional difference is found between natives and immigrants.

The analysis of life cycle patterns of net worth, assets, and debts take advantage of multiple cross-sections of data from 1984 to 2003. Immigrants arrive in the United States at different ages and accumulate wealth during their productive adult years in the United States. The analysis reveals accurate nativity gaps in life cycle patterns of wealth by following the same birth-arrival cohort over time and keeping productive adult years constant. A successive decline in net worth is found across immigrant arrival cohorts.

Do the nativity gaps in wealth holding status, wealth distribution, and life cycle patterns reflect different racial and educational differences in consumption, saving, and asset building behavior between immigrants and natives? We must keep in mind that immigrants from different countries are very different because of their migration motivations and cultural roots. In addition, wealth components such as homeownership, mortgage, and retirement accounts reveal behavioral differences more clearly than total net worth, assets, and debts. To answer the question, I therefore resort to comparisons of wealth components among immigrant groups from different countries of origin. The next three chapters address these comparisons.

= Chapter 4 =

Assets and Debts Among Latino Immigrants

T his chapter describes and analyzes the wealth of Latino immigrants from Spanish-speaking countries in Latin America and the Caribbean. Latino immigrants make up the majority of the U.S. foreign-born population and remain the fastest-growing group. In 2000, 29.5 percent of the foreign born were from Mexico and another 22.2 percent from other Latin American countries (U.S. Census Bureau 2003). Most low-skilled and unauthorized immigrants to the United States are Latino and usually work in agricultural work, manual labor, and service work. Seasonal agricultural workers move back and forth from Texas to Minnesota, plowing, planting, weeding, and harvesting (Hart 1999), often working under a piecework payment system that requires both long hours of work and the pooled efforts of family members, including school-age children. After paying for necessities, most families have little left for savings. Seasonal farm workers seldom have medical insurance or social security. Service workers, on the other hand, are often more successful. Recent news stories have described the success of immigrants who crossed the border into cities such as Las Vegas and Phoenix and, after taking on a series of jobs with progressively higher status, reached the middle class. Some start as unauthorized sweatshop workers and move on through culinary training to become qualified service personnel in upscale restaurants, acquiring along the way the emblems of middle-class life—a house, a car or two, health insurance, and a retirement plan (Steven Greenhouse, "Crossing the Border into the Middle Class," New York Times, June 3, 2004).

Despite this anecdotal evidence, we know relatively little about how most Latino immigrants fare in achieving economic security. Do these experiences differ by origin countries? How do they compare with those of native whites and Latino Americans? Do demographic characteristics such as age, marriage, number of children, and education levels determine economic security to the same degree for Latino immigrants as for native whites and native-born Latinos? How do homeownership, mortgage obtainment, bank and retirement account establishment, and consumer indebtedness among various Latino immigrants differ? This chapter answers these questions by investigating key components of assets and liabilities—homeownership, retirement accounts, interest-generating bank accounts, non-interest-bearing checking accounts, mortgages and other secured debts, consumer debt, and business ownership. The SIPP provides detailed information about country of origin more in the 1996 and 2001 panels than in earlier ones, allowing us to identify more countries of origin. Here I use seven cross-sections of the SIPP (four from the 1996 panel and three from the 2001 panel) to identify Latino immigrant groups each with a sample size of at least 175 households. Countries examined include Colombia, El Salvador, Guatemala, Mexico, Cuba, and the Dominican Republic.

Country of Origin and Demographic Differences

The demographic characteristics of Latino immigrant groups can be very different, depending on the historical and contemporary origin-destination binational structure and the economic, educational, social and cultural conditions of the origin country. Figure 4.1 (see details in table 4.1) describes the age, marital status, number of children, education level, and poverty rate of immigrants from the six Latin American countries, using native whites and native Latinos as two bases for comparison. Among native white householders, about 50 percent are twenty-five to forty-five and another 50 percent are forty-five to sixty-four, 63 percent are married, almost 50 percent are childless, about 10 percent have three or more children, 6 percent have less than a high school education, and 9 percent live below 130 percent of the official poverty line. Among Latino Americans, almost 65 percent are twenty-five to forty-four, about 55 percent are married, 35 percent are childless, 20 percent have three or more children, 22 percent have less than a high school education, and 19 percent live below 130 percent of the official poverty line. The demographic characteristics of immigrants from each of the six countries will be compared with one another and with native whites and Latino Americans after a brief review of each country's background and immigration history.

Colombia

Colombia's native language is Spanish and the predominant religion (more than 90 percent of the population) is Roman Catholic. Colombia is the third most populous country in Latin America after Brazil and Mexico. The per capita gross domestic product (GDP) was $2,035 (in 2000

Figure 4.1   Demographics by Latino Group

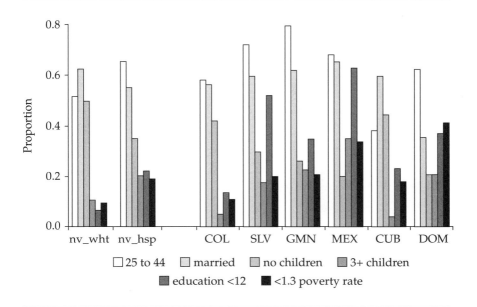

Source: Author's compilation.

constant U.S. dollars) in 2003 (World Bank 2005), placing the country in the middle to lower tier of Latin America's economic development. Recent and rapid urbanization has led to an urban population of about 75 percent of the population. Although the government mandates nine years of education, only five years are offered in rural areas (World Bank 2005). A former Spanish colony, Colombia gained its independence in 1819 (Sturges-Vera 1990). Recent decades have witnessed civil wars, insurgent movements, and guerrilla warfare. No single explanation fully addresses the deep roots of the troubles Colombia sees today, but among the contributing factors are social inequities, lack of state presence in rural areas, the expansion of illicit drug cultivation, and the violence that accompanies it.

Figure 4.1 shows that almost 60 percent of Colombian immigrant households are younger, a higher percentage than native whites but a lower one than Latino Americans, indicating that Colombians have relatively slow chain migration. The marriage rate for Colombians is lower than for native whites and higher than for Latino Americans. This may be in part due to the relatively younger age structure. The proportion having three or more children (5 percent) is also surprisingly low, even

Table 4.1 Demographic and Socioeconomic Differences by Latino Group

Group	Age (25 to 44)	Married	No Children	3 + Children	Education < 12	Poverty[a]	Sample Size
Native White	0.518	0.626	0.498	0.104	0.064	0.091	98,010
Latino American	0.655	0.552	0.352	0.204	0.222	0.190	5,179
Colombian	0.580	0.561	0.419	0.048	0.136	0.109	209
Salvadoran	0.721	0.594	0.298	0.177	0.522	0.201	422
Guatemalan	0.792	0.617	0.261	0.225	0.350	0.209	177
Mexican	0.681	0.654	0.200	0.352	0.629	0.339	4,362
Cuban	0.384	0.597	0.444	0.041	0.232	0.181	471
Dominican	0.621	0.356	0.211	0.210	0.372	0.413	317

Source: Author's compilation.
[a] Smaller than 130 percent of the official poverty line.

lower than native whites. Colombian immigrants are the best educated among the six Latino immigrant groups and better educated than native-born Latinos. About 14 percent have no high school education. Similarly, the Colombian immigrant poverty rate is the lowest among the six Latino immigrant groups and lower than that of native-born Latinos.

El Salvador

El Salvador, though a much smaller country, is similar in many ways to Colombia. It too is a former Spanish colony; it too gained independence in the early nineteenth century; its people also speak Spanish and practice Catholicism; and it too has nine years of compulsory education. The per capita GDP was $2,105 in 2003 (World Bank 2005). The impact of the 1979 to 1990 civil war on the economy was devastating. The post-war economy was a mix of boom and recession, complicated by severe damage from hurricanes. Although fleeing from civil wars and deteriorating economic conditions, Salvadorans were denied refugee status in the United States and entered mostly without documents (Rumbaut 1994). The Immigration Act of 1990 granted temporary protected status to many Salvadorans, facilitating chain migration, legal and illegal. As a result, Salvadoran immigrants are much younger than many of their counterparts—72 percent are twenty-five to forty-four (see figure 4.1). The marriage rate, however, is high—59 percent, almost the same as that of native whites. This, together with the large percentage of households with children, particularly three or more, indicates a cultural and religious value on the family. Educational attainment is low, more than 50 percent of heads of households do not have a high school education. This may mean simply that the less educated emigrate to the United States more often than their more highly educated counterparts. As a result, more than 20 percent of Salvadoran immigrant households live below 130 percent of the official poverty line.

Guatemala

Guatemala is quite different from both Colombia and El Salvador. Most of its population is rural and the per capita GDP is low ($1,718 in 2003). Although the predominant religion is Roman Catholic, 40 percent are Protestant and some are traditional Mayan (World Bank 2005). The official language is Spanish, but it is not universally spoken among the indigenous population. Guatemala gained its independence from Spain in 1821 and for the next 150 years, until the mid-1980s, it passed through a series of dictatorships, insurgencies, coups, and stretches of military rule with only occasional periods of representative government. Since then, the process of building a civil government has been tumultuous. The bleak economic and political situations have driven many Guatemalans to emigrate to the United States. Guatemalans, like Salvadorans, have been defined as economic immigrants and denied refugee status. Most have entered the United States without documents (Rumbaut 1994). Figure 4.1 shows that Guatemalan immigrants are the youngest of all—79 percent are aged twenty-five to forty-four. Their marriage and fertility rates are higher than those of Salvadorans, as are their educational levels, despite only six years of compulsory education in Guatemala. This implies that Guatemalans at various locations of the socioeconomic spectrum participate in emigration to the United States. Higher education, however, does not translate to lower poverty rate for Guatemalans as for Salvadorans.

Mexico

Mexico is predominantly Roman Catholic and most of its residents speak Spanish. Not only is it the second most populous Latin American country, with a population of 105 million, but its development level is also one of the four highest in Latin America, with the per capita GDP at $5,876 in 2003 (World Bank 2005). Mexico proclaimed independence from Spain in 1810 and achieved it in 1821. The severe social and economic problems that erupted in the revolution of 1910 to 1920 gave rise to the Institutional Revolutionary Party (PRI), which controlled Mexico's government for seventy years. The dominance of the PRI was ended by the election in 2000 of the National Action Party (PAN) candidate Vicente Fox, whose policies included promoting more legal emigration into the United States. U.S. relations with Mexico have had a direct impact on the lives and livelihoods of millions of Americans, whether the issue is trade and economic reform, drug control, or migration. Mexico is more developed than most Latin American countries, but Mexican immigrants to the United States are generally very poor.

Migration can be traced to 1848 when Mexico surrendered the present-day states of California, Arizona, New Mexico, and Texas. Because the regional population was small, the number of Mexicans living in those states at the time of the annexation was quite low, and thus nearly all of today's Mexican Americans trace their origins to those who migrated after 1848. In the nineteenth century, post-1848 migration was circular, characterized by short round trips between Mexico and the United States. Because of railroad construction and other demand for unskilled workers, the twentieth century saw mass migration until the 1930s, followed by large waves of temporary farm workers throughout the next two decades (the Bracero era). Subsequently, from 1965 to 1985, illegal migration was circular and temporary. In 1986, when the Immigration Reform and Control Act (IRCA) was put into effect, many of these unauthorized immigrants gained legal status. Since 1986, illegal migration has been less circular and more permanent because of the tightened border patrol and higher costs of migration (Massey, Durand, and Malone 2002).

Many Mexicans emigrate from rural areas not offering job opportunities to industrialized urban centers and developing areas along the U.S.-Mexico border. Cities bordering the United States, such as Tijuana and Ciudad Juarez, have seen sharp rises in population. From these cities, many cross the border and enter the United States illegally. This migration path explains why many Mexican immigrants are not well educated. However, one must remember that Mexico has an advanced educational system requiring eleven years of schooling. The increases during the past two decades have been dramatic. By 1999, 94 percent of the population between the ages of six and fourteen were enrolled. Higher education has also developed rapidly. Mexico's educational attainment is one of the highest among developing countries (UNESCO 2002).

Despite the very long history of Mexican immigration to the United States, more than two-thirds of Mexican immigrant households are aged twenty-five to forty-four (see figure 4.1). This indicates that the speed of chain migration is high, because the speed of chain migration determines the age structure among immigrants. The marriage and fertility rates of Mexican immigrants are the highest among the six Latin American countries and much higher than native whites and native Latinos. The proportion (63 percent) without a high school education is astonishingly high, putting Mexican immigrants as the least educated among the six Latino immigrant groups. This is strong evidence that out-migration largely occurs among Mexico's least educated, even though the Mexican population as a whole is much better educated. Not surprisingly, more than 33 percent of Mexican immigrant households have income lower than 130 percent of the official poverty line.

Cuba

Cuba, a Caribbean country and one of a few remaining communist states after the cold war, has little economic development. However, in terms of education, both in the pre-revolution and post-revolution periods, Cuba had one of the highest rates in Latin America (Smith and Llorens 1998). Today, Cuba has compulsory education from six to fifteen years old (UNESCO 2005). Its native language is Spanish and its predominant religion is Roman Catholic. In 1898, Cuba became the last major Spanish colony to gain independence.

The immigration experience of Cubans is in many ways different from that of other Latino immigrant groups (Pedraza and Rumbaut 1996; Castro 2002). The 1959 revolution led to the 1959 to 1962 wave of what were known as historical exiles, Cuba's rich and highly educated elite, middle-class, and skilled workers, who sought political refuge in the United States because of its proximity. The U.S. government's open arms policy welcoming all Cuban refugees led to the enactment of the 1966 Cuban Refugee Act. The 1965 to 1973 "freedom flights" were orderly departure programs made available to more than 250,000 Cubans after Castro's Communist Party's overthrow of the Cuban government. This second wave of refugees consisted of small business owners, craftsmen, and skilled and semi-skilled workers.

Later, the Refugee Act of 1980 provided a systematic procedure for the admission of all refugees for first time in history. It allowed asylum seekers, including Cubans, to adjust their status to permanent resident. In 1980, Castro opened the port of Mariel to Cuban refugees already living in the United States who wished to help relatives to emigrate, and the U.S. government welcomed what was called the Mariel boatlift. About 150,000 political prisoners (mostly young, male, and working-class) were released by Castro and sought asylum in the United States. Cuban refugees of the Mariel boatlift included criminals and other social deviants. The fourth wave arriving after 1994 were rafters, that is, immigrants on rafts or boats, most of them illegal.

More than a million Cubans migrated to the United States from 1960 to 1990. Because rafters are a relatively small group, Cuban refugee waves have wound down since 1990, making Cuban immigrants older than most. As presented in figure 4.1, only 38 percent of Cuban immigrant households are aged twenty-five to forty-four. Because the majority of Cuban immigrants are older, more are widowed or divorced, and fewer have children living at home. Twenty-three percent of Cuban household heads have no high school education and 18 percent live in poverty.

The Dominican Republic

A former Spanish colony that gained its independence in 1844, the Dominican Republic is a middle-to-low income developing country with per capita GDP of $2,428 (in 2003) and six years of compulsory education. It is the largest Caribbean economy, has the second-largest population and land mass, and is close to the United States (World Bank 2005). The economy depends on trade and tourism, and in the 1990s, was one of the fastest growing economies in the region, but the growth was not stable. In the early 2000s, it began to shrink and in the bank crisis of May 2003 almost collapsed.

Political instability, military coup and violence, economic difficulties, and failing civil services in the 1960s propelled the first wave of Dominican immigrants to the United States Urban middle-class people, fearing political persecution, left the country to seek jobs and economic advantages in the United States. The second wave of immigrants came in the 1980s because of severe economic problems. Despite the economic boom of the 1990s, Dominicans continued to emigrate in large numbers. In the ranking of sending countries to the United States, the Dominican Republic placed fifth from 1991 to 1996 and was for New York City the top sending country in 2000.

A unique characteristic of the contemporary Dominican immigrant households is the overwhelming level of female headship. Many families dissolve in reaction to the migration experience. Despite discrimination against women and immigrants in the United States, American welfare programs supporting families with dependent children give Dominican women greater autonomy in the United States than they have in their home country. Hence we hear from Dominican women that "the Dominican Republic is a country for men, the United States is a country for women" (Pedraza and Rumbaut 1996, 286). The feminization of Dominican immigration defines the occupation niche: Dominican women who are employed tend to find work in manufacturing, such as the garment industry.

More than a million Dominicans live in the United States, and many arrived illegally. The majority live in metropolitan New York City. More than 60 percent are younger, indicating that chain migration is slow but steady. Although predominantly Roman Catholic, Dominican immigrants have a very low marriage rate—only 36 percent—but a very high fertility rate, nearly 80 percent of households having children and more than 20 percent three or more. Education levels are not particularly low: 37 percent of Dominican immigrant householders do not have a high school education, far fewer than their Mexican counterparts. Despite this, Dominicans have a high poverty rate (41 percent live below 130 percent of the official poverty line) and a high welfare rate (Hao and Kawano 2001).

Of the six Latin American countries, Mexico is the most developed and Guatemala the least, but Mexican immigrants are the least educated, significantly so. As logic might indicate, the long-term political and economic instability of the less-developed El Salvador, Guatemala, and Dominican Republic propels illegal immigration. Yet it is the relatively stable and prosperous Mexico that is the major source country of illegal immigration to the United States. The political turmoil of Cuba, El Salvador, Guatemala, and the Dominican Republic created mass political refugees, but the U.S. reception of them have been very different, with Cuban refugees favored over their Salvadoran and Guatemalan counterparts. These contrasts suggest that the relationship between the conditions of a home country and the demographic characteristics of immigrants from that country are not uniformly strong. The source country's characteristics and the historical and contemporary relationships with the United States, including American military, political, economic, and cultural interventions in sending countries, shape the self selection of immigrants and open different pathways of legal or illegal immigration.

Wealth Holding Status

A qualitative measure of wealth holding, reflecting the household's degree of economic security and its consumption needs, can classify a household according to its level of net worth. A household's net worth is its total assets less its total debts, and annual household consumption is estimated using trimmed annual household income (with 130 percent of the official poverty line as the lower limit and $100,000 as the upper limit). Such a measure includes five categories: sufficient, insufficient, asset-poor, net-debtor, and paycheck-to-paycheck. Sufficient status indicates that a household has enough net worth to sustain the household's usual consumption level for twelve months without any income. Insufficient status indicates that a household has positive net worth that can cover its usual consumption needs for fewer than twelve months without any income, but can cover expenses for at least three months at the official poverty level threshold. Asset-poor status denotes those households whose net worth is positive but could not sustain the household for three months at the poverty level. Households with sufficient, insufficient, and asset-poor statuses must have positive net worth. Net-debtor status indicates that a household's debts are greater than its assets (negative net worth) or equal to its assets (zero-balanced net worth). Finally, the paycheck-to-paycheck status describes a household that has neither assets nor debts (zero net worth). Figure 4.2 shows the distributions of the five statuses of wealth holding based on the seven cross-sections of wealth data from 1996 to 1999 and 2001 to 2003 (see the corresponding table 4.2). The percentage of households in each of the five wealth holding statuses is compared among six Latino immigrant groups. These percentages are also compared with those for native whites and Latino Americans.[1] The last column of table 4.2 presents average trimmed annual income in order to reveal masked differences.

Sufficient status implies sound economic security. A much greater percentage of native whites than native Latinos achieve this status (about 56 percent vs. about 34 percent). This gap is somewhat understated because of the different trimmed income between native whites and Latino Americans ($53,000 versus $48,000, see table 4.2). If we include insufficient status, the gap between these two groups is somewhat reduced (82 percent versus 65 percent). This comparison confirms white-Hispanic inequalities of economic security in the United States.

On the issue of economic security, Cuban immigrants stand out as the

Figure 4.2   Wealth Holding Status by Latino Group

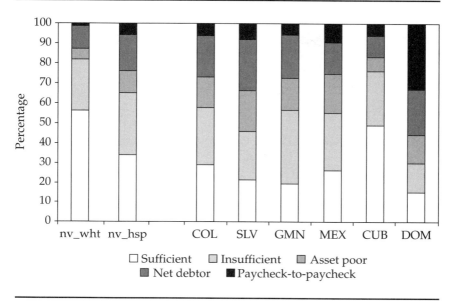

Source: Author's compilation.

top group among all Latinos, whether natives or immigrants, almost reaching parity with native whites. A hidden difference, however, lies in the relatively lower consumption levels of Cuban immigrants ($44,000) when compared to native whites ($53,000). Nonetheless, Cubans surpass native Latinos by a wide margin. It appears that nativity differences are trivial in comparison with differences by origin countries. This point is further supported by examining other Latino immigrant groups.

Economic security is hard to achieve among Latino immigrant groups other than Cubans. The least secure group is Dominican, with only 15 percent having sufficient wealth and only about 30 percent living above the asset poverty line (total net worth equals three months living expenses at the official poverty line). Colombian, Salvadoran, Guatemalan, and Mexican immigrants are better off than Dominicans but worse off than native Latinos and Cubans. These patterns suggest that when economic buffers are concerned, differences in nativity are smaller than those among Latino immigrant groups.

With an important modification of the notion that Robert Haveman and Edward Wolff first introduced (2004), asset poverty defined in this volume is the financial situation when a household owns less positive net worth than what is needed to maintain the household at the poverty

Table 4.2   Wealth Holding Status by Latino Group

	Sufficient	Insufficient	Asset Poor	Net-Debtor	Paycheck-to-Paycheck	Trimmed Annual Income[a]
Native white	0.564	0.257	0.052	0.114	0.014	$52,867
Latino American	0.341	0.310	0.110	0.181	0.058	$48,071
Colombian	0.291	0.288	0.153	0.207	0.062	$41,806
Salvadoran	0.216	0.243	0.203	0.257	0.081	$41,766
Guatemalan	0.196	0.370	0.158	0.217	0.058	$40,607
Mexican	0.263	0.288	0.195	0.158	0.095	$42,228
Cuban	0.490	0.270	0.071	0.107	0.063	$44,284
Dominican	0.152	0.147	0.141	0.228	0.331	$38,900

Source: Author's compilation.

[a] Annual income is trimmed at 130 percent of the poverty line at the bottom and $100,000 at the top.

level for more than three months without any income. Three months is often too little time to locate an alternative job, to recover from illness or injury, or to handle various emergencies—putting a significant stress on the household. Disadvantages are easily multiplied because the low level of wealth subjects such households to living in less desirable neighborhoods with fewer employment opportunities and limited access to quality medical care, thus making them vulnerable to unemployment and poor health. Therefore, despite the positive net worth, asset poverty is qualitatively different from sufficient and insufficient.

The two statuses with negative or zero net worth are net-debtor and paycheck-to-paycheck. Net debtors have no buffer for economic hardship because their asset values are less than or equal to the sum of their debts. The net-debtor condition appears worse than asset poverty. A household falls into net debt when its assets (for example, a home) depreciate or when its consumer debt is too large. The worst status is paycheck-to-paycheck. If the household head is not a single young person, living paycheck to paycheck usually indicates a poor credit history and an inability to obtain a loan, in turn predicting a gloomy financial future. We assess the three disadvantaged conditions among groups. Note that, unlike the sufficient and insufficient status, the three lower statuses are not tied to the household's consumption level.

When we combine the three disadvantaged statuses, more than 30 percent of Latino Americans live in or below asset poverty, whereas fewer than 20 percent of native whites do. Dominicans are the worst off, almost 70 percent of whom living at or below asset poverty, followed by Salvadorans, then Guatemalans and Mexicans. Cubans are the best off but still have a substantially greater proportion living at asset poverty and below (about 25 percent) than native whites.

One way to examine asset poverty alone is to condition on a similar level of zero or negative net worth, that is, the net-debtor and paycheck-to-paycheck statuses combined. Latino Americans, Colombians, Guatemalans, and Mexicans share such a condition. Among them, Latino Americans have the lowest asset poverty rate and Mexicans the highest. That is, even though these groups share a similar percentage of nonpositive net worth, Mexicans appear to have fewer resources to handle emergencies than Hispanic Americans, Colombians, and Guatemalans.

Some groups have begun asset building but run into great difficulty and sink into net debts. Salvadorans are a good example. About 26 percent of Salvadoran households have net debts, an explanation for which might be the fragmented network ties in the Salvadoran community and ethnic economy (Menjívar 2000). Guatemalans and Dominicans exhibit similar problems. On the other hand, relatively few Mexican immigrants are net-debtors, fewer than Latino Americans and whites. This, rather than being a sign of success, may reflect the fact that Mexican immigrants, many of whom are unauthorized, are less likely to incur debts greater than the value of their assets.

We learned from chapter 3 that though natives often live paycheck-to-paycheck in early life cycle stages, immigrants do so more often during later stages. The most alarming rate is that of Dominicans living paycheck-to-paycheck (33 percent), compared to 1.4 percent for native whites, 6 percent for Hispanic Americans, Colombians, Guatemalans, and Cubans, and 9.5 percent for Mexicans. Two straightforward reasons are the high rate of poverty and high rate of welfare dependency among Dominicans, described earlier. Deeper reasons, however, arise from related social forces. Unlike groups such as Cubans and Colombians, in which the majority are white, Dominicans are primarily non-white, placing them at the bottom of the American racial hierarchy. Feminization, another distinct feature of Dominican immigration, also explains their economic insecurity as immigrants. A third characteristic is that many Dominicans come to the United States illegally. Even though a substantial number have eventually obtained legal status, the illegal-to-legal transition slows down any effort toward asset building. Consequently, Dominicans carry the most severe disadvantage among the Latino immigrant population.

Overall, Latino immigrants vary in their wealth holding status. Cuban levels surpass Latino American and approach those of native whites. Cuban immigrants, the old-time refugees of both elite and ordinary background, enjoyed a positive reception, have lived in the United States for a long time, and have established a strong ethnic economy, all of which facilitate wealth attainment. Despite having relatively high education levels and few children, Colombian immigrants are in a distant second position, perhaps because the U.S. government reception is not active. Despite low education levels, unauthorized status, and many children, Mexican immigrants do better than might be expected. Well-established Mexican immigrant networks that accommodate newcomers and offer access to labor markets may explain this. Guatemalans and Salvadorans are poorer partly because they tend to be younger and have more children, less education, unauthorized status, and less developed ethnic communities. Dominicans are notably different from the other groups: despite higher education levels, they heavily rely on the welfare system, which precludes asset accumulation. More important, being black, reliant on feminized income, and illegal may contribute to their economic insecurity.

Distribution of Net Worth, Assets and Debts

An examination of the distribution of net worth, assets and debts is a quantitative supplement to the examination of wealth holding status. Be-

Figure 4.3   Percentile Distribution of Net Worth by Latino Group

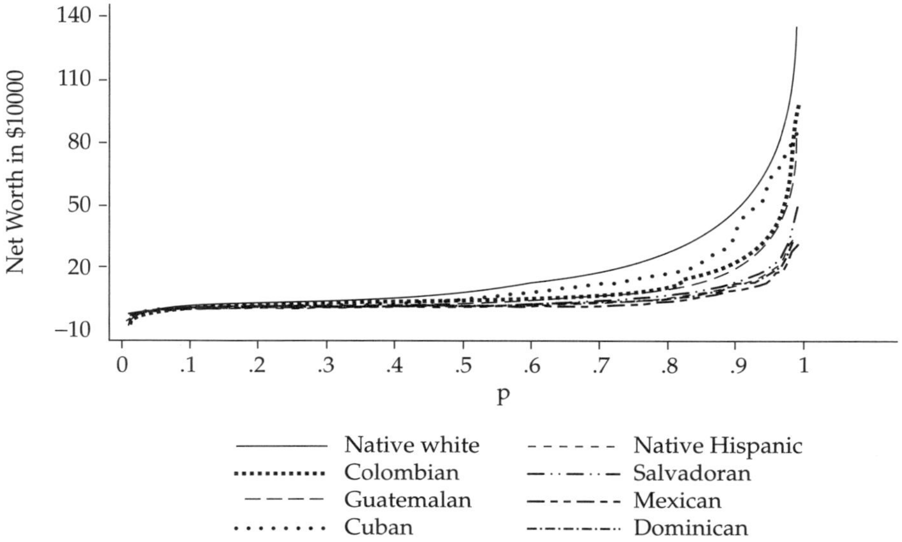

Source: Author's compilation.

cause the distributions of net worth, assets, and debts are widely spread and highly skewed, examining the distribution—rather than the mean or median—is more productive. To depict the distributions' unevenness, we first draw the percentile distribution of net worth for native whites, native Latinos, and the six Latino immigrant groups in figure 4.3. We then report three exact percentiles in the distribution—the fifth, fiftieth, and ninety-fifth percentiles—for details.

Figure 4.3 draws the 99 percentiles of net worth against the cumulative proportion of the population, for each of the groups in comparison. Because net worth is highly right-skewed, we see a relatively flat curve for the lower 70 percent of the population. The higher the position of the curve for a group, the higher the level of net worth. Native whites have the highest net worth except in the bottom 30 percent of the distribution. The Cuban curve is located not much below the native white curve, and all other group curves, including the native Latino, lie much lower than the native white. The Dominican curve is the lowest.

The left panel of table 4.3 shows the three selected percentiles of net worth. The median for native whites is about $72,000, more than four times that for Latino Americans ($16,000) and about twice that for

Table 4.3 Selected Percentiles of Net Worth, Assets, and Debts by Latino Groups

	Net worth			Assets			Debts		
	5th	50th	95th	5th	50th	95th	5th	50th	95th
Native white	−11,670	71,886	685,416	1,693	152,786	847,945	0	47,837	262,501
Latino American	−17,228	15,834	331,626	0	56,052	485,250	0	19,135	225,092
Colombian	−13,475	6,918	341,516	0	19,459	496,247	0	9,379	196,403
Salvadoran	−18,763	1,929	159,233	0	9,996	304,188	0	7,986	186,805
Guatemalan	−16,763	6,069	170,531	0	19,139	238,936	0	14,561	133,885
Mexican	−12,598	5,967	188,939	0	15,946	303,475	0	5,644	174,000
Cuban	−7,457	37,517	630,857	0	112,894	770,452	0	37,471	260,763
Dominican	−9,880	0	124,574	0	850	246,596	0	394	158,924

Source: Author's compilation.

Cubans ($38,000). All other five Latino groups have a lower median net worth than Latino Americans, with Colombians ranking first at $7,000, followed by Guatemalans and Mexicans at about $6,000, Salvadorans at $2,000, and Dominicans with zero (meaning that more than half do not have a positive net worth).

The within-group spread among Cubans is almost as wide as among native whites. At the fifth percentile, the Cuban group has a smaller negative value than that of native whites and, at the ninety-fifth percentile, also a lower net worth. The other five groups have narrower spreads than both native-born groups. These comparisons show that the variations in both median and spread of net worth are greater among Latino immigrant groups than between Latino immigrants and native whites.

The between-group discrepancies in the asset distribution are also large. The median native white has assets amounting to about $153,000, where the median Latino American's assets are worth only $56,000. Those of Cubans are lower than those of native whites but about twice those of Latino Americans. The remaining five immigrant groups have lower median assets. As for net worth, Cubans' assets have a wider spread than other Latino groups. An examination of the asset distribution reveals something hidden in the net worth distribution: the low net-worth Dominicans at the ninety-fifth percentile actually accumulate a level similar to that of Guatemalans.

Because most debts are secured, the amount of debt a household carries actually reflects its capacity to get loans to build assets. At the median, native whites have about $48,000 in debts. Cubans show a greater capacity for obtaining loans than other Latino groups. At the ninety-fifth percentile, Cubans and native whites are similarly positioned to obtain loans.

Distributions of net worth, assets, and debts add to what we learned from wealth holding status. Not only are the medians distanced, but the spreads of the distributions also differ among Latino groups. For instance, the percentile spread of net worth, assets, and loan-obtaining capacity for the Cuban group is greater than that of the native Latino group, but those of other Latino immigrant groups are smaller. This significant within-Latino variation is one of the ways in which immigration contributes to American wealth stratification, a topic examined in chapter 7.

Portfolio

Because net worth is equal to assets less secured and unsecured debts, it is informative to view them simultaneously. Net worth indicates immediately available resources. Secured debts (loans using property as collaterals) indicate loan-obtaining capacity, which may increase future assets. Unsecured debt indicates the risk of future asset liquidation, which

Figure 4.4   Net Worth and Debts as Percentage of Native White Assets by Latino Group

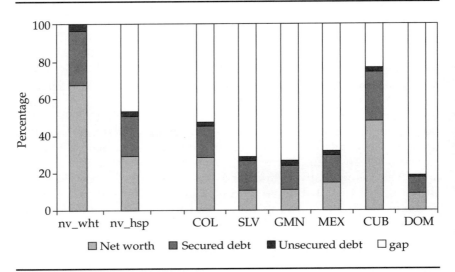

Source: Author's compilation.

may reduce future assets. I express net worth, secured debt, and unsecured debt each as a percentage of two bases—native whites' average total assets (see figure 4.4) and the group-specific total assets (see figure 4.5). Figure 4.4 facilitates between-group comparisons and figure 4.5 facilitates within-group analysis.

In figure 4.4, the three sections of the bar for native whites denote net worth, unsecured debt, and secured debt as a percentage of the total assets. For other groups, in addition to the sections for net worth, secured debt, and unsecured debt each as a percentage of native whites' total assets, the top section denotes the gap in total assets between the group and native whites. For instance, the gap between native whites and Latino Americans is nearly 50 percent, meaning that the total assets of the average Latino American household are about 50 percent those of the average native white household. Comparing a particular section (for example, secured debts) across bars reveals the absolute size differences across groups. For instance, Cubans have a lower level of net worth than native whites but both groups carry similar secured debt.

The graph shows lower absolute amounts of net worth for all Latino groups than for native whites and yet a wide variation among Latino groups. Compared with the large net worth variation, the secured debt variation is smaller. A key institutional factor in asset building is the lending market. Before 1995, when home equity loans did not yet allow loans greater than the value of home equity, secured debt indicated capacity for asset building. Since 1995, a growing number of households have taken second mortgages on their homes to cover their credit card debts, though only a minority falls in this category. Comparing the amounts of secured debts can therefore help evaluate asset building capacity. Examining between-group patterns, we see that the capacity to obtain secured debts varies, but not remarkably. The amount of secured debts is similar among the remaining Latino immigrant groups, though relatively smaller for Dominicans. This pattern indicates that all Latino immigrant groups have access to lending institutions, which may be located in either the mainstream or the ethnic economy. The amount of loans that Latino immigrants obtain is lower than native whites, but not much lower.

Unsecured debts are taken for consumption rather than for asset building. Typical unsecured debts include credit card debts, store bills, and medical bills. At the national level in 1998, 42 percent of credit card holders paid their bills monthly without being subject to any interest charges or late fees, leaving 58 percent indebted (Durkin 2000). Home equity loans complicate the situation of unsecured debts in that an increasing number of households have converted credit card debt into home equity loans. When we examine the between-group differences in unsecured debt, we need to keep in mind the propensities of various groups to shift from unsecured to secured debts. Figure 4.4 shows that the absolute amount of unsecured debts is a small portion of total assets for all groups and does not vary much across groups. In general, native whites have more unsecured debt than native and immigrant Latinos. Among Latino immigrants, Dominicans have the least unsecured debt.

With group-specific total assets as another basis, the shares of net worth, secured debt, and unsecured debt within a group describe the stage of a group's asset building within the limits of their total assets. Given an adequate amount of total assets, higher net worth provides an immediate financial buffer—a mature stage of asset building—whereas higher secured debt predicts a future financial buffer—a premature stage. Figure 4.5 compares the three sections (for net worth, secure debt, and unsecured debt) within a single bar for each group.

With the largest amount of assets among all groups, native whites have a net worth that is more than twice their secured debt. This relatively smaller share of secured debt indicates a mature stage of asset building, which offers an immediate financial buffer. Cubans, who also have higher assets, have by comparison a slightly lower net worth share and a slightly larger secured debt share, suggesting a premature stage of asset building. This predicts a future financial buffer. With significantly fewer assets among other Latino immigrant groups, their shares of net worth and secured debt cannot indicate an immediate financial buffer.

Figure 4.5   Net Worth and Debt as Percentage of Total Assets by Latino Group

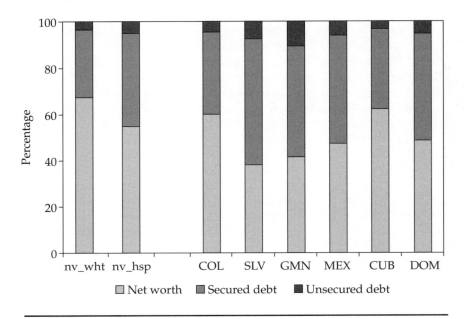

Source: Author's compilation.

Unsecured debts include consumer debt, medical bills, private debt, and loans from banks that are not for asset building. Guatemalan immigrants have the largest unsecured debt share among the groups shown in figure 4.5. However, given the low value of their total assets, their large unsecured debt share should not be taken as a sign of huge consumer debts. This portfolio examination indicates that even Latino immigrant groups who are better off do not have an immediate financial buffer and thus are not in a mature asset building stage. Those who are worse off have asset values too low for any meaningful discussion of future financial buffers.

Theoretically, a household can liquidate all its assets, pay off all its secured debt, and use the balance to cover living costs in an emergency situation. Total equity is used to mean the balance between total assets and total secured debt. Realistically, homes and retirement accounts are less liquid than other equity, such as bank accounts, stocks and bonds, and other real estate. I call home and retirement accounts quasi-liquid and the other seven components liquid. Figure 4.6 describes nine portfolio components as percentages of the specific group's total equity. Each bar consists of nine sections: home equity (home); IRA, Keogh, and 401(k) accounts (ira); interest-earning saving and checking accounts, money

Figure 4.6   Portfolio as Percentage of Total Equity by Latino Group

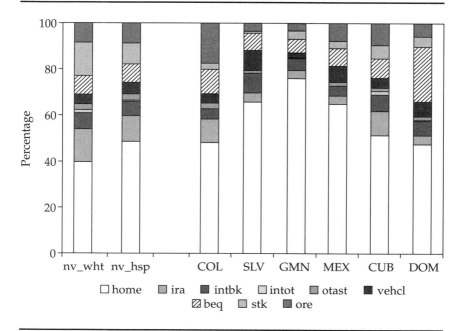

Source: Author's compilation.

market deposit accounts, and certificates of deposit (intbk); municipal bonds, corporate bonds and U.S. securities (intot); non–interest earning checking accounts, saving bonds, and other financial investment (otast); sale value of cars (vehcl); business equity (beq); stocks and mutual funds (stk); other real estate (ore). If the group's total equity is adequate, a smaller percentage of home equity indicates a higher capacity and preference for diverse financial investments. Native whites' home equity is about 40 percent of their total. The proportion for Latino Americans, Colombian immigrants, and Cuban immigrants is about 50 percent, also indicating diverse investment behavior. By contrast, given their low levels of equity, Mexican, Salvadoran, Guatemalan, and Dominican immigrants can invest only in their homes. Retirement accounts weigh more heavily for native whites than for any other group, but Latino Americans, Colombian immigrants, and Cuban immigrants also gravitate toward retirement savings. As might be expected, other Latino immigrant groups, who have a higher propensity for return migration, show a low preference for saving for old-age security, at least in the United States.

Business equity, though included here as a component, is fundamentally different from other components because it is not capital for consumption. The proportion of self-employed individuals and small business owners differs between natives and immigrants and among immigrant groups. Latino Americans are similar in this respect to native whites. Latino immigrant groups other than Guatemalans have a high share of business equity. Cuban immigrants, known for their successful entrepreneurship, as well as other groups thought to be entrepreneur-poor, such as Mexicans, own a greater share of business equity than native whites. This larger share of business equity does not equate with large businesses because of the lower levels of total equity. Nonetheless, they reflect a strategy of self employment in their economic adaptation.

The simultaneous examination of assets, debts, and net worth helps us understand the likelihood of having an immediate financial buffer (net worth) and a future financial buffer (secured debt). The data show a high degree of heterogeneity among Latino immigrant groups, with Cuban and Colombian groups faring better than others. However, none has arrived at a mature stage that offers the adequate immediate financial buffer of native whites. Portfolio analysis reveals a diverse pattern of investment across groups. The investment behaviors of Cuban and Colombian immigrants are more similar to those of native whites and Latino Americans than to other Latino immigrant groups. Although most Latino groups have been thought to have low self-employment rates, the data show that the share of total equity they invest in small businesses is similar to or greater than that of native whites, but the amount is greatly constrained by their limited total equity. This examination of equity portfolios brings us to a more detailed analysis of each component.

Homeownership

A home is the most important component of wealth. A home provides shelter without a need to pay rent. A home also symbolizes middle-class status (Oliver and Shapiro 1995). The asset value of a home is the market value of the house. The debt on a home is the mortgage, which has principal and interest to be paid off in a scheduled time window (for example, fifteen or thirty years). The interest on mortgages is tax deductible. Home equity is the market value of the home minus the remaining principal in the mortgage. A household that owns the home is in one of three possible situations: the mortgage has been paid off so the equity equals the market value of the house, the market value of the house is greater than the amount of the remaining mortgage, or the market value of the house is less than the mortgage. Here I address general issues of homeownership and leave the discussion of the third topic for later. Using native whites and Latino Americans as the benchmarks, I compare the homeownership rates of Latino immigrant homeowners.

Two reasons are behind group gaps in homeownership. One is the differences in demographic compositions of age, marital status, number of children, and education levels. I called these composition effects. The other is the potential differential effects of these demographic characteristics on cross-group homeownership. The following analysis first tackles the composition effects of demographic factors and then addresses their differential effects.

Composition Effects

To investigate whether demographic compositions explain the differences in homeownership between Latino immigrant groups and native whites and the differences among Latino groups, table 4.4 presents homeownership rates by country of origin and demographic characteristics. More than 70 percent of native white households own a home. Cubans rank at the top (63.6 percent) of the immigrant groups. Colombians and Mexicans come in a distant second (40.7 percent and 42.4 percent, respectively), and Dominicans rank at the bottom (21.7 percent).[2] The homeownership gaps between immigrant groups and native whites range from 7.2 to 49.1 percent, suggesting greater differences within Latino immigrants than between native whites and all Latino immigrants. Below I examine the extent to which each demographic composition explains these differences.

Age   Because buying a home requires a down payment, a transaction cost, and a good credit history, we would expect that younger households are less able than older households to purchase a home—a prediction suggested by the life cycle hypothesis. Given the large difference between native whites and Latino immigrants and the substantial differences among Latino immigrants, age structure may help to explain homeownership gaps. The ownership rate for younger native whites (aged twenty-five to forty-four) is 63.2 percent. Within this age group, Cuban immigrants come in first, at 48.5 percent. Mexicans rank second, at 37.4 percent. Dominicans remain at the bottom with 19.2 percent, 44 percentage points below young native whites. The middle rates range from 33 to 35 percent. The rank of older households' homeownership rates is the same as the total, indicating that older households' ranking dominates the total pattern. The gaps among older groups range from 6 to 53.3 percentage points, varying more than those for the younger groups, which range from 14.7 to 44 percentage points. The homeownership gaps within younger and older groups remain large, suggesting

Table 4.4   Homeownership by Demographic Characteristics and Latino Group

	Total	25 to 44	45 to 64	Unmarried	Married	No Children	1 to 2 Children	3 + Children	Education < 12	Education ≥ 12
Native white	0.708	0.632	0.790	0.498	0.834	0.643	0.771	0.780	0.485	0.724
Latino American	0.527	0.460	0.653	0.359	0.663	0.474	0.564	0.536	0.414	0.559
Colombian	0.407	0.329	0.513	0.315	0.478	0.311	0.457	0.682	0.430	0.403
Salvadoran	0.343	0.349	0.327	0.090	0.516	0.137	0.340	0.699	0.294	0.406
Guatemalan	0.368	0.337	0.487	0.074	0.550	0.221	0.475	0.294	0.245	0.429
Mexican	0.424	0.374	0.531	0.279	0.501	0.321	0.440	0.462	0.403	0.463
Cuban	0.636	0.485	0.730	0.447	0.763	0.577	0.662	0.944	0.543	0.663
Dominican	0.217	0.192	0.257	0.154	0.330	0.223	0.249	0.120	0.095	0.289

Source: Author's compilation.

that age structure explains only a small portion of the between-group differences and also indicating that heterogeneity within Latino immigrant groups is huge.

Marital Status   Because marriage is a wealth-enhancing institution, we expect that marital status composition might explain differences in homeownership. Because marital status varies more within Latino groups than between Latinos and native whites, we expect that marital status composition helps explain the gaps among Latino immigrant groups more than the gaps between Latino immigrants and native whites. Among unmarried households, 49.8 percent of native whites own a home. Cuban immigrants are very close to native whites. Mexican immigrants rank fifth at 27.9 percent. Unmarried Guatemalan and Salvadoran immigrants are least likely to own a home, about 7 percent and 9 percent, respectively. Among the married, native whites take the lead at 83.4 percent, 7.1 percentage points above the top Latino group—Cubans. There is little difference among Colombian, Salvadoran, and Guatemalan groups. The similarly wide gaps of unmarried and married households suggest that marital status composition does not explain much in the way of creating homeownership gaps.

Children   Having children increases saving motives, but having three or more children drains family resources. All Latino immigrants are more likely to have children than native whites, and all, except Colombians and Cubans, have more children on average than native whites. Thus, the percentages of households with no children, one to two children, and three or more children may account for homeownership gaps. Among those with no children, the gaps between Latino groups and native whites range from 6.6 percentage points for Cubans to 50.6 percentage points for Salvadorans. Among households with one or two children, the smallest gap is 10.9 percentage points for Cubans and the largest is 52.2 for Dominicans. Among households with three or more children, the gaps are −16.4 percentage points for Cubans (Cubans have higher homeownership than native whites) and 66 percentage points for Dominicans. The huge gaps within these three variables suggest that the number of children in a household does not explain homeownership gaps.

Education   Education is critical for starting wealth accumulation and maintaining a high growth rate in wealth. We therefore expect that the low education levels relative to native whites and the vast variations among Latino immigrant groups may explain the observed homeownership gaps. The rank orders of homeownership for the two educational categories (fewer than twelve years and twelve years or more) in table 4.4 differ. Less-educated Cubans actually fare better than native whites.

The order among the better-educated, on the other hand, largely mirrors that of the total population. In particular, although higher education boosts homeownership for native whites and native Latinos, it makes virtually no difference for Colombian and Mexican immigrants. This indicates the differential effects of education on homeownership between whites and Latinos and among Latino immigrant groups.

Total Demographic   How do these demographic compositions combined affect homeownership? I calculate the observed homeownership rates (the crude rates), and incrementally adjust the rates to the native white composition of age, marital status and number of children, and education levels, resulting in three sets of adjusted rates. The adjusted rates are then free of specific compositional differences. The way to adjust for demographic composition is to make each group's composition the same as that of native whites. For instance, Guatemalans are very young. Therefore, if we want to make a valid comparison between native whites and Guatemalans, we must adjust the Guatemalan age structure to make it the same as that of native whites, 51.8 percent younger and 48.2 percent older. Further adjustments will make comparisons of homeownership rates simultaneously free of the composition effects of age, marital status, number of children, and education levels. The group gaps in the fully adjusted rate reflect the differences in homeownership controlling for compositional differences.

Figure 4.7 presents four sets of rates—crude rates (the first bar), rates adjusted for age composition (the second bar), rates further adjusted for the composition of marital status and number of children (the third bar), and finally rates further adjusted for education composition (the fourth bar). The crude rate and the three adjusted rates are the same for native whites because we use their compositions as the base against which all other groups are adjusted. Comparing the changes in each additional adjustment for the Latino groups gives us an estimate of the direction and relative magnitude of the differences in the compositional effects of the additional demographic characteristics being controlled.

The differences across the fourth bar capture the homeownership gaps when the compositions of age, marital status, number of children, and education levels are held constant. When comparing the first three bars within groups, the changes are largely negligible. Compared to the third bar (controlling for age, marital status, and number of children), the fourth bar (further controlling for education levels) indicates the education composition effect. It is substantial for Guatemalans and Dominicans. Comparing the fourth bars of each Latino group to that of native whites, we see that Cubans are very close to native whites and that Guatemalans and Mexicans are a distant second. Interestingly, it is not marital status but education that improves Dominican immigrants'

Figure 4.7   Crude and Adjusted Homeownership Rates by Latino Group

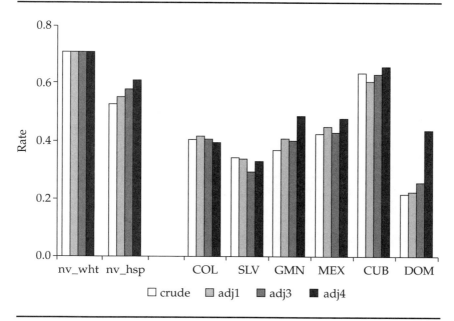

Source: Author's compilation.

homeownership. This suggests that, rather than female headship, human capital is the key to elevate this group out of poverty and welfare dependency.

As a whole, the patterns emerging from table 4.4 and figure 4.7 suggest that the compositions of age, marital status, and number of children do not help explain much of the white-Latino homeownership gaps. However, education composition does explain a substantial portion. We now turn to investigate whether each demographic characteristic affects homeownership differently within groups.

Differential Effects

The age effect captures income growth and motives to save along the life cycle. The marriage effect may differ among groups because some groups may not have the asset building advantage that married native white households have. A lower return on human capital for racial minorities and those holding foreign degrees, residential segregation by race or class, more responsibility for extended families, weaker saving

Table 4.5   Odds Ratio of Homeownership by Demographic Characteristics and Latino Group

	Age (45 to 64)	Married	No Children	3 + Children	Education ≥ 12
Native White	2.19	5.05	0.53	1.05	2.79
Latino American	2.22	3.50	0.69	0.89	1.80
Colombian	2.15	1.99	0.53	2.55	0.90
Salvadoran	0.90	10.79	0.31	4.50	1.64
Guatemalan	1.87	15.27	0.31	0.46	2.31
Mexican	1.89	2.60	0.60	1.09	1.28
Cuban	2.86	3.98	0.70	8.53	1.66
Dominican	1.46	2.72	0.86	0.41	3.86

Source: Author's compilation.

motives, and more impatient consumption behaviors can lead to lower probabilities of homeownership.

Comparing the odds of homeownership for older versus younger households or for married versus unmarried households within the same group can yield rough estimates of the group-specific age effect and marriage effect. For instance, the homeownership odds ratio of older whites to younger whites takes the ratio of older to younger whites' odds. A ratio greater than one indicates a greater probability of homeownership for older whites than younger whites; a ratio of one indicates the same probability for both groups; and a ratio smaller than one indicates a smaller probability for older whites than younger whites. In table 4.5, within each group, I examine the odds ratios for older vs. younger, married vs. unmarried, having no versus one or two children, having three or more versus one or two children, and having high school education or above versus no high school education.

Age   The odds of homeownership among older native whites are 2.19 times those of younger native whites and the comparable Latino odds are 2.22 times that of younger native Latinos, consistent with the life cycle hypothesis. The odds ratios have a wide spread among the six Latino groups. Cubans' older-younger homeownership odds ratio is even higher than native whites' (2.86), whereas Salvadorans' is 0.9, meaning that older Salvadorans are less likely to own a home than their younger counterparts. The high Cuban figure has to do with the fact that many more Cuban households are long-term U.S. residents and the low Salvadoran figure has to do with their older age at arrival. The ratios of the other Latino immigrant groups are greater than one, supporting the life cycle hypothesis, but they are all below the odds ratio of native whites, suggesting that these Latino immigrants' homeownership growth rates are lower than that of native whites and native Latinos over the life cycle.

Marriage   The married-unmarried odds ratio among native whites is 5.05, indicating a strong marriage effect on homeownership. Two Latino groups show even greater marriage effects—Salvadorans (10.79) and Guatemalans (15.27). However, with a ratio of only 3.98, Cubans, who are thought to have strong family values, do not show a stronger advantage than native whites. The Mexican ratio is also low, at 2.6. Three explanations are possible for this variation. First, our measure of marital status is being married with spouse present, which classifies many immigrants, who left their spouses behind, as unmarried. These unmarried immigrants thus have the same saving motivation as their married counterparts, as shown in the low Mexican ratio. Second, the saving motivation of married people can lead to actual homeownership when the family resources reach a certain level. Thus we see a high ratio among poorer groups such as Salvadorans and Guatemalans. Third, perhaps because of the intention of circular migration, or the wealth regime type of the home country attracts building assets in the home country, married and unmarried Mexicans tend to purchase a home in Mexico.

Children   Children are a primary reason that families need a stable and safe source of shelter. The odds of homeownership in childless households should thus be smaller than those with one or two children. The native white ratio is 0.53, meaning that the probability of homeownership is 47 percent lower than that of households with one or two children. Except for Salvadorans and Guatemalans, who are plagued by minimal resources, other Latino immigrant groups have a similar or lower ratio than native whites. These Latino immigrants are more likely than native whites to plan well in advance to have children. On the other hand, having three or more children may undermine a household's ability to buy a home, especially one that can house a large family. This is not the case for native whites, whose ratio of having three or more children to having one or two is 1.05, in part because most of these households have only three children, not more, and in part because native whites have more resources. Ratios among Latino groups vary greatly.

Education   The odds of better-educated native whites owning a home are 2.79 times those of their less educated counterparts. Five out of six Latino groups do not reach this level, suggesting two possibilities. One is that, among the better educated, many native whites are better educated (for example, a college degree) than Latino immigrants. The other is that returns to immigrants' education are lower. The Dominican ratio is high, at 3.86, which is significant for a group heavily reliant on welfare—having at least a high school education is the key to escaping welfare dependency and thus owning a home.

Using native whites as the benchmark, I have examined the differences in the effects of age, marital status, number of children, and education levels on homeownership. The results suggest that these differences are larger among Latino groups than between Latinos and native whites, with two exceptions. Having more children is not a major constraint and the return to human capital is lower for many Latino groups. In explaining homeownership gaps, differential effects play a larger role than composition effects, which are with the exception of education negligible.

Negative Home Equity

Homeownership does not guarantee home equity. The amount of a mortgage or home equity loan may exceed the market value of the house because that value is less than the mortgage. I call this negative home equity (NHE). NHE arises when the house has depreciated over time. Race- or class-based residential segregation, downward community transitions, and natural disasters may lead to house depreciation. NHE also arises when a household has taken out a home equity loan. The total value of mortgages is allowed to exceed the house's market value.

Figure 4.8 describes the crude and adjusted NHE rates among homeowners by native whites, native Latinos, and the six Latino immigrant groups (see detailed statistics in table 4.6). The crude NHE rate of native whites is lower than that of Latino Americans but not of all Latino immigrant groups. Cuban homeowners stand out as the least likely to have NHE and Salvadoran homeowners as the most likely. Controlling for age makes only a slight change in the NHE rates of Latino immigrant groups and actually increases it for Salvadorans and Dominicans. Controlling for marital status and number of children in addition to age reduces or maintains the NHE rate for all Latino immigrant groups. Further controlling for education significantly reduces it for Guatemalans and Dominicans, but increases it for Colombians, Salvadorans, Mexicans, and Cubans. With these demographics controlled, Salvadoran and Mexican immigrants are the most likely to have NHE, and Guatemalans the least likely.

The home is the most significant asset for many households. None of the six Latino immigrant groups have the same homeownership rate as native whites, but the variation among them is still huge. Compositions of age, marital status, and number of children do little to explain the differences either between whites and Latino immigrants or within Latino groups. The composition of education levels narrows the gaps, but only to a moderate degree. The education effect on homeownership appears to be smaller for Latino immigrants than for native whites. In addition,

Figure 4.8   Crude and Adjusted Negative Home Equity Rates Among Homeowners, by Latino Group

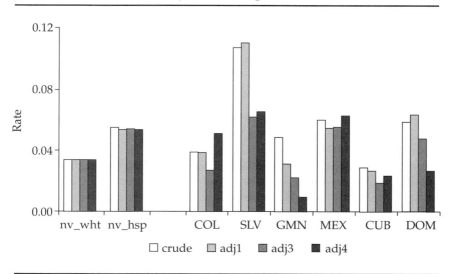

Source: Author's compilation.

marriage and children do not have much influence on Latino immigrant homeownership. When the compositions of demographic characteristics are held constant, homeownership rates are similar between Cuban immigrants and native whites but lower for other Latino immigrant

Table 4.6   Negative Home Equity Rates Among Homeowners by Latino Group

	Crude	Adj1[a]	Adj3[b]	Adj4[c]
Native white	0.034	0.034	0.034	0.034
Latino American	0.055	0.054	0.054	0.054
Colombian	0.039	0.039	0.027	0.052
Salvadoran	0.108	0.111	0.062	0.065
Guatemalan	0.049	0.031	0.022	0.009
Mexican	0.060	0.055	0.055	0.062
Cuban	0.028	0.027	0.018	0.023
Dominican	0.058	0.064	0.048	0.026

Source: Author's compilation.
[a] Adj1 adjusts for age composition.
[b] Adj3 adjusts for the composition of age, marital status, and number of children.
[c] Adj4 adjusts for the composition of age, marital status, number of children, and education levels.

groups. The NHE analysis reveals the important role of age, marital status, number of children, and education level effects, yet NHE gaps remain large when demographic compositions are held constant.

Mortgages

Households usually obtain a mortgage when purchasing a home. Over time, some households pay off their mortgages, and others take second mortgages or home equity loans. Second mortgages serve two purposes. One is to finance asset building, for instance, remodeling a kitchen to increase a home's value. The other is to finance current consumption or to convert high interest credit card debt to a second mortgage with a lower interest rate. Second mortgages accounted for less than 4 percent of outstanding home mortgage debt in 1981, but the number had risen to 12 percent by 1991 (U.S. General Accounting Office 1993). One reason for the increase was the introduction of the home-equity line of credit. This is not a traditional, fixed-term, fixed-amount mortgage but instead like a credit card account, except that the interest rate is lower. Households with this line of credit can add to their mortgage every time they make a purchase. As a result, their loan may ultimately exceed their home's value, putting them in a NHE situation. Any default on the loan can lead to the foreclosure of the mortgage and sale of the home.

Although it is ideal to distinguish between households with or without home equity loans, the SIPP does not provide this data. The information about NHE can be used to understand the distribution of the number of mortgages across groups. Table 4.7 presents the percentage distribution of three categories among homeowners—no mortgage, one mortgage, and two or more mortgages. About 20 percent of native white and Latino American homeowners have paid off their mortgages. Native Latinos are more likely than native whites to have done so. A similar percentage of Mexican immigrant homeowners are free of mortgage obligations. The percentage is lower (ranging from 5.6 percent to 17.7 percent) for other immigrant groups, with Dominican homeowners having the lowest pay-off rate. Native whites are the most likely to have second mortgages, at 12.6 percent, with Cubans trailing by about 2 percentage points. Other groups are less likely to take second mortgages. It appears that better-off groups commonly do so. The least likely are Guatemalan and Mexican immigrants (3 to 4 percent).

A better understanding of mortgage considers the length of homeownership. Three lengths are defined: short term (less than ten years), medium term (ten through nineteen years), and long term (twenty or more years). I further look at the number of mortgages and the proportion of negative home equity under different durations of homeownership in table 4.8. When the sample size of a particular length of owner-

Table 4.7   Number of Mortgages by Latino Group

	0	1	2 +
Native white	0.200	0.674	0.126
Latino American	0.217	0.700	0.083
Colombian	0.131	0.806	0.063
Salvadoran	0.145	0.788	0.068
Guatemalan	0.127	0.842	0.032
Mexican	0.210	0.746	0.044
Cuban	0.177	0.713	0.110
Dominican	0.056	0.879	0.065

Source: Author's compilation.

ship is less than ten, the statistics are unstable, indicated in the table as NA. The left panel shows the proportion of households falling in each length of homeownership. More than 70 percent of all Latino immigrant homeowners except Cubans bought their houses within ten years. More than 16 percent of Cuban homeownerships are long term, similar to the native white proportion. Small sample sizes are found for Colombian, Salvadoran, Guatemalan, and Dominican homeowners in the long-term category, and Guatemalan and Dominican homeowners in the medium-length category.

When do households start to take more than one mortgage? From the middle panel of table 4.8, the native white pattern is curvilinear with a higher rate at the medium-length and lower rates at the short- and long-term ownership. This pattern repeats for native Latinos, as well as for the two immigrants groups (Mexicans and Cubans) among the three with sufficient sample sizes. Among new homeowners, two or more mortgages are most likely to occur with native whites and Guatemalans and Mexicans are least likely to take second mortgages. It appears that Latino immigrants have certain but limited access to the lending market.

NHE occurs more often in the short term than in the medium or long term (see the right panel of table 4.8). The proportion of new homeowners with a NHE is higher than that of long-term homeowners for all Latino immigrant groups (except Cubans). This helps us pinpoint the timing of financial risk facing these immigrant homeowners.

Because the first mortgage represents the initial step of purchasing a home, it is informative to describe the terms of the first mortgage. Buying a home is a big step in asset building. For more than fifty years, government policies have helped Americans achieve homeownership. Federal income tax laws provide incentives to taxpayers of all income levels. The Federal Housing Administration (FHA) and Veterans Benefit Administration (VBA) provide loan guarantee programs to low income

Table 4.8 Mortgages and NHE by Years of Ownership and Latino Group

	Proportion			2+ Mortgages			Prop. NHE		
	< 10	10 to 19	20 +	< 10	10 to 19	20 +	< 10	10 to 19	20 +
Native white	0.580	0.245	0.175	0.129	0.151	0.080	0.053	0.033	0.017
Latino American	0.618	0.213	0.170	0.075	0.136	0.045	0.083	0.062	0.045
Colombian	0.785	0.192	0.022	0.070	0.041	n.a.	0.091	0.065	n.a.
Salvadoran	0.793	0.168	0.038	0.085	0.000	n.a.	0.129	0.032	n.a.
Guatemalan	0.750	0.146	0.104	0.011	n.a.	n.a.	0.130	n.a.	n.a.
Mexican	0.712	0.180	0.108	0.041	0.062	0.031	0.101	0.048	0.037
Cuban	0.563	0.276	0.161	0.074	0.247	0.000	0.038	0.044	0.012
Dominican	0.750	0.111	0.140	0.085	n.a.	n.a.	0.100	n.a.	n.a.

Source: Author's compilation.
Note: n.a. indicates a cell size < 10.

Table 4.9   **Program and Interest Rate of First Home Mortgage by Latino Group**

	FHA/VA	Interest Rate < 7.0	Interest Rate ≥ 8.5
Native white	0.200	0.331	0.172
Latino American	0.370	0.289	0.218
Colombian	0.285	0.228	0.191
Salvadoran	0.187	0.305	0.203
Guatemalan	0.416	0.213	0.265
Mexican	0.321	0.255	0.238
Cuban	0.196	0.203	0.300
Dominican	0.447	0.305	0.241

Source: Author's compilation.

households. These programs may have contributed to the homeowner-ship growth from 44 percent in 1940 to 64 percent in 1990 for the whole population (Masnick 2001). Do immigrants benefit equally from these programs? Table 4.9 combines the FHA and VA programs into one cate-gory and separately shows the proportion of the first mortgage under low or high interest rates. As expected, higher-income groups, such as native whites and Cuban immigrants, are less likely to use FHA and VA loans (20 percent or lower) whereas lower-income groups, such as Lati-nos, are more likely (29 to 45 percent). The FHA-VA program participa-tion rates are largely in tandem with poverty status. About 41 percent of Dominican immigrants live below 130 percent of the official poverty line and their FHA-VA participation rate is 45 percent. Similarly, the high poverty rate among Mexicans (34 percent) corresponds to a higher rate of FHA-VA participation (32 percent). This indicates that immigrants have adequate access to government policies. However, Salvadorans ex-hibit the lowest usage rate (18.7 percent), which may reflect less favor-able reception from the federal government.

An important aspect of mortgages is the interest rate because, in addi-tion to principal, it determines the amount of the monthly loan payment. A low interest rate significantly reduces monthly mortgage costs and makes the payment easier to handle in a financial crunch. In contrast, a high interest rate greatly increases monthly payments, which can be-come hard to manage during an unemployment spell. Literature has documented the consistent and pervasive racial disparities and concen-tration of unfair lending in minority communities and to minority bor-rowers at all income levels (National Predatory Lending Task Force 2000; Bradford 2002). The help of white parents with down payments and the costs of points on mortgages are proposed as a major reason that white homeowners enjoy relatively low mortgage interest rates compared to blacks (Charles and Hurst 2002). That white homeowners are better able to pay refinancing fees compounds their advantage in mortgage rates. Less is known about mortgage terms for immigrants. Table 4.9 uses three categories of interest rates on the first mortgage—less than 7 percent on the lower end and 8.5 percent and above at the upper end. Among native whites, more than 30 percent have low interest rates. Proportions with low-interest mortgages are much lower for all immigrant groups, particularly Cuban and Guatemalan homeowners. Note that the FHA and VA programs do not necessarily offer the lowest interest rate available in the conventional market. Of those paying the high-end interest rates, the percentage of native whites is not only the lowest but also significantly lower. The high percentage among Cuban immigrants may reflect that many more purchased homes earlier, when interest rates were higher. The high rates of other groups are consistent with past findings, which suggests that high rates result from lending market discrimination.

This section examines the patterns of homeowners with paid-off mortgages, second mortgage holdings, and the NHE proportion under different lengths of homeownership, FHA-VA loans, and mortgage interest rates. Mexican immigrant homeowners reach parity with native whites in having no mortgage obligation. Cuban homeowners approach parity in taking second mortgages. Many new immigrant homeowners have a higher prevalence of NHE than native whites. Latinos in general are subject to higher interest rates. These idiosyncratic patterns suggest that Latino immigrants differ even more in mortgage holding than in homeownership. More generally, we must examine debt differences to fully understand wealth differences.

Liquid Financial Assets

Among forms of liquid assets, financial assets are those that are easiest to liquidate without high transaction costs or penalties. Because withdrawing money from retirement accounts before age fifty-nine and a half incurs high penalties, I consider retirement accounts to be quasi-liquid financial assets, which will be discussed in the next section. Liquid financial assets discussed here include stocks and mutual funds, interest-earning savings and checking accounts, bonds, securities, and non-interest-earning checking accounts. I focus on whether households have these items rather than on the value of the items. I also consider the ownership of at least $20,000 in combined liquid financial assets, the amount considered necessary for any household emergency fund (Gale and Scholz 1994).[3]

Stocks and mutual funds are modern financial investments offering greater opportunities for capital and income growth than traditional savings and checking accounts. However, there are fluctuations and risks associated with these investments. Stocks for specific companies are the most risky whereas mutual funds usually diversify investments so that the risks are averaged over a variety of stocks and bonds. In any case, stocks and mutual funds follow cyclical market movements. Therefore, households knowledgeable about financial markets and long-term financial strategies are more likely to invest in stocks and mutual funds. Immigrants may need time to acquire this knowledge. In addition, immigrants from countries with less-developed financial markets may instead trust traditional investment, such as real estate or lending to family members and friends. They need time to grow trust in modern financial markets. Fees and commissions may reduce the attractiveness for individuals who have little to invest. For these reasons, I expect that Latino immigrants are less likely to own stocks and mutual funds.

Figure 4.9 (see details in table 4.10) presents group percentages of stocks and mutual funds, interest-earning bank accounts, non-interest-earning bank checking accounts among those who have no interest-earning bank saving account, and the crude and adjusted ownership of at least $20,000 liquid financial assets. Although ownership of stocks and mutual funds is underreported in the SIPP, the group differences are not distorted. I therefore focus on group differences rather than absolute percentages. Group differences in stocks and mutual funds (see the first bar for each group in the graph) are large between native whites and other groups and among Latino immigrant groups. Among immigrant groups, Colombians and Cubans have a higher percentage, and Salvadorans and Mexicans a lower percentage.

The easiest way to withdraw cash with few transaction costs is to use bank accounts. Writing checks to pay for household utility charges, telephone services, and children's school fees is part of the typical American household's financial management routine. Withdrawals from bank accounts can provide the fastest cash in a household emergency such as layoff or illness. A lack of access to banks can be a terrible predicament. The second bar of figure 4.9 shows the percentage differences in interest-earning bank account holding among groups. The percentage for native whites is greater than for all other groups. Salvadoran, Mexican, and Dominican immigrants have limited access to financial institutions. The late 1990s and early 2000s saw a growth in bank practices that allowed unauthorized immigrants to open non–interest-earning checking accounts with identification documents from their home country. The third bar further examines the percentage of households without interest-earning accounts who have non–interest-earning checking accounts. Non–interest checking accounts provide only the most basic access to financial institutions. Salvadorans, Mexicans, and Dominicans still have low percentages with this basic access.

In the face of an emergency such as unemployment or illness, can a

Figure 4.9   Financial Asset Rates by Latino Group

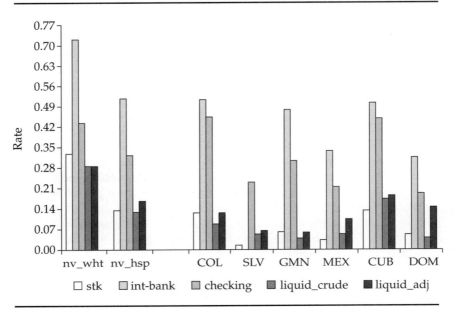

Source: Author's compilation.

household pool $20,000 from their liquid financial assets to pay for their essential needs? The last two bars for each group present the crude rate of owning liquid assets of at least $20,000 and the corresponding rate adjusted for the composition of age, marital status, number of children, and education levels. Native whites (the baseline group) are the most likely to have at least $20,000 in liquid assets (28.4 percent). The crude rates for all other groups are much lower. Cuban immigrants rank a distant second at 17.4 percent but higher than Latino Americans at 12.7 percent. The rates for other immigrant groups are very low, particularly Salvadorans, Guatemalans, Mexicans, and Dominicans, all lower than 6 percent. After adjusting for demographic composition, all nonwhite groups improve, with Dominican immigrants seeing the greatest increase (from 3.7 to 14.3 percent).

Overall, all Latino immigrant groups seem to lag behind native whites in their rates of investing in the modern financial economy in the forms of stocks and mutual funds. Perhaps the most striking finding is that Latino immigrant households have much lower levels of liquid financial assets even when their demographic compositions are comparable to those of native whites. This makes Latino households financially vulnerable.

Table 4.10   Ownership of Liquid Financial Assets by Latino Group

	Stock and Mutual Fund	Int. Bank Account	Non-Int Checking[a]	$20,000 or More Combined	
				Liquid Crude	Liquid Adj4[b]
Native white	0.328	0.720	0.434	0.284	0.284
Latino American	0.136	0.517	0.321	0.127	0.165
Colombian	0.125	0.514	0.456	0.088	0.124
Salvadoran	0.013	0.351	0.230	0.053	0.064
Guatemalan	0.059	0.479	0.304	0.037	0.056
Mexican	0.032	0.336	0.213	0.052	0.104
Cuban	0.134	0.503	0.447	0.174	0.186
Dominican	0.052	0.316	0.193	0.037	0.143

Source: Author's compilation.
[a] Among those who have no interest-earning bank accounts.
[b] Adj4 adjusts for the composition of age, marital status, number of children, and education levels.

Retirement Accounts

The most popular retirement accounts are individual retirement accounts (IRAs), Keogh plans, and 401(k) plans. IRAs were first established in 1974 to help employees without pension plans save for retirement. IRAs feature tax-deductible contributions up to an annual limit and tax-free accrual of interest. In 1981, IRA eligibility was extended to all taxpayers and the contribution limits were raised (up to $3000 in 2001). A retirement program particularly designed for self-employed workers is a Keogh plan, in which contributions are deductible from income and taxes on interests are deferred. The 401(k) plan is a deferred compensation plan, in which an employee can elect to have the employer contribute a portion of his or her wages to a plan on a pre-tax basis. These deferred wages are not subject to income tax withholding at the time of deferral but are subject to social security, Medicare, and federal unemployment taxes. An employee can contribute more ($12,000 in 2003) to a 401(k) plan than an IRA. Employers sometimes match employee contributions but are not required to do so. The major advantages of 401(k) plans are tax deferral and possible employer matches. Self-employed workers can also set up a 401(k) plan. In general, before the account holder reaches the age of fifty-nine and a half, early withdrawal from retirement accounts is subject to substantial penalties (Gale and Scholz 1994).

Figure 4.10 (table 4.11) shows the distribution of retirement accounts by groups. I combine IRA and Keogh accounts into one category because

Figure 4.10   Crude and Adjusted Retirement Account Rates by Latino Group

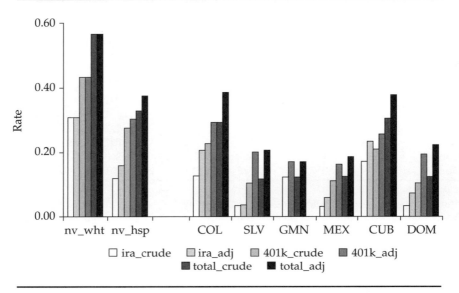

Source: Author's compilation.

neither IRAs nor Keoghs include employer contributions. I maintain 401(k) accounts separately because they often include employer contribution. Households in which the head is older than fifty-nine or households with liquid assets in excess of $20,000 are more likely to own retirement accounts (Gale and Scholz 1994). The early withdrawal penalty discourages young households or households with limited liquid financial assets from setting up retirement accounts because of the high transaction costs when early withdrawal is likely. Thus, a more valid group comparison must adjust for the composition of these two characteristics. Figure 4.10 shows both the crude rates and the rates adjusted for the composition of head of household's age (younger or older than fifty) and household's liquid financial assets (less or more than $20,000).

Among native whites, the crude rate of IRA-Keogh ownership is 30.8 percent, much higher than any other group. The Cuban immigrant rate is 16.8 percent, which though a low second is far above the remaining groups. At the bottom are Guatemalan, Salvadoran, Mexican, and Dominican immigrants, with rates ranging from 0 to 3 percent. Adjusting for the composition of age and liquid financial asset compositions leads to a large increase in the adjusted rates for Latino Americans, Colombian, Mexican, Cuban, and Dominican immigrant groups and virtually no change for Salvadoran immigrants.[4]

Table 4.11   Retirement Account Ownership by Latino Group

	IRA-Keogh		401k		Total	
	Crude	Adj[a]	Crude	Adj[a]	Crude	Adj[a]
Native white	0.308	0.308	0.434	0.434	0.568	0.568
Latino American	0.117	0.159	0.274	0.303	0.328	0.375
Colombian	0.125	0.204	0.225	0.292	0.292	0.386
Salvadoran	0.032	0.034	0.102	0.199	0.113	0.207
Guatemalan	0.000	0.000	0.121	0.168	0.121	0.168
Mexican	0.030	0.057	0.108	0.160	0.121	0.184
Cuban	0.168	0.231	0.208	0.254	0.305	0.378
Dominican	0.032	0.069	0.102	0.192	0.120	0.221

Source: Author's compilation.
[a] Adj adjusts for the composition of age and ownership of $20,000 liquid financial asset.

Because 401(k) plans offer greater tax incentives than IRAs and Keoghs and unique saving incentives as some employers match employee contributions, we expect that at the population level, more households have 401(k) accounts than IRA or Keogh accounts. In figure 4.10, all groups show higher rates of 401(k) ownership than IRA-Keogh ownership. Again the percentage of native whites who own 401(k) accounts is the greatest. The three groups least likely to have IRA or Keogh accounts are also at the bottom in the 401(k) ranking, but are not as distant from the higher ranked groups. After being adjusted for the composition of age and liquid financial asset, the rates of all disadvantaged groups increase considerably, suggesting that age and liquid financial asset compositions contribute substantially to the observed 401(k) gaps. Nonetheless, Latino groups are not reaching parity with native whites, and Latino immigrants, including Cubans, are not reaching parity with Latino Americans. These gaps may be attributable to the kinds of jobs that nonwhite workers most commonly hold. We expect that a worker is more motivated to contribute to a retirement account if the employer matches the contribution. If employers of Latino workers, particularly Latino immigrant workers, are less likely to make matches, it is not surprising that these immigrants' 401(k) ownership rates are lower even after being adjusted to the same composition of age and liquid financial asset compositions for native whites.

Combining IRA-Keogh and 401(k) provides an overall picture of saving for retirement. The Latino-white gaps are large: where 56.8 percent of native whites have some sort of retirement account, among Latino immigrants the high is 30.5 percent for Cubans and the low is 11.3 percent for Salvadorans. Except for Cuban immigrants, whose preparation for old-age security is similar to that of Latino Americans, Latino immigrant groups are less prepared for their old-age security. Adjusting for the composition of age and liquid financial assets narrows the gaps, particularly for Colombians, Cubans, and Dominicans, but the gaps remain substantial.

For households in which the head is aged twenty-five to fifty-four, saving for retirement is a long-term effort. Only a small percentage of Latino immigrants are following such a plan. Even after controlling for age composition and liquid financial assets, Latino immigrants are much less prepared to financially support themselves in old age. If these conditions persist and these immigrants stay in the United States on a permanent basis, they will be a large group in need of public assistance.

Life Insurance

Life insurance is for survivors, who may include a spouse, children, or other family members. When a person is younger and healthier, life insurance costs are lower. Some employers provide life insurance for their employees and others do not. By looking at employer-provided and self-bought life insurance policies, I hope to uncover patterns showing whether immigrants have stronger motives for providing for family members. Figure 4.11 (table 4.12) presents the group rates of employer-provided, self-bought, and total life insurance. Both crude rates and rates adjusted for the composition of age, marital status, number of children, and education levels are presented.

The employer-provided life insurance rate is 56.4 percent for native whites, followed by 43.4 percent for native Latinos, 40 percent for Cuban immigrants, and 38 percent for Colombian immigrants. Only about 20 percent of Salvadoran, Guatemalan, Mexican, and Dominican immigrants have life insurance provided by their employers. This pattern is similar to the 401(k) pattern, because, except for Colombians and Cubans, Latino immigrants are less likely than natives to find jobs that offer good benefits. Adjusting for the composition of age, marital status, number of children and education levels increases the rates of the Mexican and Dominican groups more than other groups.

People with or without employer-provided life insurance may buy life insurance. About 46 percent of native whites bought their own life insurance. Salvadoran, Guatemalan, Mexican and Dominican immigrant rates are less than 20 percent. Controlling for age, marital status, number of children, and education levels increases the self-bought rate of all groups except for Colombian and Guatemalan immigrants.

Regardless of the policy provider, 78.4 percent of native whites own a life insurance policy and 60 percent of Latino Americans do. Cuban and Colombian immigrants are 9 percentage points behind Latino Americans. Guatemalan, Mexican, and Dominican immigrants are the least

Figure 4.11   Crude and Adjusted Life Insurance Rates by Latino Group

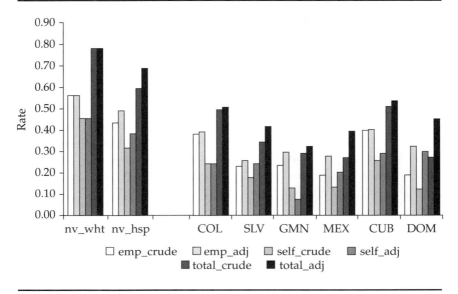

Source: Author's compilation.

likely to be insured. Adjusting for the demographic compositions of native whites narrows the life insurance gap somewhat, but it still remains large. The overall low rates of life insurance ownership among Latino immigrants reflect that some of them plan an eventual return to their countries and therefore feel no need to purchase this type of insurance in the United States.

Table 4.12   Life Insurance by Latino Group

	Employer-Provided		Self-Bought		Total	
	Crude	Ad4j[a]	Crude	Adj4[a]	Crude	Adj4[a]
Native white	0.564	0.564	0.457	0.457	0.784	0.784
Latino American	0.434	0.493	0.317	0.384	0.598	0.690
Colombian	0.380	0.392	0.241	0.241	0.496	0.507
Salvadoran	0.228	0.257	0.177	0.240	0.346	0.417
Guatemalan	0.233	0.294	0.126	0.071	0.291	0.324
Mexican	0.188	0.275	0.132	0.202	0.269	0.393
Cuban	0.400	0.402	0.254	0.289	0.510	0.537
Dominican	0.187	0.322	0.122	0.297	0.270	0.451

Source: Author's compilation.
[a] Adj4 adjusts for the composition of age, marital status, number of children, and education levels.

Consumer Debts

Consumer debts include credit card debts and shop bills. During the 1980s and 1990s, credit card use expanded into the middle and working classes and among college students and the elderly. Credit card users fall into one of two categories. Convenience users benefit from credit card use without being subject to any fees or interest payments because they pay the bill in full each month. Paying a monthly credit card bill simplifies finances as one needs to write only one check per month for all purchases. Another type of user, however, is often trapped in risky financial situations. Revolvers, who revolve from card to card when they approach a card's limit, pay various fees and high interests on cumulated consumer debts. Consumers become revolvers for different reasons. Job losses, sicknesses, injuries, or divorces often foster a reliance on credit cards as a way to get through a difficult economic time. College students may be lured to spend their future income without a conscious financial plan. The elderly may spend their retirement savings on their grandchildren. Other consumers, though a minority, fit the stereotype of reckless shopping sprees and impulsive consumption, overspending on extravagant gifts, meals, vacations, and things they already have or will never use and cannot afford. Unleashed by the federal government's deregulation and spurred by the manipulation of deceptive low short-term interest rates and low minimum payments, the credit card industry has aggressively targeted those at financial risk (Manning 2000). An increasing number of people are trapped in credit card debts with high interest rates and fees. Universal default is a legal contract term the credit card industry manipulates to indicate a potential slight increase in the financial risk a card holder presents to the industry. This increase can result from a late payment, high balance, or even a late payment for another debt. Classification under universal default leads to escalating credit card interest rates and various fees, which are unregulated and unlimited (Warren and Tyagi 2003). The use of credit cards has greatly expanded and so have credit card debts. In 2000, approximately 78 million households had at least one bank credit card, and the average credit card debt for indebted households was almost $7,000 (Warren and Tyagi 2003).

Do immigrants have less access to credit cards and thus lower consumer debts? Immigrants can be either more or less likely to have consumer debts than natives. On the one hand, less-educated Latino immigrants face greater job instability than natives. Credit cards can help them overcome short-term economic hardship, but they can subsequently be trapped in financial crisis if they find themselves unable to pay the high interest rates on large accumulated consumer debt. On the other hand, immigrants from developing countries are unfamiliar with the modern credit market and have moderate, controlled consumption habits.

Figure 4.12   Crude and Adjusted Rates of Consumer Debts by Latino Group

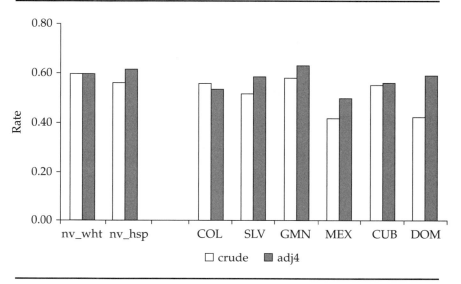

Source: Author's compilation.

The SIPP survey asks whether a household owes money on credit cards or store bills. Store bills have declined as a source of consumer debt, and information collected from this question refers mainly to credit cards. Figure 4.12 (table 4.13) presents the statistics on consumer debts by groups: crude rate, rate adjusted for the composition of age, marital status, number of children, and education, average debt, and trimmed average debt (eliminating the very small and very large amounts). The most striking feature of figure 4.12 is the similarities, rather than the differences, among groups. Looking at the crude rates, though all Latino immigrant groups have lower consumer debt rates, the differences are small. Native whites have the highest rate at 59.8 percent and Mexican and Dominican immigrants have the lowest at about 42 percent. With the adjustment for the composition of age, marital status, number of children, and education levels, Guatemalan immigrants rise to the top in consumer debt. These statistics reflect the national trend of sweeping consumer debts in all segments of the population, including presumably prudent immigrants.

The third column of table 4.13 shows the average amount of consumer debt for indebted households. From 1996 to 2003, the average amount of consumer debt per indebted household ranged from $4,668 for Dominican immigrants to $7,828 for Mexican immigrants. The native-white av-

Table 4.13   Unsecured Debts by Latino Group

	Crude	Adj4[a]	Credit Card Debts Amount	Trim. Amount
Native white	0.598	0.598	$6,141	$5,658
Latino American	0.560	0.615	$5,704	$5,642
Colombian	0.559	0.534	$5,922	$4,915
Salvadoran	0.517	0.585	$5,489	$5,622
Guatemalan	0.580	0.628	$5,184	$5,220
Mexican	0.416	0.497	$7,828	$4,474
Cuban	0.550	0.560	$6,587	$6,343
Dominican	0.421	0.589	$4,668	$4,726

Source: Author's compilation.
[a] Adj4 adjusts for the composition of age, marital status, number of children, and education levels.

erage of $6,141 is close to the national average of $6,648 (Federal Reserve Statistical Release 2000). Worth noting is the particularly large average consumer debt among Mexican immigrant households that carry debt. Examining the full distribution, I find that the high average amount results primarily from four households being indebted more than $100,000 each. To document the consumption debts for most households, I eliminated the top 0.02 percent (more than $50,000) and the bottom 1.63 percent (less than $100) and recalculated the trimmed average debt (see the last column). This trimming effectively reduces the average amount for Mexican and Colombian immigrants as well as for native whites. Mexican immigrants are now the group with a lower average amount, but Cuban immigrants still have a relatively high ranking. As for consumer debt status, the consumer debt amount does not vary much across groups. On this point, we should not forget that the recent trend of taking home equity loans disguises consumer debt. Because native whites are more likely to take home equity loans, some of their consumer debts may be transferred to second mortgages.

These data show that approximately half of all households in each group incur consumer debts. The rate and the amount of this debt do not vary much across groups. Together, the rate and average debt reflect the national trend of all populations accumulating consumer debt. This similarity presents a completely different pattern than do other asset and debt comparisons, in which gaps are huge and the spread is wide.

Business Ownership

Most ethnic enterprises are founded in retail and service sectors. The risks are high because of their smallness and newness. Entrepreneurs often combine resources in innovative ways and handle the risks strategically. Some ethnic groups face more favorable opportunity structure than others (Aldrich and Waldinger 1990). For example, with their long immigration history and existing ethnic economy, contemporary Asian immigrants have greater access to business ownership than their Latino counterparts. Group characteristics also determine entrepreneurship. For instance, the first wave of Cuban immigrants had high education, adequate capital, previous business experiences, and high motivations, giving them an edge in establishing ethnic economy that continues to benefit later Cuban immigrants (Portes and Bach 1985). Jimy Sanders and Victor Nee (1996) further examine the role of family social capital and human capital in facilitating self employment. Between Latino and Asian immigrants, the major difference lies in the level of human capital, which explains why Latino immigrants have lower business ownership than their Asian counterparts.

The business ownership data from the SIPP is used to examine ethnic patterns of small businesses among Latino immigrants, against native whites and Latino Americans.[5] Note that business ownership data in the SIPP tend to be underreported but again the group patterns are not distorted. Figure 4.13 (table 4.14) shows that the crude rate is .158 for native whites and .087 for Latino Americans. However, the crude rates vary greatly among Latino immigrants. For Colombian immigrants, it is even higher (.202) than for the entrepreneurship-rich Cuban immigrants (.183). It is rather surprising to find that Guatemalan immigrants rank third. The Mexican immigrant rate is the lowest, at .082. After age (a proxy for experiences) is adjusted, Guatemalan and Mexican rates increase moderately and other rates remain steady. Marital status and number of children capture family social capital that facilitates small businesses. After family social capital is also adjusted, the high Colombian rate plunges and the low Dominican rate becomes even lower but the Guatemalan rate increases. Finally, education captures human capital, which also facilitates small businesses. When education is further adjusted to the native white composition, the increase in business ownership rates is seen for the three less-educated groups—Salvadoran, Guatemalan, and Mexican. The fully adjusted rate for Guatemalans is .192 and is the highest, higher than Cuban immigrants and native whites. The fully adjusted rate for Mexicans is .121 higher than the rate for Latino Americans and moving close to the rate for native whites.

This analysis shows the huge heterogeneity in small business ownership among Latino immigrants. Even with younger ages and lower education, Colombian and Guatemalan immigrants have business ownership rates that are similar to or higher than native whites. If Latino immigrants have the same demographic and educational characteristics as native whites, all Latino immigrant groups, except for Dominicans,

Figure 4.13   Crude and Adjusted Rates of Business Ownership by Latino Group

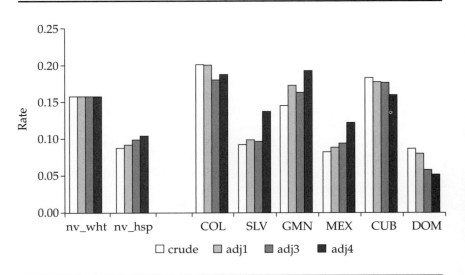

Source: Author's compilation.

have a business ownership rate close to that of native whites, or even greater than native whites. The low entrepreneurship for Salvadoran and Mexican immigrants can be greatly enhanced by improving their educational levels.

Table 4.14   Business Ownership by Latino Group

	Crude	Adj1[a]	Adj3[b]	Adj4[c]
Native white	0.158	0.158	0.158	0.158
Latino American	0.087	0.092	0.099	0.105
Colombian	0.202	0.201	0.181	0.188
Salvadoran	0.092	0.098	0.096	0.137
Guatemalan	0.145	0.172	0.163	0.192
Mexican	0.082	0.088	0.093	0.121
Cuban	0.183	0.177	0.177	0.159
Dominican	0.086	0.078	0.056	0.050

Source: Author's compilation.
[a] Adj1 adjusts for age composition.
[b] Adj3 adjusts for the composition of age, marital status, and number of children.
[c] Adj4 adjusts for the composition of age, marital status, number of children, and education levels.

The Likelihood of Cross-Border Asset Ownership

Thus far we have examined the wealth of Latino immigrant groups in comparison to native whites and native Latinos based on the SIPP data. All surveys with available wealth data implicitly ask questions about wealth in the United States because no questions ask about wealth outside it. Although we can envision wealthy native-born Americans owning assets abroad, both well-off and working-class immigrants have incentives to build part of their assets in their homeland. Reasons for immigrants' incentives to own wealth in the home country are discussed in chapter 2, including family and kinship obligations, networks with the home country, and the home country's type of wealth regime.

Before moving onto a discussion about the differential possibilities of cross-border asset ownership, it is important to bring up the issue of remittances, which are sometimes incorrectly equated with asset building. Recently, much attention has been paid to the rapid growth in remittances sent by immigrants. Lindsay Lowell (2002) notes that remittance flows from the United States to Mexico and Central American have increased at an uninterrupted high rate since 1990 even during the slowed American economy of 2000 and 2001. Annual remittances to Latin America have risen from about $4 billion in 1990 to almost $20 billion in 2002. These data are provided by banks and do not include nonbank forms of transfer. Studies have found consistent evidence supporting that family ties motivate much of the remittances, suggesting that a significant proportion of those dollars were spent on sustaining the consumption of family members left behind (Lucas and Stark 1985; Agarwal and Horowitz 2002). An ethnographic study of 302 Latino immigrants by the Pew Hispanic Center (Suro et al. 2003) `suggests that remitters come disproportionately from the working poor and many are in the United States illegally. Approximately $200 to $300 are sent to family in the home country every two weeks to pay ordinary living expenses, such as rent, utilities, and food, rather than for saving or to support a business endeavor. Once sent, remittances are seldom under immigrants' control. More formally, Ralph Chami, Connell Fullenkamp, and Samir Jahjah (2003) posit that immigrants care about the well-being of their family left behind in the home country. They send remittances to help the family avoid shortfalls created by a poor economy, making remittances compensatory transfers countercyclically. Based on 113 countries from 1970 to 1998, Chami and his colleagues find that remittances are not a source of capital for economic development. All these findings suggest that remittances are largely for cross-border consumption and have little impact on the possibility of immigrants having asset ownership in the homeland. For remittances to be productive, they must be used as capital for investment, such as operating a business or buying a house, though they seldom are. Despite the high aggregate levels of remittances, they are the sum of individual, private, small amount of transfers, and thus should not be taken as part of the cross-border investment of immigrants.

The likelihood of cross-border asset ownership is assessed using the concept of wealth regime and its measurement developed in chapter 2. The wealth regime classifies countries according to the relative development level, the investment environment, the expected future returns to investment, and the power of the U.S. currency. Based on data primarily from the World Bank for 199 countries from 1991 to 2003, I have constructed quantitative measures of the four dimensions: annual measures of relative development level (the GDP-capita gap between a country and the United States); annual measures of investment environment (a composite of the size of the domestic credit market, the degree of property rights protection, and political instability, all in relative terms against the corresponding U.S. measure); the past five-year growth rate and the standard deviation of the annual growth rate within the past five years; and the ratio of the market exchange rate of one U.S. dollar for a specific country to the corresponding purchasing power factor (PPP). I then made three categories based on each quantitative measure, and from these created a nine-category typology for the wealth regime.

Figure 4.14 shows the wealth regime typology and the selected countries falling under each type in 2002. The six Latin American sending countries examined in this chapter belong to different wealth regime types. Colombia and Cuba have very low levels of investment environment due to high political instability in Colombia and low property rights protection in Cuba. An unfavorable investment environment discourages emigrants of these two countries from making investments and building assets in their homelands. Mexico, El Salvador, and Guatemala have a medium level of investment environment. Their low development levels indicate the heavy obligation immigrants feel to support family members who remain in the home country. Immigrants' U.S. earned wages, with the overshooting of the U.S. dollars in the market exchange, can buy many more assets in the home country than they can in the United States. All these factors create incentives for emigrants to invest back in the homeland. However, growth rates are low in both countries, lowering expected future returns to investment. The Dominican Republic has an investment environment and development level similar to El Salvador and Guatemala, but exhibits a higher growth rate and stable growth, increasing expected future returns to investment.

What implications does the wealth regime typology have for immigrant decisions on cross-border investment? We must consider the impact of the wealth regime alongside the self selection of immigrants. For

Figure 4.14   The Wealth Regime Typology, 2002

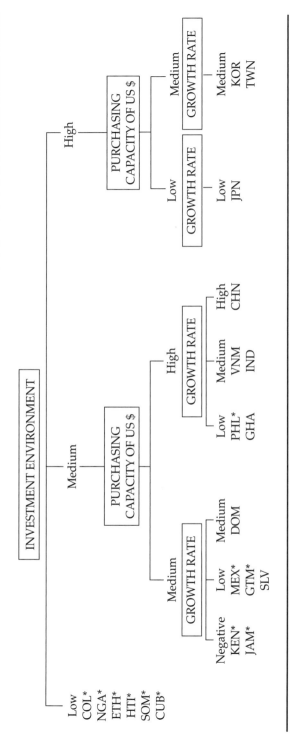

Source: Author's compilation.
Notes: The wealth regime typology is constructed based on 199 countries 1997 to 2002. The graph shows only the types that characterize the sending countries examined in this volume.
* Indicates unstable growth: 2 to 5 negative annual growth during 1997 to 2002.

example, Salvadoran and Mexican immigrants tend to have less education than those who remain, and Dominican immigrants are more likely to be single mothers with dependent children. In addition, a larger proportion of Mexican immigrants are circular migrants, usually intending to build assets in Mexico. Dominican immigrants, on the other hand, tend to stay in the United States permanently. Therefore, both the binational structure in terms of the wealth regime and the specific immigrant group's self-selection should be accounted for in assessing the likelihood of cross-border asset ownership.

First, the unfavorable investment environment of Colombia and Cuba determines that the likelihood of investment in the home country among these two countries' emigrants is low, despite that Cuban and Colombian immigrants fare quite well. Given the medium investment environment, low growth rate, and advantage of U.S. earned wages, Mexican, Salvadoran, and Guatemalan immigrants would have moderate probability of investment in their homeland. The family support obligation among Mexican and Salvadoran immigrants may be greater than among Guatemalans because Mexican and Salvadoran immigrants are more likely to come from the lower end of the home-country income distribution. In addition, the favorable conditions of the Dominican Republic in the wealth regime do not lead to a significant investment in the home country among those immigrants. The feminization of Dominican immigration, the financial constraints of single-mother families, and the intention of permanent stay dominate the favorable wealth regime conditions of the Dominican Republic, making the likelihood of cross-border investment low.

Thus, though we do not have the actual data on immigrant investments in their home countries, we can use the wealth regime concept to pinpoint the bias in the wealth patterns based on survey data. For example, we would expect the wealth of Mexican immigrants to be underestimated and that of Colombian, Cuban, and Dominican immigrants to be more accurate.

Summary

Because the perpetuation of chain migration from Latin America will continue for generations (Massey, Durand, and Malone 2002), a better understanding of assets and debts among Latino immigrants can help identify issues related to their immediate and long-term economic security.

The country of origin determines an immigrant's language, cultural, and religious roots. However, the economic and educational development and the social and political situation of an origin country are not uniformly associated with the demographic characteristics of its immigrants. Latino immigrants provide a good example of self-selection.

Among the six Latin American countries examined here, Mexico is the most developed. But among Latino immigrant groups, Mexicans are the least educated. A relatively low development level combined with long-term instability and severe catastrophes in El Salvador, Guatemala, and the Dominican Republic have propelled illegal emigration from these countries. Unauthorized immigrants from the relatively stable, prosperous Mexico seem to be of a subpopulation not representative of the whole. Primarily from underdeveloped rural areas, the vast majority of Mexican immigrants are from the lowest social stratum and their journey to the United States is the last step in their rural-urban migration. U.S. refugee policies can profoundly affect the prospects of refugee immigrants. Cuban and Salvadoran immigrants provide a good comparison. The political situations in both countries created several massive-scale influxes of refugees, but the U.S. reception of the two groups has been very different, favoring Cuban refugees over Salvadoran.

Latino immigrants begin their new lives in the United States with differences in cultural traditions, migration motives, self selection, and the receptiveness of the U.S. government and labor market. Under these conditions, comparisons among Latino immigrant groups, Latino Americans, and native whites require a distinction between the compositional differences in demographic characteristics and the differences in the effects of these characteristics on asset and debt obtaining behaviors. Observed patterns and patterns controlled for compositional differences are both presented to isolate the compositional effects in shaping observed group differences.

Several patterns emerge from the analysis in this chapter regarding both heterogeneity and homogeneity among Latino immigrants. Cuban, and sometimes Colombian immigrants are better off than other Latino immigrant groups in many aspects. Mexicans, the largest and least educated Latino immigrant group, usually fall in the middle. Other illegal-immigrant-concentrated groups fare poorly. Latino immigrants as a whole have two things in common—their rates of retirement account ownership are lower than the rate of native whites and their consumer debt is similar to the rates of native whites.

Cubans are the best off among Latino immigrant groups in many respects. In terms of economic security (measured by owning the amount of net worth that could cover the household's consumption for one year without income), they surpass Latino Americans and approach parity with native whites. They show a larger dispersion of net worth, total assets, and secured debts than native whites. At the ninetieth percentile, they have greater net worth, assets, and loan-obtaining capacity than native whites, whereas at the tenth percentile Cubans are more disadvantaged. Cuban immigrants have reached a more mature stage of asset building; their net worth measured as a proportion of total assets is larger than those of other Latino immigrant groups, though it falls short of the native white proportion. Cuban immigrant homeownership rates also approach those of native whites. In addition, Cuban immigrants lead in taking up second mortgages, having bank accounts, having at least $20,000 in liquid financial assets, and having employer-provided life insurance. They also have high rate of business ownership, higher than native whites.

This optimistic picture of Cuban immigrants, however, is countered by other facts. Cuban immigrants have low rates of owning either retirement accounts or investments in stocks and mutual funds. Home equity seems to be their choice for economic security. Although real estate is not a bad investment, home equity is not easy to liquidate in the face of an emergency or on retirement. In addition, diversifying investments and keeping up to date with the modern financial market may be key to greater capital and income growth and to greater success in asset building. The wealth regime analysis toward the end of the chapter suggests that the measures of Cuban immigrant wealth are unlikely to be underestimated because the incentive to invest back in Cuba is so low.

With good education, fewer children, and a low poverty rate, Colombian immigrants take second place in many aspects of wealth, including levels of net worth and assets, homeownership, stock and mutual fund ownership, retirement account ownership, life insurance ownership, liquid financial assets, and business ownership. They are the most likely to have bank accounts and the most able to avoid high interest rates on their first home mortgages. However, they still rank far behind their Cuban counterparts. This picture is unlikely, as with Cuba, to be downwardly biased because of the scant opportunity to invest in Colombia.

With the least education and the most children, Mexican immigrants have the second-highest poverty rate among Latino immigrants. Their most impressive accomplishment is their sufficient wealth holding status: they rank third. This can be partially explained by their high rate of poverty, that is, their sufficient wealth holding status is determined by their poverty-level consumption. They also do relatively well in levels of net worth and total assets, homeownership rate, and liquid financial assets. Mexican homeowners successfully avoid having NHE, taking second mortgages, and paying high interest rates on home mortgages. However, Mexican immigrants do not fare well in many other respects. They have a high paycheck-to-paycheck rate, little access to financial institutions, little life insurance ownership, and little business ownership. The low rate of business ownership can be explained by low levels of education. Their wealth situation, however, is actually better than what it might be given their demographic and educational characteristics. This may be explained at least in part by their well-established networks accommodating newcomers and offering access to labor markets. Their overall situation may be related to the fact that many are likely to eventually return to Mexico, and the wealth regime analysis suggests that actual wealth holding may be higher than what survey data report.

The remaining Latino immigrant groups fare poorly. Salvadoran and Guatemalan wealth holdings are lower than Mexican even though the three groups have similar demographic characteristics: younger ages, more children, less education, and frequent illegal status. Well-established Mexican networks may have provided Mexicans with advantages. Therefore, a steady development of ethnic communities, such as Salvadoran communities in the Washington, D.C., area, may enable other Latin American immigrants to follow the Mexican trajectory. Guatemalan immigrants are found to have a high rate of business ownership. Improving their education could further boost this group's prospect of small business success. Dominicans stand apart: the households are likely to be female-headed, poor, and reliant on welfare, aspects that show them to be the poorest of Latino immigrant groups.

The analysis in the chapter has established heterogeneity among Latino immigrants. At the same time, evidence for the homogeneity among Latino immigrants is strong in two respects. First, retirement account ownership rates are low, regardless of whether they plan to stay in the United States. They have prepared less for old-age than their native-born counterparts, who already lag far behind native whites. Latino immigrants are less likely than native whites and Latino Americans to have primary labor market jobs that offer pensions or employer contributions to retirement accounts. Many Latino immigrants, including those planning an eventual return to their home countries, will ultimately stay in the United States. Thus the very low rates of retirement account ownership of Latino immigrants will eventually present a serious challenge to this group and to public programs. Financing this fast-growing population's retirement years will become a pressing problem in the near future.

Further adding to the gloomy side of the financial situation, consumer debts among Latino immigrants are catching up to those of native whites, despite immigrants' presumably prudent consumption. The penetration of credit card use into every segment of the population has had a sweeping impact on all Americans, native- and foreign-born alike. The fragile wealth foundation among Latino immigrants makes them more vulnerable to financial risks. They can easily slip into universal default in the face of unstable jobs or unemployment, both chronic problems for many of them. Universal default status can create a financial time bomb, which can destroy the American dream that led so many Latino immigrants to the United States in the first place.

= Chapter 5 =

Assets and Debts Among Asian Immigrants

The Asian immigrant population is growing rapidly. From 1990 to 2000, it grew by 52.4 percent, catching up to the growth rate of 57.9 percent for Latino immigrants (U.S. Census Bureau 2003). Although the numbers of Asian immigrants are relatively small today, the population's high growth rate will lead to a more substantial Asian presence in the near future. Understanding how Asian immigrants prepare for their economic security today will help us to predict how their growing presence will change the nation's wealth distribution in the future. For simplicity, in this chapter the word country is used to include a separate group that combines Hong Kong and Taiwan, because those two populations have different conditions and immigration histories than mainland China.

Much literature has documented dramatic differences in economic attainment between Asian and Latino immigrants (Borjas 1999; Bean and Stevens 2003). U.S. immigration policy limited immigration from Asian countries from the Immigration Act of 1924 to the Immigration and Nationality Act Amendments of 1965, but Latin American countries were never subjected to such a restriction. Asian countries today are primarily sources of professionals, small business owners, and service workers, whereas Latin American countries are primarily sources of manual laborers and agricultural workers. Whereas many Latino immigrants have no legal status and plan to return to their home countries, most Asian immigrants are legal and plan to stay in the United States. All this gives rise to differences in demographic characteristics and consuming and saving behaviors between Asian immigrants and Latino immigrants, which in turn mean differences in assets and debts between the two groups.

Despite differences between Asian and Latino immigrants, variations among Asian immigrants from different countries may be even greater. Although Asian immigrants from all countries face similar U.S. immigration policies, differences in home country conditions and immigration histories may be major determinants for who is selected to emigrate and how they adapt to the host society. Wealth differences among Asian immigrant groups may arise from these conditions.

Traditionally, Americans have viewed Asian immigrants through the lens of a Chinatown, a community of many tightly packed small businesses that serves a coethnic and American clientele. Today, ethnic economies, such as newly emerging Korean towns and Little Saigons, continue to thrive, embracing wave after wave of newcomers, many of whom will enter the mainstream within a decade or a generation. Many people are also aware of Asian immigrant professionals, such as Chinese, Indian, Japanese, and Korean scientists and engineers, Indian doctors, and Filipino nurses and physical therapists. These professionals seldom rely on ethnic economies, but join the American mainstream just as contemporary western European immigrants do. As a result, huge variations in assets and debts exist among Asian immigrant groups, even among immigrants from the same country. The task here is to provide a better understanding of asset and debt patterns and their relationship to demographic characteristics and country of origin.

This chapter describes and analyzes the wealth of immigrants from seven Asian countries and regions—Mainland China, Hong Kong and Taiwan, India, Japan, South Korea, the Philippines, and Vietnam. Detailed information about asset and debt components comes from the six cross-sections of the 1996 and 2001 SIPP panels. The choice of origin countries is based on the data's providing an adequate sample size of immigrants from each country. The SIPP's 1996 and 2001 panels distinguish country of birth for mainland China, Hong Kong, and Taiwan, unlike the pre-1996 panels. This distinction is important for an accurate depiction of Chinese immigrants' wealth because of the vast differences between mainland China on the one hand and Hong Kong and Taiwan on the other.

Country of Origin and Demographic Differences

Asian immigrants' demographic characteristics are examined in relation to the historical and contemporary economic, geopolitical, educational, social, and cultural conditions of their origin countries. The discussion also includes migration motives, U.S. immigration policy pertaining to the specific sending country, and the reception of the American labor market to each of the seven groups.

Figure 5.1 (see details in table 5.1) compares the age structure, marital status, number of children, education levels, and poverty status of immigrants from the seven Asian countries to that of Asian Americans as well as native whites, the basis of comparison for all immigrant groups. Asian American households are remarkably similar to native white households in all demographic characteristics except age—some 65 percent have heads younger than forty-five, compared to 51.8 percent of native whites. Although the SIPP does not identify their ancestry, Asian Americans aged twenty-five to sixty-four between 1996 and 2002 were born from 1932 to 1977, so a majority of them are most likely the second or third generations of the early Asian immigrants from mainland China, Japan, and the Philippines. They appear to have assimilated successfully, in that they have attained as much or more education than native whites. In addition, a similarly low proportion of Asian Americans and native whites live below 130 percent of the official poverty line, and the two groups exhibit similar demographic characteristics regarding marital status and number of children. To compare native whites and Asian Americans with each of the Asian immigrant groups, it is important to review each origin country's background and history of sending immigrants to the United States.

Mainland China

With 1.3 billion people in 2003, China is the most populous country in the world, accounting for a quarter of the world's population. Despite its low GDP per capita ($1,209 in 2003), China's high economic growth rate

Figure 5.1   Demographics by Asian Group

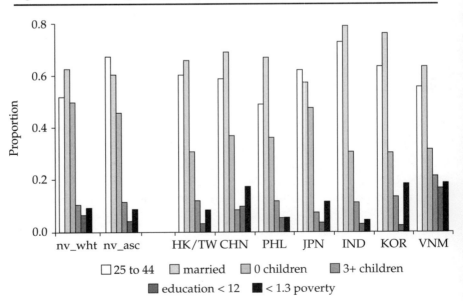

Source: Author's compilation.

Table 5.1   Demographic and Socioeconomic Differences by Asian Group

	Age (25 to 44)	Married	0 Children	3 + Children	Education < 12	Poverty[a]	Sample Size
Native white	0.518	0.626	0.498	0.104	0.064	0.091	98,010
Asian American	0.674	0.605	0.459	0.115	0.040	0.086	943
HK–Taiwan Chinese	0.603	0.661	0.307	0.120	0.029	0.083	276
Mainland Chinese	0.590	0.693	0.369	0.082	0.096	0.173	448
Filipino	0.492	0.671	0.361	0.116	0.052	0.053	659
Japanese	0.622	0.574	0.479	0.074	0.038	0.115	168
Asian Indian	0.729	0.791	0.307	0.110	0.028	0.044	548
Korean	0.637	0.764	0.304	0.133	0.023	0.185	363
Vietnamese	0.557	0.638	0.318	0.213	0.168	0.187	462

Source: Author's compilation.
[a] Less than 130 percent Poverty Level.

since the 1990s predicts its growing importance in the world economy. Its urbanization level is relatively low: people engaged in industry and commerce make up only about 25 percent of the population, whereas those engaged in agriculture and forestry make up 60 percent. Most urban areas are able to provide the nine years of education required by law, but rural areas face many resource constraints. Although the literacy rate is 86 percent, only 2.0 percent of the Chinese population aged twenty-five and above had received postsecondary degrees in 1990 (UNESCO 2002). Although the country has emphasized learning English in recent years, the population's English knowledge as a second language is low, even among the college educated.

In varying ways and to different degrees, Confucianism constitutes a large part of the cultural heritage of China, as well as Japan, Korea, and Vietnam, leading some to say that Confucianism is to East Asia what Christianity is to western Europe. Confucianism is a social ethic, according to which the cardinal Five Relationships—those between ruler and minister, father and son, husband and wife, brothers, and friends—form the intricate and organic web of relations into which everyone is born. The central cultural features derived from Confucianism are high values placed on hard work, frugality, education, and the willing sacrifice of individual benefit for the collective good. Confucianism was repressed during the first forty years of the Chinese communist regime but has revived since the economic reforms of the 1980s. The cultural features derived from Confucianism play an important role in influencing Chinese immigrants' adaptation and wealth accumulation in the United States.

China has a long U.S. immigration history. Two types of immigrants have typically arrived from China—working-class and scholar-professional. The earliest wave of working-class immigrants arrived during the 1850s when laborers were recruited from southern rural areas in China for railroad construction and agricultural, mining, and manufacturing work (Lyman 1974). In the 1860s, about one in three western miners in the United States were Chinese. The significant presence of Chinese laborers led to the Chinese Exclusion Act of 1882, which barred laborers from China, and the subsequent Immigration Act of 1924 that cut off all immigration from Asia and denied citizenship to Asian immigrants. The Chinese population dwindled from a high of 107,000 in 1890 to 61,000 in 1920. The repeal of the Chinese Exclusion Act in 1943 recognized China's position as an ally in World War II. The United States started to allow a token quota of entrants and to make Chinese permanent residents eligible for citizenship. The Brides Act of 1946 permitted entry to wives and children of citizens and permanent residents, allowing male Chinese immigrants to have their families in the United States. The 1965 Immigration and Nationality Act brought in an even larger influx of working-class Chinese through its family reunification clause. The country quota has allowed 20,000 entrants per year since 1965; more than half of these entrants can be classified as working class.

The scholar-professional Chinese immigrants have a shorter history. The older group arrived as students in the 1940s and 1950s and stayed. The younger group entered under the employment based preference system of the 1965 act. Before the Chinese economic reforms and market transition of the 1980s, a small percentage of the population received higher education. However, the large absolute number of the highly educated and China's recent open-door policy have made the country a more significant source of professional immigrants to the United States. A significant proportion of professional, managerial, and white-collar immigrants trained in China, however, experience a drop to blue-collar and service status because of language and licensing difficulties. In contrast, Chinese immigrants trained in the United States have gained an increasing presence in professions such as engineering, computer sciences, physical sciences, and academia. The Immigration Act of 1990 increased the number of visas for priority workers and professionals with U.S. job offers and legalized Chinese refugees who were living in the United States in 1990. A special order also allowed Chinese students who had arrived before the 1989 Tiananmen Square event to stay.

The SIPP data show that of those born from 1932 to 1978, 68 percent of the sampled mainland Chinese immigrant householders ($n = 448$) came to the United States after 1984 and only 9 percent arrived before 1965. After 1965 and particularly after 1990, immigration policies favored professional immigrants, so the sample includes relatively more professional and fewer working-class Chinese.

The fourth set of bars in figure 5.1 shows the demographic and socio-economic characteristics of immigrants from mainland China. Almost 60 percent of the heads of households are aged twenty-five to forty-four. Although on average Chinese immigrants are younger than native whites, they are older than Asian Americans. Almost 70 percent of Chinese immigrants were married, 6 and 9 percentage points higher than comparable rates for native whites and Asian Americans, respectively. Chinese immigrants are less likely to be childless than native whites and Asian Americans (37 percent versus 50 percent and 46 percent). Mainland Chinese immigrants, however, are also less likely to have three or more children (8.2 percent versus 10.4 percent and 11.5 percent). This is inconsistent with development theories, which posit that fertility rates are higher in developing countries than developed countries. The one-child policy of China makes the country a unique case among developing nations. Some immigrants from mainland China may have more children after coming to the United States because there is no policy constraint against it. Others may consider their potential resources to invest in their children and thus decide to have smaller families.

Because Chinese immigrants are a mixture of professionals and laborers, the proportion with no high school education (9.6 percent) is much higher than for native whites and Asian Americans (6.4 percent and 4.0 percent, respectively). The proportion of those with less education is not as high as that for some observed Latino immigrant groups. The mix of classes also leads to the relatively high poverty rate among mainland China immigrants, with 17.3 percent below 130 percent of the official poverty line, compared to about 9 percent for native whites and Asian Americans.

Hong Kong and Taiwan

Some Chinese immigrants came from Hong Kong or Taiwan. The population of these two regions is much smaller than mainland China's. In 2003, the population of Hong Kong was 6.8 million and in Taiwan 22.7 million, compared to 1.3 billion in mainland China. More important, the development level and immigration history of these two regions are notably different from mainland China.

Hong Kong had come under British colonial rule in 1842, which ended in 1997 when it became a special administrative region of China. The 155 years of colonial history make Hong Kong distinctive from mainland China in a number of respects. Hong Kong's GDP per capita was $26,236 in 2003, twenty-one times that of China. The literacy level was 92 percent and 90 percent of the population completed either high school or vocational school. The official language is English and until recently English was also the instructional language in many secondary schools and in a majority of colleges and universities. Hong Kong has strong economic ties with the United States, which is one of Hong Kong's principal investors and trading partners.

Taiwan became a Dutch colony in the 1600s, then seceded, became a province under various Chinese dynasties, and finally became a Japanese colony. Since the end of the World War II, it has been under the rule of the Nationalist Chinese, the political opponent of the communist regime in mainland China. During the past half century, Taiwan has transformed from an agricultural to a commercial, industrial economy. Its GDP per capita was $13,925 in 2003, 53 percent of Hong Kong's and 1200 percent of mainland China's. The literacy rate was 97 percent. Taiwan stipulates nine years of compulsory education and boasts an attendance rate of 100 percent. Colleges and universities in Taiwan have high admission standards. Taiwan-U.S. economic, political, and military ties were very strong in the cold war era and have remained strong since then. A deep U.S. influence in Taiwan derives from large-scale U.S. foreign aid, technical assistance, trade, and direct investment, which have opened gateways for many professionals and university students to come to America.

The cultural root of Confucianism in Hong Kong and Taiwan has been preserved better than it has in mainland China. Confucian institutions, worship rituals, secondary-school curriculum, and active government promotion of Confucianism have sustained a stronger adherence to Confucianism among people in Hong Kong and Taiwanese than among those in mainland China.

Immigration from Hong Kong and Taiwan got under way when the educated arrived in the 1940s and 1950s as students and stayed after obtaining their degrees. The 1965 immigration law allowed new professionals, investors, and relatives of professionals and investors to immigrate to the United States. Before the 1997 conversion of Hong Kong's political power, a large influx of immigrants from Hong Kong had arrived.

The SIPP data show that an overwhelming 96 percent of the sampled immigrants from Hong Kong and Taiwan arrived after 1965 and that 80 percent arrived after 1974. The third set of bars in figure 5.1 shows the characteristics of sampled immigrants from Hong Kong and Taiwan combined. More than 60 percent of them are aged twenty-five to forty-four, about 65 percent are married, 30 percent have no children, and 12 percent have three or more children. Compared with their mainland Chinese counterparts, immigrants from Hong Kong and Taiwan have a slightly lower marriage rate, which may be because they are younger. But they also have more children than mainland immigrants, perhaps because they were not subject to the one-child policy in China.

Although demographic characteristics are quite similar among all Chinese immigrants, the socioeconomic status of those from Hong Kong and Taiwan is much higher than that of those from the mainland. Only 2.9 percent of immigrants have no high school education, compared to 9.6 percent of those from the mainland, and only 8.3 percent live below 130 percent of the official poverty line, compared to 17.3 percent of those from the mainland. In fact, the socioeconomic status of immigrants from Hong Kong and Taiwan is higher than that of mainland immigrants and almost identical to that of Asian Americans.

Japan

Japan is a smaller country than China, with a population of 127.7 million in 2004. It is the second-largest economy in the world after the United States, with a GDP per capita $37,651 in 2003. That year also, 99 percent of the population was literate and 90 percent had completed high school. The post–World War II years saw tremendous economic growth in Japan. Its industrial leadership, well-educated work force, high saving rates and investment rates, and intensive promotion of industrial development and foreign trade have produced a mature industrial economy. Japan is one of the three major players in the global market economies, along with North America and western Europe. In addition to high education and high saving and investing rates, Confucianism was considered as one of the important factors in Japan's economic miracle.

Like those from mainland China, Japanese immigrants have a long history of emigrating to the United States, beginning with laborers going to Hawaiian plantations in the mid-nineteenth century. By 1919, Japanese workers made up 54.7 percent of the total plantation labor force. Many Japanese moved from Hawaii to the U.S. mainland. After the Chinese Exclusion Act of 1882, American industrialists sought to replace Chinese immigrants with Japanese. The presence of Japanese immigrants in the continental United States increased until the so-called Gentlemen's Agreement of 1907, which curtailed labor immigration from Japan but permitted wives and children of laborers to enter the country. The Immigration Act of 1924 curtailed any immigration from Japan. During World War II, Japanese immigrants were sent to internment camps. Significant Japanese immigration did not again begin until the Immigration and Nationality Act of 1965, and most recent Japanese immigrants have been highly educated professionals.

The SIPP data shows that sampled Japanese householders arrived in different periods: more than 16 percent before 1965 and about half after 1984. The sixth set of bars in figure 5.1 describes Japanese immigrant characteristics. Marriage and fertility patterns, for example, are notably different from other Asian immigrant groups. Only 57.4 percent of Japanese immigrants are married, the lowest rate among Asian immigrants, native whites, and Asian Americans. The percentage of those who are childless is also the highest among all Asian immigrants and similar to that of native whites. Following patterns similar to those in Japan, Japanese immigrants have the lowest fertility rate among all as well, with only 7.4 percent having three or more children. Only 3.8 percent of Japanese immigrants have no high school education. Their poverty rate of 11.5 percent, however, is not the lowest, indicating that some Japanese immigrants do not fare well.

The Philippines

The Philippine population, 76.5 million in 2000, is somewhat smaller than Japan's but much smaller than China's. The Philippine GDP per capita was $1,045 in 2003, similar to that in China. The literacy rate was 92 percent and compulsory education was six years. Only 65 percent of the age-appropriate population is enrolled in secondary education. However, private colleges have recently mushroomed and produced a greater college-educated labor force than the Philippine economy requires. Although Pilipino—which is based on a principal indigenous language, Tagalog—has recently been promoted as a national and instructional language in all schools, English remains the official language. Nearly all professionals are English proficient. After the Spanish colonial period, which spanned the sixteenth through the nineteenth centuries to 1898, the Philippines became an American colony until it gained its independence in 1946. The Spanish period saw the conversion to Roman Catholicism. The fifty years as an American colony saw a pervasive Americanization in the development of an American-style education system and the adoption of English as an official and instructional language. After World War II, the Republic of Philippines slid from being one of the richest countries in Asia (following Japan) to one of the poorest. Because of their historical and cultural links, U.S.-Philippine relations are strong. An estimated two million Americans of Philippine ancestry live in the United States.

The Philippines also has a long history of emigration, American colonization having opened a pathway for an exodus of Filipinos to the United States. Educated Filipinos came as government scholars to study in American universities, and many of them stayed. At the same time, less-educated Filipinos came as a cheap migrant labor supply for Hawaii plantations. By the 1930s, Filipinos had replaced the Japanese as the largest ethnic group of plantation workers. When in the 1920s California's agricultural economy needed a steady supply of migrant labor, Filipinos arrived in California in large numbers to work under the contract system. By 1930, Filipino immigrants became a substantial presence in California. Most of these workers eventually adopted the United States as their new homeland. The 1924 Immigration Act that curtailed all other Asian immigrants did not affect Filipinos because of the colonial relationship. The citizenship rate was high among Filipino immigrants in part because many had fought side by side with the Americans during World War II and subsequently become American citizens. Employment in the military became a special niche for Filipino immigrants and about half of the Filipino labor force in San Diego was employed by the U.S. Navy (Rumbaut 1994).

The Immigration and Nationality Act of 1965 allowed for a new and different wave of Filipino migration. Thousands of professionals, mostly doctors, physical therapists, and nurses, arrived with their spouses and children. The number of Filipinos in the United States multiplied to 1,406,770 in 1990. The Immigration Act of 1990 increased the number of visas for priority workers and professionals with U.S. job offers, leading to the Philippines' position as second in the list of sending countries.

According to the SIPP data, almost all sampled Filipino householders arrived after 1965 (96.2 percent), but their arrival was gradual. Because the Filipino inflow had not been interrupted, the age structure of Filipino immigrants is similar to that of native whites: 49 percent aged twenty-five to forty-four (see the fifth set of bars in figure 5.1). Perhaps because of Catholicism, the marriage rate among Filipino immigrants is 67 percent, higher than that of native whites and Asian Americans. A smaller percentage than native whites have no children (36 percent), but the percentage having three or more (11.6 percent) is similar to that of native whites and Asian Americans. The education level of Filipino householders is also high. Only 5.2 percent have no high school education. Their poverty rate is low as well, with only 5.3 percent living below 130 percent of the official poverty line. Taken together, these demographic and socioeconomic characteristics are similar to those of native whites, and in the case of education of poverty are even better than native whites.

India

India is the second most populous country in the world, following China, with a population of 1.05 billion in 2003. It is also one of the poorest countries in Asia, with a GDP per capita of $552 in 2003. The urbanization level is low, 70 percent of the population lives in villages and the literacy rate is only 55 percent. The most practiced religion is Hinduism. India makes a great educational effort by providing nine years of compulsory education, an academic system that is the oldest and largest in the developing world. In 1991, 7.3 percent of the Indian population aged twenty-five and above received postecondary education (UNESCO 2002), a much greater percentage than in China. Because India's population is so large, the number of highly educated Indians is also large. In India, English is the official and instructional language, so that English proficiency is high among the well educated even though the majority of people speak Hindi.

The British influence on India can be traced to the early seventeenth century. Under formal British colonial rule beginning in 1857, India gained independence in 1947 and became a republic of the Commonwealth. The long British influence contributed to both the wide use of English and the large higher education system. With some 65 percent of its economy in agriculture, India is still in the process of industrialization. The United States is its largest trading partner. Large-scale U.S. foreign aid, technical assistance, trade, and direct investment have created a strong U.S. influence and opened channels for many professionals and university students to come to America. The rapidly growing software sector in India is boosting service exports and modernizing India's economy.

In 1899 the first significant presence of Indian immigrants in the United States arrived from the province of Punjab. These were barely educated, poor agricultural workers. In 1913, students and political dissenters began to arrive. The Immigration Act of 1924 barred Indian immigrants altogether. The Immigration and Naturalization Act of 1965, with its quota of 20,000 immigrants from each country, allowed Indian professionals to come, though subsequently many more arrived under family reunification preferential categories. By 1975, the number of Asian Indians in the United States had risen to well over 175,000. According to an estimate in 1993, some 4 percent of doctors in the United States were Indian. Although there are more professionals among Indians than any other ethnic group, the number of Indian taxi drivers, gas station owners and attendants, and subway newsagent vendors has continued to grow.

Virtually all of the sampled Indian immigrant householders arrived after 1965 and 64 percent of them after 1984. It is thus not surprising that they are the youngest among the seven Asian groups, with almost 75 percent aged between twenty-five and forty-four (see the seventh set of bars in figure 5.1). The Indian value on marriage is very high. Despite younger ages, the marriage rate of 79 percent is the highest among the seven Asian groups. The fertility rate is similar to the those of Hong Kong, Taiwan, and the Philippines. Educational levels are very high: only 2.8 percent lack a high school education. Not surprisingly, their poverty rate is low, at 4.4 percent.

South Korea

With a population of 48.3 million, a GDP per capita of $12,245 in 2003, a 98 percent literacy rate, nine years of compulsory education, and a high school graduation rate of 95 percent, South Korea is a rapidly developing country. Unlike its neighbors with traditional Asian religions, the majority of South Koreans are Christians. Koreans, however, are also deeply influenced by Confucianism.

The Korean peninsula was a Japanese colony from 1910 until 1945, when it was divided into U.S. and Soviet military zones of administration. The invasion of South Korea by North Korean forces marked the start of the Korean War, which involved UN intervention led by the United States and, later, Chinese intervention. The end of the Korean War maintained the division between North and South Korea. The United States has established a strong security relationship to help South Korea defend itself against external aggression. Economically, South Korea received large amounts of U.S. foreign aid until 1980. The United States and South Korea have also established strong economic ties in trading and investing. The South Korean economy has achieved spectacular growth in the past thirty years, helping it rise from one of the poorest countries to the eleventh-largest economy in the world.

Immigrants from South Korea are a significant presence in the United States. Like Japanese immigrants, Korean Americans first migrated in the late 1800s and early 1900s, primarily as contract laborers for Hawaiian plantations. Others migrated as a result of United States-Korean interaction during the Korean War, when American solders stationed in Korea married Korean women, often called war-brides or peace-brides. In addition, thousands of Korean children orphaned by the war were adopted by American families. Korean immigrants after 1965 tend to be professionals such as doctors and engineers. In 1975, more than 32,000 Koreans entered the United States. Between 1980 and 1990, the Korean population more than doubled. By 2005, it was approximately 1,200,000. Because many of the new immigrants could not speak English fluently, they were often not able to enter the professions for which they had been trained in Korea, despite graduate degrees and highly skilled backgrounds. As a result, the new immigrants chose to run small businesses. Korean-owned groceries, restaurants, and dry cleaners have mushroomed throughout the country.

Almost all sampled South Korean immigrants arrived after 1965, about half between 1965 and 1984 and the other half after 1984. Korean immigrants share certain characteristics with Indian immigrants but are distinct in others. Both are likely to be married (more than 75 percent), to have one or two children, and to be highly educated (only 2 percent lack a high school education). However, Koreans are older than Indians (some 65 percent aged twenty-five to forty-four compared to 75 percent for Indians) and are much more likely to be poor (18.5 percent compared to 4.4 percent for Indians). In fact, their poverty rate is the highest among the seven Asian immigrant groups. I will examine this puzzle later in this chapter.

Vietnam

Vietnam is one of the poorest countries in Asia, with a population of 80.7 million, a 91 percent literacy rate, and a $471 GDP per capita in 2003. The majority of Vietnamese practice Buddhism and follow Confucianism. Vietnam's history includes the Chinese dynastic rule era, independence, the French colonial period, Japanese occupation, and the north-south division after World War II. The Vietnam War started in 1961 and lasted until 1973.

Vietnam's history of immigration to the United States is relatively short. The significant presence of Vietnamese immigrants began during the Vietnam War. Before 1975, most Vietnamese in the United States were spouses and children of American servicemen. The end of the Vietnam War prompted the first wave of emigration. Approximately 125,000 highly skilled and educated people left Vietnam during 1975, airlifted by the U.S. government to American bases and subsequently transferred to various refugee centers in the United States under a special status. From 1978 to the mid-1980s, a second wave of about 2 million fled Vietnam in small, unsafe, and crowded boats. They were generally less educated and less skilled than those in the first wave. Between 1981 and 2000, the United States accepted 531,310 Vietnamese refugees and asylum seekers. The Vietnamese government now allows people to leave Vietnam legally for family reunions and humanitarian reasons. Many Vietnamese immigrants are ethnic Chinese and serve as a bridge between Vietnamese immigrants and Chinese immigrant communities. The majority of Vietnamese immigrants are small business owners of restaurants, beauty salons, barber shops, and auto repair businesses. In the 1990s, Vietnam ranked third in the list of sending countries.

This background leaves Vietnamese immigrants with very different characteristics than those of other Asian groups. Very few of the sampled Vietnamese immigrants arrived before 1965, and almost 60 percent did so between 1974 and 1985. Figure 5.1 shows that they are relatively older—55.7 percent aged twenty-four to fifty-five, similar to the age structure of native whites. Fewer than 65 percent are married, a relatively low marriage rate that may be the result of widowhood and the Vietnam War. Although approximately 33 percent of Vietnamese immigrants have no children, those who do have more than their counterparts in all comparison groups: 21.3 percent have three or more children, double the percentage of other Asian immigrant groups, Asian Americans, or native whites. Some 16.8 percent have no high school education, reflecting the low education levels of the second wave of refugees. The poverty rate of 18.7 percent is not high given the low education levels of this group.

Asian immigrants share four characteristics—high marriage rates, low fertility rates, high education levels, and low poverty rates—in stark contrast with those of many non-Cuban Latino immigrants. Deeply rooted cultural values from Confucianism may govern the adaptation and wealth accumulation behaviors of immigrants from East Asia. However, despite these commonalities, each of the seven groups is unique.

The various attributes of Asian immigrants reflect the conditions of their home countries and their immigration history, which contribute to their self-selection and migration motives. These factors, together with the treatment immigrants received in the United States, continue to play a major role in how the immigrants adapt to and integrate into American society.

Wealth Holding Status

The five wealth holding statuses noted in earlier chapters measure qualitative differences in economic security among households. A household is considered as having sufficient economic security if its net worth can sustain the household's usual consumption for twelve months without any income. Those in the insufficient group can cope with hardship for fewer than twelve months. The other three classifications are at or below the asset poverty line: asset poor (having positive net worth but at or below the asset poverty line), net-debtor (having greater debts than assets) and paycheck-to-paycheck (having no assets or debts). Figure 5.2 shows the wealth status distribution among the seven Asian immigrant groups, compared with native whites and Asians Americans (see table 5.2 for details). The consumption levels on which the sufficient status is based are captured by the average trimmed annual household income (trimmed at 130 percent of the official poverty line for households at the lower limit and $100,000 at the upper limit, also see the last column of table 5.2).

Native whites and Asian Americans are two bases for comparison. The differences between these two groups mirror those observed in chapter 3 for whites and Asians. Native whites are better off than Asian Americans, having a higher sufficient percentage and a lower paycheck-to-paycheck percentage. The heterogeneity among Asian nationality immigrant groups is obviously greater than the difference between native whites and Asian Americans.

Among the seven Asian immigrant groups, immigrants from Hong Kong and Taiwan achieve the highest percentage with sufficient wealth holding (68.5 percent). This is 12 percentage points higher than native whites and 16 points higher than Asian Americans. In addition, the average trimmed annual income of Hong Kong and Taiwanese immigrants is a little higher than that of native whites ($54,000 versus $53,000). The great advantage of this group may be partially explained by the fact that their rates of marriage and levels of education are higher than those of native whites. Including those with insufficient wealth holding, 89 percent of immigrants from Hong Kong and Taiwan are not asset poor, the best-off of those examined in this volume.

The next best-off are immigrants from mainland China. More than half, 55 percent, have sufficient wealth holding, a slightly lower percentage than native whites and slightly higher than Asian Americans. The trimmed annual income for mainland Chinese immigrants, $52,000, is nearly as high as for native whites. In addition, 25 percent of mainland Chinese immigrants are in the insufficient wealth holding status, giving 80 percent of this group some economic buffer. However, mainland Chinese immigrants exhibit the highest paycheck-to-paycheck rate (5.9 percent) among the seven Asian immigrant groups. The higher paycheck-to-paycheck percentage is associated with this groups' relatively higher poverty rate. Labor immigrants from mainland China may live without economic security for a long time before an upturn.

Although the sufficient share for Japanese immigrants is lower than that for their mainland Chinese counterparts, 49 percent, the insufficient share is high at 37 percent. Thus, 86 percent of this group have some economic buffer against hardship, similar to those from Hong Kong and Tai-

Figure 5.2   Wealth Holding Status by Asian Group

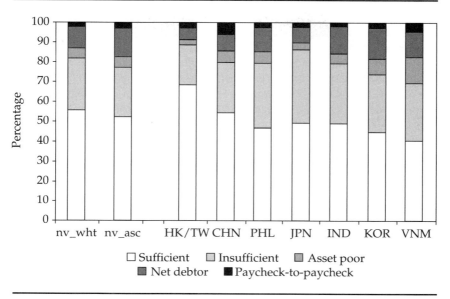

Source: Author's compilation.

wan. The trimmed annual income of Japanese immigrants ($57,000) is higher than that for immigrants from Hong Kong and Taiwan. Among the 14 percent of Japanese households at financial risk, only 2.4 percent live paycheck to paycheck. The wealth holding status of Japanese immi-

Table 5.2   Wealth Holding Status by Asian Group

	Sufficient	Insufficient	Asset Poor	Net-Debtor	Paycheck-to-Paycheck	Trimmed Annual Income[a]
Native white	0.564	0.257	0.052	0.114	0.014	$52,867
Asian American	0.523	0.251	0.055	0.147	0.024	$57,359
HK–Taiwan Chinese	0.685	0.202	0.027	0.061	0.025	$54,010
Mainland Chinese	0.549	0.250	0.060	0.082	0.059	$52,394
Filipino	0.468	0.325	0.059	0.124	0.023	$54,759
Japanese	0.491	0.373	0.037	0.076	0.024	$56,984
Asian Indian	0.491	0.302	0.053	0.137	0.016	$58,720
Korean	0.451	0.290	0.079	0.159	0.022	$49,184
Vietnamese	0.407	0.287	0.131	0.131	0.045	$51,613

Source: Author's compilation.
[a] Annual income is trimmed at 130 percent poverty line at the bottom and $100,000 at the top.

grants indicates that their economic attainment is higher than suggested by their relatively high poverty rate (shown in figure 5.1). Among Indian immigrants, almost 50 percent have sufficient and 30 percent have insufficient wealth holdings, meaning that about 80 percent have at least some economic buffer. Two reasons behind this seemingly less-advantaged situation are the younger ages of Indian immigrants—75 percent are aged twenty-five to forty-four—and a high trimmed annual income average, $59,000, the highest of all groups examined here. Indian immigrants, however, are at greater financial risk than Chinese and Japanese immigrants. Net debtors comprise 13.7 percent of Indian immigrants, the reasons for which will be examined later in this chapter (see the sections about negative home equity, mortgages, and consumer debts).

Filipino immigrants are in a situation similar to that of Indian immigrants. The percentages of the five wealth holding statuses are very similar, although Filipino immigrant trimmed annual income is $55,000, $4,000 lower than that of Indian immigrants.

With the lowest trimmed annual income ($49,000) among the seven Asian groups, Korean immigrants have lower percentages with an economic buffer: 45 percent of Korean immigrants hold sufficient wealth and 29 percent hold insufficient wealth. These percentages are lower than they are for the other groups examined so far, and Korean immigrants' trimmed annual income is also lower.

Only about 40 percent of Vietnamese immigrants hold sufficient wealth, the lowest percentage among the seven Asian groups. Their asset poor share is the largest of all, 13 percent. Their trimmed annual income ($516,000), however, is not the lowest, and the percentage of Vietnamese immigrants living paycheck-to-paycheck (4.5 percent) is not the highest.

Although the within-Asian immigrant gaps in wealth holding status are substantial, they cannot compare with the within-Latino immigrant gaps described in chapter 4. Each of the seven Asian immigrant groups has relatively sound economic security and low financial risk, and has closed the gap with or even surpassed native whites and Asian Americans. This pattern is in a stark contrast with the pattern of some Latino immigrant groups (Mexicans, Salvadorans, Guatemalans, and Dominicans) but is similar to that of Cuban immigrants.

Distribution of Net Worth, Assets, and Debts

To complement the examination of qualitative wealth holding status, this section focuses on the quantitative distribution of net worth, assets and debts. The percentile distribution of net worth for native whites, Asian Americans, and the seven Asian immigrant groups are shown in

Figure 5.3   Percentile Distribution of Net Worth by Asian Group

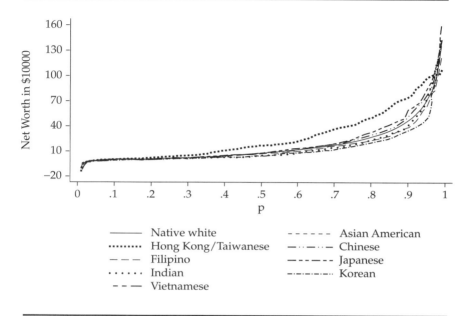

Source: Author's compilation.

figure 5.3. With one exception, all groups' percentile function seems to cluster in close neighborhood. The Hong Kong and Taiwan group is above the others, particularly over the population proportion of .3 to .95.

Using three percentiles—the fifth, fiftieth, and ninety-fifth—captures the location and spread of the distribution of net worth, assets, and debts, shown in table 5.3. The differences in the median (fiftieth percentile) indicate the central location differences among groups and the ranges between the fifth and ninety-fifth percentiles indicate the spread differences among groups. The median net worth for native whites is about $72,000, less than half of that for those from Hong Kong and Taiwan ($162,000) and is also lower than that for Chinese and Indian immigrants, but is double that for Korean and Vietnamese. The spread of net worth is similar for native whites and Chinese and Indian immigrants. It is widest for those from Hong Kong and Taiwan, Asian Americans, and Japanese immigrants, in that order. The narrowest distribution is among Korean immigrants. These comparisons show that not only the median differences but also the spread differences are greater among Asian immigrant groups than between Asian immigrants and native whites.

The amount of assets gauge future financial security, assuming that debts are eventually paid off. The asset distribution is widest for Asian

Table 5.3 Selected Percentiles of Net Worth, Asset, and Debt by Asian Group

	Net Worth			Assets			Debts		
	5th	50th	95th	5th	50th	95th	5th	50th	95th
Native white	−11,670	71,886	685,416	1,693	152,786	847,945	0	47,837	262,501
Asian American	−18,247	66,085	816,792	706	161,054	1,037,901	0	63,996	336,680
HK–Taiwan Chinese	−807	161,254	956,785	3,667	305,769	1,010,827	0	93,788	369,831
Mainland Chinese	−8,267	74,642	756,422	0	160,304	977,757	0	23,599	287,977
Filipino	−13,025	56,900	607,440	1,729	173,979	820,307	0	83,678	322,829
Japanese	−13,546	42,484	716,746	1,309	134,365	977,894	0	39,378	341,603
Asian Indian	−16,911	76,250	632,971	2,658	158,477	871,203	0	55,150	320,930
Korean	−16,221	31,576	475,782	2,282	93,438	640,419	0	24,020	284,100
Vietnamese	−15,330	30,851	693,123	0	100,500	952,600	0	28,220	281,945

Source: Author's compilation.

Americans and the narrowest for Korean immigrants. Debts, particularly secure debts, indicate the ability to obtain loans. Immigrants from Hong Kong–Taiwan and China appear to have the highest ability and Koreans the lowest.

The distributions of net worth, assets, and debts provide information on something that might be missed if only net worth is examined. Not only are the medians distanced, but the spreads of the distributions also differ among Asian groups. In all accounts—median and spread of net worth, assets, and debts—immigrants from Hong Kong and Taiwan rank first (above the two native-born groups) and from Korea rank last. This great within-Asian variation motivates a further investigation using a systematic analysis, provided in chapter 7.

The net worth, asset, and debt distributions of Asian immigrant groups have higher medians and wider spreads than those of any Latino immigrant group except Cubans (described in chapter 4). Cuban immigrants fare better than their Korean and Vietnamese counterparts but worse than other Asian immigrant groups. These three immigrant groups differentiate members within Asian and Hispanic groups and blur the Asian-Hispanic divide.

Portfolio

To examine the relationships among net worth, assets, and debts, net worth, secured debts, and unsecured debts are expressed as percentages of total assets. Because different groups have different levels of total assets, it is important to place the analysis in a relative framework, such as immigrant groups to native whites. Figure 5.4 shows the average total assets of each group as a percentage of native white average total assets. Figure 5.5 shows secured debts, unsecured debts, and net worth of each group as percentages of its own total assets. Figure 5.5 should be examined in the context of figure 5.4.

In terms of the average level of total assets (per household), native whites rank third from the bottom, higher only than Korean and Vietnamese immigrants (see figure 5.4). The Hong Kong and Taiwan immigrant average asset level is almost twice that of the native whites. Asian Americans take a distant second place, followed by Indian immigrants. Mainland Chinese, Filipino, and Japanese immigrants have a similar average assets level, one higher than that of native whites.

Not only do they have the highest average assets level, Hong Kong and Taiwan immigrants also have the highest percentage of net worth and lowest of unsecured debts, a superior state of economic security. Compared to Hong Kong and Taiwan immigrants, Asian Americans have lower net worth and higher secured and unsecured debts, which may be a result of their younger average age. The same statement applies

Figure 5.4   Net Worth and Debts as Percentage of Hong Kong and Taiwan Assets by Asian Group

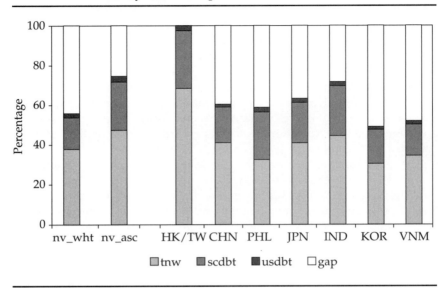

Source: Author's compilation.

Figure 5.5   Net Worth and Debt as Percentage of Total Assets by Asian Group

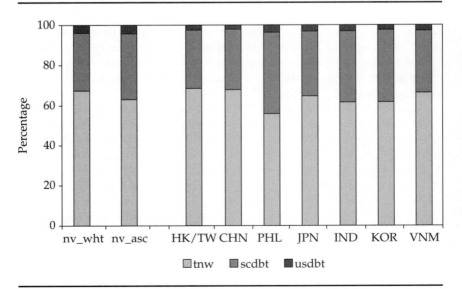

Source: Author's compilation.

Figure 5.6   Portfolio as Percentage of Total Equity by Asian Group

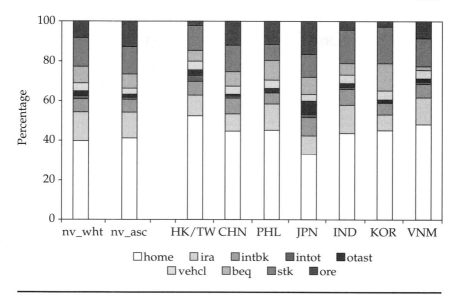

Source: Author's compilation.

to Indian immigrants. Although mainland Chinese, Filipino, and Japanese immigrants have similar total assets, the low secured and unsecured debts and high net worth of Chinese immigrants provide them with a more secure buffer than either Filipino or Japanese immigrants. In the two least advantaged groups, Korean immigrants have fewer average assets and a lower percentage of net worth than their Vietnamese counterparts.

Because secured debts are obtained using particular asset components as collateral, one way to examine portfolios is to use equity components, that is, the value of an asset less its secured debts. For example, home equity is a home's market value less any mortgages. Each equity component is expressed as the percentage of total equity. In figure 5.6, each equity component is expressed as a percentage of the total equity, and all equity components add to 100 percent for each group.

One guiding principle to examine figure 5.6 is to determine whether home equity (home) occupies an overwhelming percentage of total equity, an indicator of lack of diversity in portfolios. All Asian groups exhibit a diverse portfolio because home equity counts for no more than half of the total equity, except Hong Kong and Taiwan immigrants, for whom it is slightly more than half . All Asian immigrant groups have a substantial percentage in a number of components: retirement accounts (ira), indicating sufficient old-age security; interest-earning bank accounts (intbk), indicating sufficient liquid assets for emergency use; and stocks and mutual funds (stk), indicating modern investment strategies seeking high growth in wealth. These patterns are similar to those of native whites and Asian Americans.

Unique portfolio patterns are observed for Japanese, mainland Chinese, Filipino, and Korean immigrants. Japanese immigrants exhibit the lowest home equity percentage, which may be driven by their diverse investment preferences, for example, Japanese immigrants invest most heavily in real estate (ore). Mainland Chinese and Filipino immigrants are the other two groups that invest more in real estate than other groups. The highest percentage in business equity (beq) is found for Korean immigrants.

These portfolio descriptions show that despite gaps among them, Asian immigrant groups have much in common but are very different from Latino immigrants examined in chapter 4. Most Asian immigrant groups have more average assets than native whites. For most Asian immigrants, home equity is not the majority of total equity. Rather, their investments are diversified. In contrast, all Latino immigrant groups have fewer average assets than native whites. For Latino immigrants, home equity is the major component of total equity and their investments are not as diverse as those of Asian immigrants. In the long run, these portfolio differences between Asian and Latino immigrant groups may further widen the gap in wealth between them.

Homeownership

What are the homeownership differences among Asian immigrant groups? The answer, as with Latino immigrants, is demographics (age, marriage, and children). Education also plays an important role. However, because the proportion with no high school education is very small among nearly all Asian groups examined here, it is difficult to perform the same analysis as in chapter 4. Two sets of effects of these factors will be examined here. One includes composition effects, meaning that different groups have different proportions with advantageous demographic characteristics, and total homeownership rates may therefore differ. The other includes the potential differential effects of age, marital status, and number of children on homeownership by groups.

Table 5.4 shows the homeownership rate both for the total and by demographic characteristics and thus the composition effect for each of the demographic characteristics. The first column lists the rate for the total. The rate is the highest among Hong Kong and Taiwan immigrants (74 percent), higher than native whites (70.8 percent). Next is the rate for Filipino immigrants (64.2 percent), followed by Asian Americans (63.6 percent), then mainland Chinese immigrants, Indian, Vietnamese, Japanese, and Koreans, in that order.

Although homeownership rates are higher for older individuals, the growth rates differ by groups. For example, in the younger age group, Japanese immigrants rank last (ninth place) and Vietnamese fourth, whereas in the older group, the Japanese rank fifth and the Vietnamese eighth, indicating a greater growth rate for Japanese than for Vietnamese. Not only does the age effect vary, but the age composition also affects the total ranking. The very low homeownership rate at young ages and a relatively high proportion (62 percent) of young Japanese immigrants contribute to their low ranking overall. Likewise, the very low homeownership rate and relatively high proportion of older Vietnamese immigrants contribute to their low overall ranking even though at younger ages their homeownership rate is not that low.

Married households are more likely than unmarried to own their own homes. This is true for all comparison groups but the married-unmarried gaps differ by groups. Indian immigrants exhibit the highest gap whereas Korean immigrants exhibit the lowest gap. The marriage rate of Japanese immigrants is the lowest of all and their homeownership rate is not high among the unmarried, contributing to their low overall ownership rate. On the other hand, the high marriage rate of Korean immigrants does not enhance their total homeownership rate because of the low homeownership rate among married Korean immigrants.

Having children also promotes homeownership. However, when the financial situation of a household is tight, having more children has an adverse effect. Table 5.4 shows that households with no children have the lowest ownership rate in all groups and that those with three or more have the highest ownership rate, with two exceptions: Asian Americans and Vietnamese immigrants. Asian Americans have fewer children and those who have three or more are less likely to own a home than those who have one or two. The homeownership rate of Vietnamese households with three or more children is much lower than it is for those with one or two, dropping to the rate of childless households.

When examined separately, both differential effects and composition effects play a role in determining Asian immigrant homeownership. Figure 5.7 answers the question how rates differ among Asian immigrant groups if they have the same demographic composition as native whites. Presented are crude rates (observed), the rates adjusted for the native white age composition, for marital status and number of children, and for education composition. No Asian group exhibits substantial changes from the crude to the adjusted rates, indicating that the combined composition effects of age, marriage, and children on Asian immigrants' homeownership are negligible.

The potential differential effects of age, marital status, and number of

Table 5.4 Homeownership by Demographic Characteristics and Asian Group

	Total	25 to 44	45 to 64	Unmarried	Married	0	1 to 2 Children	3 +	Education < 12	Education ≥ 12
Native white	0.708	0.632	0.790	0.498	0.834	0.643	0.771	0.780	0.485	0.724
Asian American	0.636	0.559	0.796	0.451	0.758	0.533	0.754	0.612	0.648	0.636
HK–Taiwan Chinese	0.740	0.664	0.855	0.513	0.857	0.464	0.842	0.960	0.404	0.750
Mainland Chinese	0.570	0.527	0.631	0.373	0.657	0.425	0.653	0.665	0.231	0.606
Filipino	0.642	0.529	0.751	0.476	0.723	0.608	0.639	0.760	0.623	0.644
Japanese	0.503	0.376	0.713	0.390	0.587	0.362	0.591	0.888	0.596	0.499
Asian Indian	0.551	0.510	0.662	0.252	0.630	0.301	0.640	0.778	0.331	0.557
Korean	0.490	0.459	0.546	0.445	0.504	0.448	0.467	0.685	0.853	0.482
Vietnamese	0.548	0.547	0.549	0.383	0.642	0.450	0.674	0.419	0.264	0.603

Source: Author's compilation.

Figure 5.7   Crude and Adjusted Homeownership Rates by Asian Group

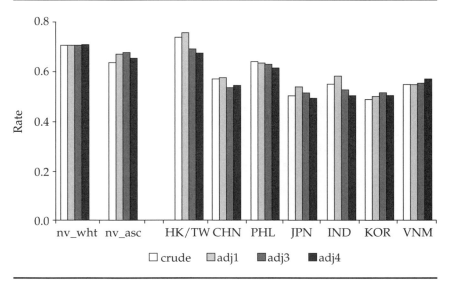

Source: Author's compilation.

children can be seen through the odds ratios of homeownership in table 5.5. Take the age effect as an example. For each group, the older-to-younger ratio of homeownership is the ratio of the odds for older households to those for younger households. When the odds are greater for the older than for the younger, the ratio is greater than 1. When the odds are the same, the ratio is 1. When the odds are smaller for the older than for the younger, the ratio is less than 1. Thus, when comparing odds ratios across groups, the larger the odds ratio, the greater the age effect.

The effects of demographic characteristics are quite different among Asian groups. The age effect is strongest for Japanese immigrants, with an odds ratio of 4.13, meaning that older Japanese immigrant households are more than four times as likely as their younger counterparts to own a home. The weakest effect is among Vietnamese immigrants, whose ratio is 1.01, meaning almost no difference. The marriage effect varies even more widely. It is the strongest for Hong Kong and Taiwan immigrants, whose ratio of 5.68 is higher than that that of native whites (5.05). Korean immigrants have the weakest effect: married households are only 27 percent more likely to own a home than their unmarried counterparts. The children effect also differs substantially among groups. Hong Kong and Taiwan immigrants have the strongest no-child effect: the likelihood of owning a home is 84 percent (1 minus 0.16) less than for households with one or two children. The effect is the weakest for Korean immigrants,

Table 5.5   Odds Ratio of Homeownership by Demographic Characteristics and Asian Group

	45 to 64	Married	0 Children	3 + Children	Education ≥ 12
Native white	2.19	5.05	0.53	1.05	2.79
Asian American	3.07	3.81	0.37	0.51	0.95
HK–Taiwan Chinese	2.98	5.68	0.16	4.51	4.42
Mainland Chinese	1.54	3.21	0.39	1.06	5.10
Filipino	2.68	2.88	0.88	1.79	1.09
Japanese	4.13	2.23	0.39	5.51	0.67
Asian Indian	1.89	5.04	0.24	1.97	2.54
Korean	1.42	1.27	0.92	2.48	0.16
Vietnamese	1.01	2.89	0.40	0.35	4.24

Source: Author's compilation.

whose ratio is close to 1 (0.92). For some groups, having more children has a promoting effect, which is the strongest for Japanese immigrants. For others, such as native whites and mainland Chinese immigrants, it has little effect, whereas for Asian Americans and Vietnamese immigrants, it has a detrimental effect. Education, too, promotes homeownership for some groups, including Hong Kong–Taiwan, mainland Chinese, Vietnamese, and Indian immigrants, but has either no effect or a negative one for Filipino, Japanese, and Korean immigrants.

In sum, the differential effects of age, marital status, number of children, and education are much more important than composition effects in explaining homeownership gaps among Asian immigrant groups, native whites, and Asian Americans. Although the gaps observed within Asian immigrant groups are smaller than those within their Latino counterparts, the conclusion about a small role of composition effects and the large role of differential effects of demographics holds for both.

Negative Home Equity

Some homeowners have mortgages that exceed the current market value of the home, that is, negative home equity (NHE). NHE is a hidden risk among the middle class. Figure 5.8 (details in table 5.6) examines the crude rate and three adjusted rates of NHE among homeowners. Filipino and Japanese immigrants stand out in that their NHE doubles all other groups shown. After adjustments are made for the composition of marriage and number of children, Japanese immigrants show the elevated NHE rate. This uniqueness may suggest an excessive use of home equity loans. It is worth noting that it is not the less-advantaged groups such as

Figure 5.8   Crude and Adjusted Negative Home Equity Rates Among
Homeowners by Asian Group

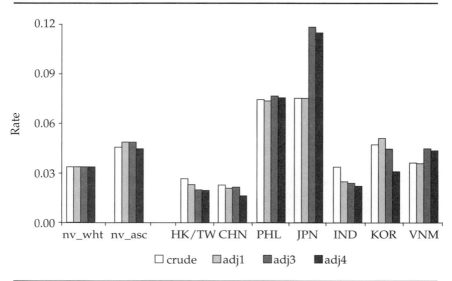

Source: Author's compilation.

Table 5.6   Negative Home Equity Rates Among Homeowners by
Asian Group

	Crude	Adj1[a]	Adj3[b]	Adj4[c]
Native white	0.034	0.034	0.034	0.034
Asian American	0.046	0.048	0.049	0.045
HK–Taiwan Chinese	0.027	0.023	0.020	0.019
Mainland Chinese	0.023	0.021	0.022	0.016
Filipino	0.075	0.074	0.077	0.076
Japanese	0.076	0.075	0.118	0.115
Asian Indian	0.034	0.025	0.024	0.022
Korean	0.047	0.051	0.045	0.031
Vietnamese	0.036	0.036	0.045	0.044

Source: Author's compilation.
[a] Adj1 adjusts for age composition.
[b] Adj3 adjusts for the composition of age, marital status, and number of children.
[c] Adj4 adjusts for the composition of age, marital status, number of children, and education levels.

Korean and Vietnamese immigrants but instead the relatively well-off groups (Filipino and Japanese) who exhibit the NHE problem.

Mortgages

Some homeowners have paid off their mortgages, and others have not. Although most take a single mortgage, in the past two decades more and more have taken either second mortgages or home equity loans. Because home equity loans do not have a fixed term or a fixed amount, a homeowner using then to cover consumption debt may end up with negative home equity or even face foreclosure of the loan and sale of their home. Table 5.7 classifies Asian immigrant households into three categories: those who have paid off mortgages, those with one mortgage, and those with second mortgages or home equity loans. Similar to native whites, about 20 percent of Chinese immigrants have paid off their mortgages. The percentage for all other groups who have paid off mortgages is lower. For all groups, more than 65 percent are paying one mortgage. The proportion of second mortgages is 12.6 percent among native-white homeowners and 14.6 percent among Asian Americans, reflecting the trend of increasing financial risk among the middle class. For Japanese immigrant homeowners, the figure is 20 percent, and for Filipino it is 12.9 percent. These relatively high rates among are a reason for the higher NHE rates documented earlier. By contrast, among mainland Chinese immigrants the proportion taking second mortgages is only 6.1 percent. Immigrants from Hong Kong, Taiwan, India, Korea, and Vietnam also take out fewer second mortgages than native whites.

Mortgages can be better understood with the duration of homeownership, examined in table 5.8. About 65 percent of all Asian immigrant homeowners had bought their home within the previous ten years.

Table 5.7   Number of Mortgages Among Homeowners by Asian Group

	0	1	2+
Native white	0.200	0.674	0.126
Asian American	0.136	0.718	0.146
HK–Taiwan Chinese	0.191	0.724	0.085
Mainland Chinese	0.180	0.759	0.061
Filipino	0.067	0.805	0.129
Japanese	0.065	0.734	0.201
Asian Indian	0.069	0.818	0.113
Korean	0.149	0.756	0.095
Vietnamese	0.164	0.766	0.070

Source: Author's compilation.

Table 5.8 Mortgages and NHE among Homeowners by Years of Ownership and Asian Group

	Proportion			2 + Mortgages			Prop. NHE		
	<10	10 ~ 19	20 +	<10	10 ~ 19	20 +	<10	10 ~ 19	20 +
Native white	0.580	0.245	0.175	0.129	0.151	0.080	0.053	0.033	0.017
Asian American	0.670	0.216	0.114	0.142	0.154	0.161	0.059	0.060	0.027
HK–Taiwan Chinese	0.713	0.245	0.042	0.075	0.077	0.309	0.052	0.018	0.000
Mainland Chinese	0.700	0.199	0.101	0.037	0.117	n.a.	0.027	0.000	0.043
Filipino	0.633	0.269	0.098	0.098	0.180	n.a.	0.104	0.069	0.000
Japanese	0.642	0.298	0.060	0.147	0.296	0.298	0.104	0.070	0.000
Asian Indian	0.789	0.184	0.027	0.113	0.129	n.a.	0.054	0.000	n.a.
Korean	0.691	0.253	0.056	0.075	0.168	0.000	0.082	0.034	0.000
Vietnamese	0.752	0.217	0.031	0.065	0.071	n.a.	0.060	0.015	n.a.

Source: Author's compilation.
Note: n.a. indicates a cell size < 10.

Small sample sizes are found for most Asian immigrant homeowners in the long-term category. The middle panel of table 5.8 identifies when households start to take more than one mortgage. The native white pattern is curvilinear with a higher rate during the medium-length and lower rates during the short- and long-term ownership. The pattern is monotonic, however, for Hong Kong–Taiwan immigrants. For other groups with limited data, owning a home for more than ten years increases the probability of taking multiple mortgages. The timing of NHE (see the right panel of table 5.8) is more often during the first ten years of ownership. This is particularly true for immigrants.

The U.S. government has offered assistance to working class families and servicemen in purchasing a home. The two most popular programs are the Federal Housing Administration (FHA) program for working class families and the Veterans Benefit Administration (VBA) program for servicemen. Do Asian immigrants have the same access to these programs? Table 5.9 shows the percentage participating in the FHA or VA program in obtaining a first mortgage, as opposed to obtaining a conventional first mortgage. The percentage for FHA-VA participation is about 20 percent for native white and Asian American homeowners. The percentage for Filipino immigrant homeowners is 27 percent, 7 percentage points higher than the two native groups. Some earlier Filipino immigrants fought side by side with native-born Americans in World War II. This history may have an effect on Filipinos' contemporary participation in military services and veterans' programs. Vietnamese immigrants also have a high access to FHA-VA, 24.6 percent, indicating the active reception the U.S. government has given to this group. The FHA-VA participation rates of other Asian immigrant groups are much lower, in the 10–14 percent range.

In general, lower-income homeowners are saddled with higher mortgage interest rates. Are Asian immigrants similarly burdened? Table 5.9 presents the percentage of homeowners with lower and higher interest rates for their first mortgage. Among native whites, 33 percent have lower rates and 17 percent have higher rates. A slightly better rate distribution is found among Asian American homeowners. Among Hong Kong and Taiwan immigrant homeowners, 42.9 percent enjoy low interest rates and only 6.6 percent bear high rates. Among Indian immigrants, the numbers are 51.3 percent and 7.1 percent. Filipino and Korean immigrant homeowners are less likely to have lower interest rates than the two native groups; 26.1 percent of Filipinos and 27.7 percent of Koreans see relatively low rates and 21.2 percent and 13.3 percent relatively high rates, respectively.

Examining mortgage behaviors can improve our understanding of homeownership and NHE. Heavier use of second mortgages and home equity loans may explain NHE among Filipino and Japanese immigrants.[1] Immigrant access to government programs that help finance home purchasing varies. Immigration history and the home country

Table 5.9   Program and Interest Rate of First Home Mortgage by Asian Group

	FHA–VA	< 7.0	≥ 8.5
Native white	0.200	0.331	0.172
Asian American	0.205	0.371	0.102
HK–Taiwan Chinese	0.104	0.429	0.066
Mainland Chinese	0.131	0.399	0.147
Filipino	0.270	0.261	0.212
Japanese	0.111	0.345	0.200
Asian Indian	0.132	0.513	0.071
Korean	0.133	0.277	0.133
Vietnamese	0.246	0.401	0.123

Source: Author's compilation.

play important roles here. Filipino and Vietnamese immigrants, for example, are more likely to participate in the government programs than native whites. High mortgage interest rates are not always a problem for immigrants. In fact, some groups, such as Hong Kong, Taiwan, and Indian immigrants are generally able to obtain lower interest rates than native whites. In short, mortgage behaviors among Asian immigrant groups vary widely, much more so than homeownership.

Compared to Latino immigrants (see chapter 4), Asian immigrants are more likely to take second mortgages, but they are less likely to have NHE. Although high poverty rates may explain the high FHA-VA participation of many Latino immigrant groups, it is the immigration history that seems to explain the high participation among Filipino immigrants, whose poverty rate is low, and Vietnamese immigrants, whose poverty rate is high but not higher than that of many Latino immigrant groups. A most noteworthy difference between Asian and Latino immigrants is that the proportion of all Latino groups shouldering high interest rates is greater than that of most of their Asian counterparts. Filipino and Japanese proportions are comparable with those of Latino immigrants.

Liquid Financial Assets

Financial emergencies are unavoidable. Households with enough liquid financial assets are more secure than those with no assets or only illiquid or quasi-liquid assets. This section examines assets such as stocks, mutual funds, interest-earning savings and checking accounts, bonds, and securities, and non-interest-earning checking accounts. These are liquid assets families can draw on in an emergency. In this sense, both the probability of having such assets and enough of them are important to assessing financial security. Using a cutoff of $20,000 as sufficient, the dif-

Figure 5.9   Financial Asset Rates by Asian Group

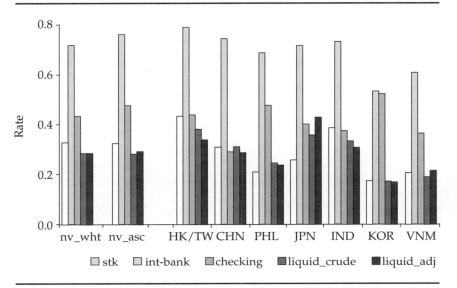

Source: Author's compilation.

ferences in such a status among Asian immigrant groups are examined, using both crude and adjusted rates. Figure 5.9 describes whether and how Asian immigrant groups are prepared for financial emergency.

Figure 5.9 (see details in table 5.10) shows large group differences in stocks and mutual funds (see the first bar for each group in the graph). Among immigrant groups, Hong Kong–Taiwan and Indian immigrants have a higher percentage of owning stocks and mutual funds and Filipino, Korean, and Vietnamese immigrants a lower percentage. The prevalence of owning bank accounts is high among most Asian immigrants, with Korean and Vietnamese lagging more than 10 percentage points. Korean immigrants are more likely to have non–interest-earning checking accounts. These liquid components lead to the total liquid assets, resulting in low percentages of owning $20,000 liquid financial assets among Korean and Vietnamese immigrants. Adjusting for demographic composition does not have much of an effect on the distribution of owning sufficient liquid financial assets among Asian immigrant groups.

In short, liquid financial assets are another area in which substantial heterogeneity among Asian immigrant groups appears. Similar to the patterns of total assets, total equity, and total net worth, Hong Kong, Taiwan, and Indian immigrants are consistently more advantaged than native whites, and Korean and Vietnamese immigrants more disadvantaged. Although Filipino and Japanese immigrants are more likely to

Table 5.10   Ownership of Liquid Financial Assets by Asian Group

	Stock Mutual Fund	Int. Bank Account	Non-Interest Checking[a]	$20,000 or More Combined	
				Crude	Adj4[b]
Native white	0.328	0.720	0.434	0.284	0.284
Asian American	0.323	0.764	0.477	0.281	0.292
HK–Taiwan Chinese	0.438	0.795	0.443	0.383	0.339
Mainland Chinese	0.309	0.748	0.290	0.310	0.285
Filipino	0.209	0.690	0.478	0.245	0.235
Japanese	0.258	0.719	0.404	0.361	0.430
Asian Indian	0.388	0.735	0.376	0.336	0.308
Korean	0.174	0.537	0.528	0.172	0.167
Vietnamese	0.206	0.611	0.365	0.190	0.216

Source: Author's compilation.
[a] Among those who have no interest-earning bank accounts.
[b] Adj4 adjusts for the composition of age, marital status, number of children, and education levels.

have NHE, their liquid financial security is sound, meaning that they are less likely to be at risk of losing their homes.

A remarkable difference between Asian and Latino immigrants (see results from chapter 4) is the economic security of the former and the vulnerability of the latter. Evidence of this difference includes the higher percentages of Asian immigrants who own stocks and mutual funds, easy-withdrawal accounts in financial institutions, non–interest-earning checking accounts, and an adequate amount of liquid financial equity.

Retirement Accounts

Liquid financial assets are used to cope with emergencies. Retirement accounts are for old-age security. Even among the well-educated in the mainstream economy, the average immigrant works fewer adult productive years in the United States (PAYUS) than the average native. It is therefore important to assess how prepared Asian immigrants are for their retirement support. Figure 5.10 presents the crude and adjusted rates of two types of retirement accounts—IRA and Keogh combined, which are funded by individual contributions, and 401(k)s, which are funded by both employee and employer contributions, and the total retirement accounts (see table 5.11 for detail).

Retirement accounts are an area where the native advantage is clear but the native-immigrant gap is nonetheless remarkably small. The crude rate of IRA-Keogh ownership is highest for Asian Americans, with

Figure 5.10   Crude and Adjusted Retirement Account Rates by Asian Group

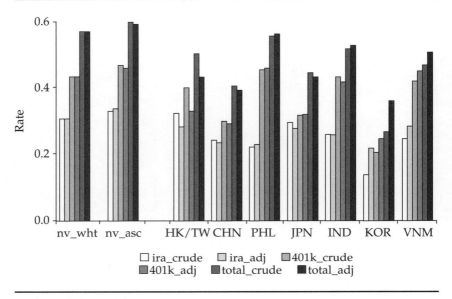

Source: Author's compilation.

Filipino and Korean immigrants having a lower rate. Adjusting for the composition of age and liquid financial assets raises the rate only for Koreans. The rate of 401(k) ownership is high for four groups: native whites, Asian Americans, Filipino immigrants, and Vietnamese immigrants. The Korean immigrant rate remains the lowest. This pattern suggests that the types of jobs Filipinos and Vietnamese hold tend to make

Table 5.11   Retirement Account Ownership by Asian Group

	IRA–Keogh		401k		Total	
	Crude	Adj[a]	Crude	Adj[a]	Crude	Adj[a]
Native white	0.308	0.308	0.434	0.434	0.568	0.568
Asian American	0.330	0.337	0.467	0.459	0.595	0.590
HK–Taiwan Chinese	0.322	0.282	0.400	0.329	0.500	0.430
Mainland Chinese	0.242	0.233	0.297	0.290	0.404	0.393
Filipino	0.222	0.229	0.453	0.458	0.552	0.560
Japanese	0.293	0.275	0.317	0.318	0.444	0.428
Asian Indian	0.258	0.257	0.430	0.414	0.515	0.526
Korean	0.138	0.218	0.204	0.244	0.267	0.358
Vietnamese	0.245	0.282	0.420	0.450	0.464	0.503

Source: Author's compilation.
[a] Adj adjusts for the composition of age and ownership of $20,000 liquid financial asset.

contributions to employee retirement accounts but those of Koreans do not. When the total retirement accounts are compared, Korean immigrants are the most disadvantaged, followed by mainland Chinese immigrants. Adjusting for the composition of age and the ownership of sufficient liquid financial assets improves the Korean immigrant situation significantly.

Overall, Asian immigrants are more prepared for old-age security than their Latino counterparts. They have not, however, yet achieved parity with native whites. This is clearly an immigrant deficit, the only so far in our examination of assets and debts among Asians.

Life Insurance

Where retirement accounts are for one's old-age security, life insurance is for survivors' economic security. This issue is especially important for immigrants who intend to stay in the United States for generations. The majority of Asian immigrants are permanent immigrants. This section examines whether Asian immigrants are well prepared for intergenerational transfers that enable future generations to establish permanent roots in the United States. Figure 5.11 presents the percentage distribution of employer-provided life insurance, a benefit attached to some jobs, individual-bought life insurance, which costs a premium and annual contribution, and the two types combined (see table 5.12 for detail).

Native whites and Filipino immigrants have the highest employer-provided life insurance rates, both employer-subsidized and self-bought, than other groups. Among Asian immigrants, Indian immigrants are close to the top. Other groups trail native whites, particularly Koreans, Vietnamese, and mainland Chinese. Households may purchase life insurance on their own. Mainland Chinese immigrants seem to make some effort to compensate for their disadvantages in employment benefits. The percentages of individual-bought life insurance do not differ much among most groups.

When all life insurance is considered together, almost 80 percent of native whites have at least one form of life insurance, the highest among all groups. Filipino and Indian immigrants trail native whites closely and Korean, Vietnamese, and mainland Chinese immigrants lag furthest behind. Adjustment for the composition of age, marital status, and number of children does not change the ranking much, suggesting that these factors are not decisive in determining ownership of life insurance. Because most Korean, Vietnamese, and mainland Chinese immigrants become permanent residents, this finding suggests that life insurance may not be a major measure for intergenerational transfers among permanent immigrants. Income constraints and different strategies of intergenerational transfers may play a role in determining gaps in life insurance ownership.

Figure 5.11   Crude and Adjusted Life Insurance Rates by Asian Group

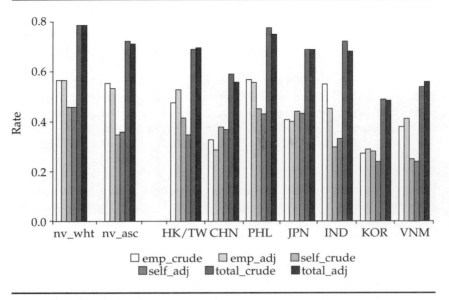

Source: Author's compilation.

A major difference between Asian and Latino immigrants is the Asian advantage in obtaining employer-provided life insurance. Except for Koreans, many of whom are self employed, a higher percentage of nearly all Asian immigrant groups have employer-provided life insurance than their Latino counterparts, reflecting more ability to obtain jobs with de-

Table 5.12   Life Insurance by Asian Group

	Employer-Provided		Self-Bought		Total	
	Crude	Adj[a]	Crude	Adj[a]	Crude	Adj[a]
Native white	0.564	0.564	0.457	0.457	0.784	0.784
Asian American	0.553	0.534	0.349	0.361	0.722	0.710
HK–Taiwan Chinese	0.475	0.527	0.414	0.348	0.686	0.693
Mainland Chinese	0.328	0.288	0.378	0.368	0.591	0.556
Filipino	0.566	0.556	0.452	0.430	0.775	0.746
Japanese	0.406	0.402	0.441	0.432	0.685	0.687
Asian Indian	0.548	0.451	0.300	0.331	0.719	0.677
Korean	0.273	0.288	0.281	0.239	0.488	0.482
Vietnamese	0.378	0.410	0.247	0.238	0.536	0.556

Source: Author's compilation.
[a] Adj4 adjusts for the composition of age, marital status, number of children, and education levels.

cent benefits. To a lesser degree, more Asian immigrants bought their own life insurance, which reflects differential income constraints. Overall, Asian immigrants are better prepared for intergenerational transfers, supporting the idea that life insurance is one of many ways to ensure the well-being of succeeding generations.

Consumer Debts

In the past two decades, an increasing number of middle-class Americans have been trapped in consumer debt because of the variable, high interest rates imposed by credit card companies. Do Asian immigrants follow this pattern and accrue high consumer debt, or are they more prudent and avoid it? Figure 5.12 presents the crude and adjusted rate of having credit card debts (see detailed statistics and trimmed average amount of credit card debts in table 5.13).

Nearly 60 percent of native white and Asian American households carry consumer debt. The only Asian immigrants surpassing this rate are Filipinos, at 65.5 percent. Given their middle-class levels of net worth and total assets, this suggests assimilation into middle-class America and its consumption behavior. Chinese groups have the lowest rates— 42.6 percent for Hong Kong and Taiwan immigrants and 37.8 percent for mainland Chinese—even though Hong Kong and Taiwan immigrants have higher levels of net worth and total assets than native whites. That Korean immigrants have a relatively high rate of debt (51 percent) suggests that they may use credit card debts to cope with economic difficulties, given their lower net worth. Although compositions of age, marital status and number of children may affect the needs of consumption, they do not seem to be decisive in credit card debts—the adjustment for these compositions does not alter the rate of consumer debts substantially.

The amount of consumer debt indicates the financial risk a household faces. The last two columns of table 5.13 show the observed average amount and the trimmed average amount among those who incur consumer debts. The observed average amount is $6,100 for native whites and $6,800 for Asian Americans. The observed average amount varies widely among Asian immigrant groups, ranging from $11,000 for Hong Kong and Taiwan to $5,800 for mainland Chinese. After they are trimmed at a lower bound of $100 and a higher bound of $50,000, the group variations drop dramatically, and all Asian immigrant groups show a higher average trimmed amount than native whites. Thus, though most Asian immigrant groups (except Filipinos) have less credit card debt when measured using the trimmed amount, those who do have debt borrow more than native whites. This finding is contrary to our expectation that Asian immigrants may be more prudent in taking on consumer debts.

Figure 5.12   Crude and Adjusted Rates of Consumer Debts by Asian Group

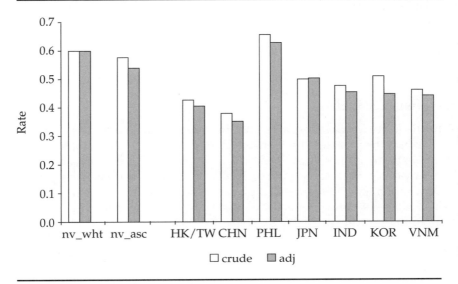

Source: Author's compilation.

Consumer debt is the one of a few areas in which Asian and Latino immigrant groups are notably similar. All groups have a substantial rate and a similar amount of consumer debt. In the sense of consumption assimilation, both Asian and Latino immigrants have "successfully" assimilated to the American consumer debt culture.

Table 5.13   Consumer Debts by Asian Group

	Credit Card Debts			
	Crude	Adj4[a]	Amount	Trim. Amount
Native white	0.598	0.598	$6,141	$5,658
Asian American	0.578	0.539	$6,840	$6,704
HK–Taiwan Chinese	0.426	0.404	$11,175	$5,729
Mainland Chinese	0.378	0.351	$5,863	$6,177
Filipino	0.655	0.627	$7,349	$6,769
Japanese	0.498	0.501	$8,749	$7,740
Asian Indian	0.475	0.453	$7,150	$6,623
Korean	0.510	0.447	$6,513	$6,460
Vietnamese	0.461	0.440	$6,270	$6,339

Source: Author's compilation.
[a] Adj4 adjusts for the composition of age, marital status, number of children, and education levels.

Business Ownership

Asian immigrants are often described as rich in entrepreneurship (Light 1972; Light and Bonacich 1988). From long-standing Chinatowns to newer and fast-growing Korean small businesses everywhere, many Asian immigrants take a detour to upward mobility through entrepreneurship, bypassing more traditional occupational ladders (Portes and Rumbaut 1996). Asian immigrant success in small business manifests the important role of ethnic networks. At the same time, successful immigrant entrepreneurship influences subsequent immigrant inflows (Light and Bhachu 1993).

Business ownership patterns are derived from the 1996 to 2002 SIPP data. Asian immigrant patterns are compared with each other and against those of Asian Americans and native whites. Figure 5.13 (see table 5.14 for detail) shows that the crude rate is .158 for native whites and .161 for Asian Americans. However, the crude ownership rates vary greatly among Asian immigrants. Those from Korea and Hong Kong–Taiwan take the lead (.252 and .247 respectively). Mainland Chinese, Japanese, and Vietnamese are each similar to Asian Americans (.164 to .181). The Asian Indian rate (.146) follows. The Filipino rate is lowest (.077), less than half that of native whites. After age (a proxy for experiences) is adjusted to native whites, the rates for Asian Indians and Koreans increase noticeably. Marital status and number of children capture family social capital that facilitates small businesses. After family social capital is also adjusted, the rates of those from Hong Kong and Taiwan, Korea, and Vietnam drop significantly, indicating the important role of family social capital in ethnic enterprises among these groups. Finally, education captures human capital, which also facilitates small businesses. When education is further adjusted, the business ownership rate significantly increases for Vietnamese, the least educated group, but drops for all others. None of the adjustments have much effect on the Filipino business ownership rate, which is the lowest. After all adjustments, Asian immigrant groups except Filipinos have a slightly higher small business ownership rate than native whites.

This analysis shows that Asian immigrants are not homogeneous in their business ownership. With financial capital, ethnic networks, and human capital, many from Hong Kong and Taiwan engage in businesses and, judging from their wealth holding status, achieve upward mobility. With both ethnic networks and human capital, Korean immigrants' success in entrepreneurship predicts continuing growth. Judging from their wealth holding status, however, Korean immigrant small businesses are less successful than their Hong Kong–Taiwan counterparts. Other Asian immigrant groups do not demonstrate any dramatically higher entrepreneurial propensity than native whites. Future examinations of contem-

Figure 5.13   Crude and Adjusted Rates of Business Ownership by Asian Group

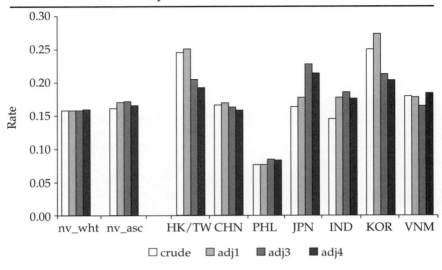

Source: Author's compilation.

porary Asian immigrant ethnic businesses will better our understanding of the relative importance of financial, social, and human capital in ethnic entrepreneurship.

The relatively high education levels and relatively low wealth levels

Table 5.14   Business Ownership by Asian Group

	Crude	Adj1[a]	Adj3[b]	Adj4[c]
Native white	0.158	0.158	0.158	0.158
Asian American	0.161	0.171	0.173	0.165
HK–Taiwan Chinese	0.247	0.253	0.206	0.193
Mainland Chinese	0.167	0.170	0.163	0.159
Filipino	0.077	0.076	0.085	0.084
Japanese	0.164	0.179	0.229	0.215
Asian Indian	0.146	0.179	0.188	0.176
Korean	0.252	0.275	0.214	0.205
Vietnamese	0.181	0.179	0.166	0.185

Source: Author's compilation.
[a] Adj1 adjusts for age composition.
[b] Adj3 adjusts for the composition of age, marital status, and number of children.
[c] Adj4 adjusts for the composition of age, marital status, number of children, and education levels.

among Korean immigrants present a perplexing case. I examine a few areas outside the focus of this chapter that might contribute to their lower levels of wealth: timing of arrival, occupation, and small business scale. Korean immigrants are similar to Filipino in arriving earlier than Chinese and Indian immigrants. Earlier timing is an advantage rather than a disadvantage because of less competition and a longer period for business expansion. Despite having more education, Korean immigrants are less likely to engage in managerial and professional occupations (33 percent) than both the equally well-educated Hong Kong–Taiwan Chinese (47 percent) and Indians (51 percent) and the less educated mainland Chinese immigrants (35 percent). Korean immigrants are by contrast more likely to engage in sales (23 percent) than all other Asian immigrant groups examined here, reflecting their propensity for self-employment. Similarly, the Korean immigrant self-employment rate is 28 percent, more than double the overall population rate (12.7 percent) and higher than other entrepreneur-rich Asian immigrant groups (for example, 15 percent of Chinese and Japanese and 14 percent of Vietnamese). The most revealing fact is that the ratio of assets owned by the self-employed to the employed is the lowest among Korean immigrants—about 1.5 versus greater than 3 for most other Asian groups. The ratio of debts (common for business operation) owed by the self-employed to the employed is about 1.1 but 2 for the other groups. This asset-debt pattern suggests that the business scale of Korean immigrant business is small, limiting expansion. In sum, the relative low engagement in managerial and professional occupation and high engagement in small-scale businesses may act as a double disadvantage among Korean immigrants.

The Likelihood of Cross-Border Asset Ownership

A wealth regime typology was used in chapter 4 to ascertain the likelihood of cross-border asset ownership among Latino immigrants (see figure 4.14). The seven Asian sending countries and regions examined here belong to different wealth regime types. The Philippines has a medium investment environment. Its low income indicates the heavy obligation immigrants feel to support family members in the home country and U.S. wages can buy far more assets in the home country than they can in the United States. All these factors promote investment in the homeland. However, the growth rate is low in the Philippines, lowering expected future returns to investment. India, Vietnam, and China have a similar investment environment and development level, but medium to higher growth rates and stable growth, increasing expected future returns to investment. The highly skilled Indian and Chinese immigrants have a unique niche in the growing economy of their home countries, especially those involved in information technology. In contrast Korea, Taiwan, and Japan present a case where the investment environment is excellent, but the economic growth rate is low to medium, and the U.S. currency capacity is low to medium, offering little advantage to investment over the United States.

The wealth regime typology provides an understanding of the necessary conditions under which Indian, Chinese, Vietnamese, and Filipino immigrants are more likely to invest in their homeland than other Asian immigrant groups. The sufficient condition, however, depends on the self-selection of these immigrants. An important distinction between Vietnamese immigrants and all others is the refugee status. Earlier waves of Vietnamese escaped from the war and have become long-term settlers, reducing the likelihood of cross-border investment. Later waves, however, came for family reunification. Reform in Vietnam has led to market transition that increasingly attracts investment from abroad, including Vietnamese emigrants. Although the Philippine growth rate is low, the large waves of professional emigration and the accompanied mandate of remittances may sustain a continuous cross-border investment. Both highly skilled and less skilled Chinese emigrate to the United States. This differential selection according to education suggests different investment behavior across the national border. Highly skilled Chinese, particularly those working in high-tech areas, are increasingly operating businesses and acquiring assets in China (Saxenian 2006), whereas their less skilled counterparts may focus on building a permanent stay in the United States based on a moderate income. The majority of Indian immigrants are professionals with very high levels of education. Many are in high-tech occupations. I anticipate that cross-border economic activities, including operating businesses and acquiring assets, will increase among the highly skilled.

Note that the SIPP does not provide data on immigrants' investments in their home countries. This analysis gives us reason to believe that the level of wealth for Filipino, mainland Chinese, Indian, and younger Vietnamese immigrants may be significantly higher than what the SIPP measure.

Conclusion

Asian immigrants as a whole stand out as younger, reflecting their continuous chain migration and fast growth rates. They are more likely to be married, reflecting a strong cultural value on the family. They are more likely to have children but fewer of them, reflecting the fertility behavior of their home countries. They are also more likely to be well educated, reflecting their response to the skilled preference of the 1965 immigration law.

At the same time, the variations in demographic characteristics among Asian immigrants are substantial. The differences in language, culture, and education among Asian immigrants across groups stem from a combination of factors—particularly home country geopolitical positions, historical conditions, current economic and educational development levels, and population sizes. The colonial history of the Philippines under U.S. rule and India and Hong Kong under British rule is the reason that emigrants from these countries have English skills, which pave the way for massive professional immigration and entrance into the U.S. mainstream. Even with lower economic and educational development, the large size of the Indian population enables massive professional immigration to the United States. The impact of colonial history on religion takes a different route. It is Spanish colonial influence that leads to the Catholicism of Filipinos. British colonial influence, however, did not change the majority of Indians' original religion, Hindu, or Hong Kong people's belief in Confucianism. Missionary influence, on the other hand, shaped South Korean Christianity.

Although colonial history determines differences in Asian immigrants' language barriers, Western influence determines—to a large degree—differences in higher education systems, the connection between curriculum and technology, and the transferability of education obtained in the home countries. Taiwan was never a U.S. colony but is nonetheless under strong U.S. influence. Immigrants from Taiwan are well educated and generally find it easy to transfer their education to the American labor market. Being a competitive economic power, Japan sends emigrants to the United States with transferable education, very different from the earlier Japanese labor migrants. Mainland China is in a completely different situation. With its very different political system, China has experienced the least U.S. influence of all Asian countries and regions examined. The self-selection of mainland Chinese immigrants seems to take two different paths. Even with low educational development, the large population makes it possible for China to become a major source of highly educated immigrants having little in common with early Chinese immigrants. Chinese education is, however, difficult to use directly in the American labor market and pushes highly educated Chinese immigrants to obtain additional degrees in the United States. The strong structural push forces in China also propel many with little education, a group having more in common with the early Chinese immigrants, to emigrate. Vietnamese immigrants represent still another situation—refugees of a war, in which the United States was involved. Like Cuban refugees, both elite and common Vietnamese people were actively received, leading to high within-group heterogeneity. A number of factors then—long immigration history, strong structural push forces, and high migration costs among them—drive Asian emigration.

In many respects, immigrants from Hong Kong and Taiwan fare the best. With very high education, low poverty, high marriage rates, high child presence, and low fertility, their economic security is soundly established. They exhibit strong wealth holding, higher net worth and assets, consistent homeownership, lower negative home equity, lower mortgage interest rates, and higher liquid assets, more secure old-age security, and more life insurance ownership. Another significant edge is their high rate of business ownership. These numbers are comparable, and sometimes better than, those among native whites and Asian Americans.

Indian immigrants are the youngest, the most likely to be married, the best educated, and the least likely to be poor. Their financial situation is not as favorable as that of their counterparts from Hong Kong and Taiwan but is better than others in many respects, including diverse portfolios, low NHE rates, high liquid financial assets, and retirement accounts.

Filipino immigrants have one significant demographic characteristic—they are older. This uniqueness stems from their U.S.-colonial history and continual immigration, having not experienced the fifty-year ban imposed on all other Asian immigrants. Earlier immigrants are more likely to have jobs with greater benefits, such as 401(k) employer contributions and life insurance. They also have greater participation in federal programs to assist with homeownership. Because of this, Filipino immigrants are the best prepared for retirement and intergenerational transfers using life insurance. Although they invest considerable amounts in their homes, they are also more likely to have NHE because they tend to take home equity loans and have high mortgage interest rates. They also are more likely to have a high rate and high amount of consumer debt. In addition, their business ownership rate is very low. All this signals a relatively less sound economic basis.

Mainland Chinese immigrants have a long history in the United States. The distribution of education and poverty among the immigrants of today is bimodal. The percentage with little education and that with high education are each higher than that of native whites. The poverty rate is double that of native whites. As a group, mainland Chinese immigrants have achieved reasonably sound economic security. They fare less well in homeownership because they are less likely to participate in federal homeowner programs and shoulder relatively higher mortgage rates. They are also less prepared for old-age security in terms of retirement accounts and intergenerational transfers using life insurance. These factors combined signal a long-term risk. On the other hand, these immigrants demonstrate prudent consumption and cautious use of credit cards, given that they are the least likely either to take home equity loans or to have credit card debts. They also have the lowest credit card debt.

Korean immigrants—despite their typically advanced education, high prevalence of marriage, and few children—see less success. Their poverty rate is relatively high, approximately two and a half times that of native whites. They also rank low in all aspects of wealth except business ownership. One possible explanation is that their language barrier leads them to undertake small business operation rather than to use the skills for which they were trained at home. The profits of their small businesses may not be high. Ivan Light and Edna Bonacich (1988) found that 22 percent of Koreans in Los Angeles in 1980 were self-employed and that they employed another 40 percent of Korean workers. I speculate that the relatively low engagement in managerial and professional occupations and high engagement in small-scale businesses are a double disadvantage.

Immigrants from Vietnam came first as political refugees and later for family reunification. This group includes both elite and common people from a less-developed country. The active reception they experienced on arrival played an important role in integrating them into the American society. The minimal development, small population, and war-stricken circumstances of their home country shaped the lower socioeconomic characteristics and high fertility rates of Vietnamese immigrants. In general, their economic security is worse than that of most of the other Asian immigrant groups. They do relatively better in preparing for retirement. They also exhibit prudent behavior by avoiding home equity loans and high consumer debts.

Japanese immigrants, who also have a long history of immigration to the United States, have transformed primarily to professional immigrants. Given the high development level in their home country, it is surprising that Japanese immigrants lag behind Hong Kong and Taiwan immigrants. They have a higher poverty rate, less wealth holding, less net worth and assets, lower homeownership, and lower ownership of retirement accounts and life insurance policies. Their rate of second mortgages and home equity loans is the highest among all Asian immigrant groups examined. They also have a relatively high rate and amount of consumer debt.

The variations in wealth among Asian immigrants are nonetheless smaller than the vast variations in wealth among Latino immigrants described in chapter 4. Most are comparable with native whites, and in some respects Hong Kong, Taiwan, and Indian immigrants fare even better. Only one or two Asian immigrant groups lag significantly behind native whites and are comparable with their Cuban counterparts.

= Chapter 6 =

Assets and Debts Among
Black Immigrants

B lack immigrants to the United States come from two parts of the world: the Caribbean and Africa. The SIPP data from 1996 to 2003 allow the identification of immigrants from two Caribbean countries, Haiti and Jamaica. Because of the relatively small sample from specific African countries in the SIPP, for the purpose of analysis, sub-Saharan Africa is taken as a region. Thus, immigrants from Arab countries in northern Africa, such as Egypt, Libya, and Morocco, are excluded. In addition, nonblack immigrants from South Africa are excluded. The major black immigrant sending countries in sub-Saharan Africa are Nigeria, Ethiopia, Kenya, Ghana, and Somalia.

Black immigrants account for only a small percentage of the U.S. foreign-born population. In 2000, 2.1 percent were from Haiti and Jamaica and 2.5 percent were from sub-Saharan African countries (U.S. Census Bureau 2003). Some black immigrants are well educated, for example, economists from Nigeria, engineers from Kenya, and school teachers from Jamaica, and others are near illiterate, for example, nomadic pastoralists and farm workers from Somalia and peasants from Haiti. Black immigrants include professionals, entrepreneurs, laborers, and refugees.

Although heterogeneous, black immigrants and African Americans have two things in common: their historical experience of slavery and their contemporary experience of racial discrimination in the United States. Thus, despite their small group size, black immigrants provide a unique opportunity to better understand the impact of the American racial ethnic hierarchy and various immigrant statuses on the economic attainment of black residents in the United States.

Many studies on British Caribbean immigrants, also called West Indians, provide important insights into the process of the adaptation and assimilation of black immigrants (Harrison 1992; Waters 1999). Although Caribbean blacks have a history of slavery, they have had greater economic opportunities during and after slavery. A racial majority in their

180

home countries, they have developed a higher achievement orientation than African Americans (Glazer and Moynihan 1963; Lewis 1983). This cultural advantage, however, does not benefit Caribbean blacks in the United States after the first generation. A central message from previous studies is that even though the first generation of British Caribbean immigrants achieve upward economic mobility and outperform African Americans, the stubborn U.S. racial hierarchy confines them to the lowest tier. Caribbean immigrants lose ground because of the downward succession of neighborhoods and communities and the downward assimilation of the second generation.

This chapter incorporates African immigrants into the study of native and immigrant blacks. Africa has sent steadily growing waves of immigrants since the 1965 immigration law and particularly since the 1980s (Rumbaut 1994). African immigrants have demonstrated more of an orientation to higher achievement and a stronger work ethic than their American and Caribbean counterparts. One reason is self-selection, given that many African immigrants are highly educated. Another is that the institutional basis for slavery in Africa is very different from that for slavery in America. Some scholars argue that though slavery existed in Africa, and still does today, slavery of Africans by other Africans often means ownership of labor, rather than of the person, and slaves have rights and opportunities for advancement (Curtin 1976). African slaves were seldom considered the simple commodities they were in America. Suzanne Miers and Igor Kopytoff (1977) maintain that kinship relations in Africa gave people social existence that divided insiders from outsiders and that outsiders had the same meaning of slaves. This institution thus gave rise to enslavement of those captured in warfare. Males were less likely to adjust to their captivity and therefore were put up for trade, including those traded to America. Women were more likely to be absorbed by local communities and kinship through subordinate positions such as concubine. Gradually, women and children become the insiders of the kinship, evading intergenerational transmission of slave status. In addition, because of the racial homogeneity in most African societies, race did not significantly determine status. In America, it did. In America, slavery was a racial phenomenon. The institutional rules from the property rights of the colonial period to the "one-drop" rule of the Jim Crow era determined the intergenerational transmission of slave status. These distinct setups contribute to very different orientations of African Americans and African immigrants.

After giving some background on Haiti, Jamaica, and major African sending countries, I compare wealth components and wealth accumulation behaviors among black immigrants from these countries. I then make comparisons against two native-born groups: native whites and African Americans. These comparisons will provide answers to the question of whether black immigrants are favored over native-born blacks. The comparisons will also address the question of whether negative racial stereotypes of African or Caribbean black immigrants impede their achievement orientations and work ethic.

Country of Origin and Demographic Differences

Black immigrant groups differ greatly from other racial ethnic immigrant groups in their demographic characteristics (see figure 6.1 and table 6.1). Compared to native whites, all black groups are relatively younger—they have a higher percentage of householders aged twenty-five to forty-four. Immigrants from sub-Saharan Africa are particularly young: about 76 percent fall into that age bracket. Other black immigrant groups are younger than African Americans, who in turn are younger than native whites. Whites, followed by Jamaicans, have the highest marriage rate and African Americans have the lowest. Haitians and African immigrants are the most likely to have three or more children (27 percent and 34 percent, respectively). The percentages of having three or more children for native whites, African Americans, and Jamaicans are in the teens. All black groups have lower education levels than native whites. Among black groups, African immigrants have the highest educational level, coming close to that of native whites, whereas Haitians have the lowest. Jamaicans are similar to those of African Americans. Poverty patterns do not follow those of education. That is, the high educational level of African immigrants does not translate to a low poverty rate. Jamaicans, who have less education than Africans, are more likely to escape poverty. African Americans are the least able to translate their education to economic well-being; their poverty rate is almost double their high school dropout rate.

I use these group-specific demographic characteristics in examining wealth components and wealth accumulation behaviors. First, however, I briefly describe the background and immigration history of Haiti, Jamaica, and major sub-Saharan African sending countries.

Haiti

Haiti, which gained its independence from France in 1804, is the least-developed country in the western hemisphere and is one of the poorest in the world. Its per capita GDP was only $441 in 2003 (World Bank 2005) and it has just six years of compulsory education. Only 63 percent of those enrolled complete the six years of primary school. In Haiti, those of African descent make up 95 percent of the population. The majority practice Roman Catholicism and speak Creole, a form of French.

Figure 6.1   Demographics by Black Group

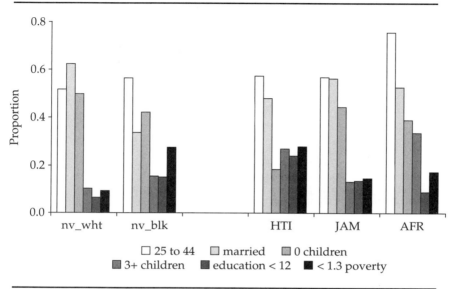

Source: Author's compilation.

Most waves of Haitian immigration to the United States have arisen from the country's political and economic instability (Pedraza and Rumbaut 1996). The first group of Haitian immigrants arrived during the American occupation of Haiti at the beginning of the twentieth century. In the late 1950s and early 1960s, upper-class Haitians came to the United States fleeing dictatorship, resulting in a brain drain. The large wave of uneducated peasants and urban residents who escaped the country's repression and violence during the late 1970s and early 1980s arrived in small boats, and were therefore known as the boat people. The 1981 U.S. policy to interdict Haitian immigrants made them unwelcome economic refugees subject to deportation. A coup in 1991 killed many Haitians and created another large-scale exodus from the country. More than 40,000 came to the United States by boat in 1991 and 1992. In 1992, U.S. policy dictated deportation of Haitians without screening, an order supported by the Supreme Court in 1993. Economic embargos, diplomatic isolation, and economic problems continued to sustain large-scale emigration. This has created a large overseas Haitian population: about one out of every six Haitians lives abroad. About 420,000 Haitian immigrants were living in the United States in 2000, many of whom were unauthorized.

Figure 6.1 shows that the age structure of Haitian immigrants is fairly balanced—58 percent are in the younger group, between twenty-five

Table 6.1   Demographic and Socioeconomic Differences by Black Group

	25 to 44	Married	0 Children	3 + Children	Education < 12	Poverty[a]	Sample
Native white	0.518	0.626	0.498	0.104	0.064	0.091	98,010
African American	0.564	0.338	0.421	0.155	0.150	0.275	14,322
Haitian	0.575	0.482	0.183	0.272	0.240	0.279	204
Jamaican	0.567	0.562	0.443	0.132	0.134	0.145	247
African immigrant	0.755	0.526	0.388	0.335	0.087	0.173	184

Source: Author's compilation.
[a] Less than 130 percent poverty level.

and forty-four—indicating a slow rate of chain migration. The marriage rate is relatively low, the fertility rate is relatively high, 24 percent do not have a high school education, and the poverty rate is the highest among all black groups compared here.

Jamaica

Although more than 90 percent of the Jamaican population is of African descent, similarities with Haiti end there. Jamaica is an English-speaking country, its per capita GDP was $3,203 in 2003 (World Bank 2005), and education is compulsory to age fourteen. Spain's occupation brought in the first African slaves but in the seventeenth century Jamaica became a British colony, and Britain abolished slavery in the mid-nineteenth century. Jamaica gained independence in 1962 but has remained a member of the British Commonwealth since then. This history explains why Jamaicans speak English and generally practice Anglican, Baptist, and other Protestant religions. After the 1962 independence, the United States began a neocolonial relationship with Jamaica through military intervention, media penetration, tourism, and antidrug activities.

Historically, Jamaican emigration to the United States has been heavy because of both the island's nearness and U.S. economic power. Before the 1924 immigration restriction laws, the United States allowed unlimited immigration from the western hemisphere. The first immigration wave from Jamaica got underway at the turn of the twentieth century and peaked in the early 1920s. Because at the time the United States required a literacy test from immigrants on arrival, the first wave of Jamaicans was highly selected and consisted mostly of professionals. Even after the 1924 laws, Jamaicans under British rule were within the quota for Britain and continued to emigrate until the Great Depression began. Immigration resumed following World War II, but the quota became very small because Jamaica was no longer a British colony. In the 1960s, the United Kingdom restricted immigration from Jamaica. Facilitated by America's 1965 Immigration Law, the major flow of Jamaican emigrants went to the United States. Since 1965, about 20,000 Jamaicans have come to the United States each year. New York, Miami, Chicago, and Hartford, Connecticut are among the U.S. cities with significant Jamaican populations. The size of the Jamaican immigrant population in the United States is larger than 20 percent of the island's population (U.S. Census 2003). Remittances from expatriate communities in the United States make increasingly significant contributions to Jamaica's economy.

Figure 6.1 shows a balanced age structure, a slightly lower marriage rate than native whites, and a slightly higher fertility rate. The 13 percent of less-educated householders is the second lowest rate among the four black groups examined, but the poverty rate is the lowest.

Africa

Contemporary sub-Saharan Africa is characterized by a large population, deep poverty, and high levels of unemployment and underemployment. The average per capita income has been low and stagnant for the last three decades. These indicators suggest that Africa's economic crises are serious and widespread. Colonial history, postcolonial political instability, and inadequate development policies are the deep roots of these crises. Thus the push forces of African emigration are strong. We do not see massive emigration, however, because it is not simply absolute poverty but a complicated web of factors that determine emigration. Economic crises, for example, dramatically reduce employment opportunities for the more highly educated. The immigration policies of destination countries define where emigrants go, however. Leaving aside the colonial slave trade, immigration from African countries was unusual until 1965, when the United States passed its employment- and family-based immigration law. The top five black immigrant sending countries, as mentioned, are Nigeria, Ethiopia, Kenya, Ghana, and Somalia.

Nigeria, which lies to the west, has a population of 130 million, making it the most populous country in sub-Sahara Africa. That it was a British colony from 1914 to 1960 contributed to its having English as its official language and Christianity as the second-largest religion after Islam. After it gained its independence, it slowly transitioned to democracy, witnessing many years of military governments until a democratic government was elected in 1999. Economic development has been hindered by an unhealthy dependence on oil extraction and by a neglect of agriculture and manufacturing that started with the oil boom of the 1970s. One of the twenty poorest countries in the world, Nigeria had a per capita GDP of $387 in 2003, a literacy rate of only 45 percent, and an urbanization rate of 25 percent (World Bank 2005). Over the last three decades, political instability, economic stagnation, high unemployment, and extreme inequality have sustained emigration and a brain drain.

Ethiopia, which lies to the east, is the second most populous , with a population of about 70 million. The two major religions are Islam and Ethiopian Orthodox (the only pre-colonial Christian church of sub-Saharan Africa). Many languages are spoken, but English is the major foreign language taught in schools. Except for a five-year occupation by Italy from 1936 to 1941, successive Ethiopian empires controlled the country until the revolution of the 1970s, when a socialist regime was established. Subsequently, the country experienced military coups, uprisings, and refugee problems until 1991, when a democratic government was established. Unfortunately, border wars with Eritrea, natural disasters, and induced famine created large-scale waves of refugees, some of whom settled in the United States. Being an agricultural society and one of the poorest countries in the world, Ethiopia has a low GDP per capita of $120 in 2003, a low literacy rate of 42 percent, and a low urbanization rate of 20 percent (World Bank 2005). The civil unrest and depressing economic situation are major push forces for emigration.

Kenya, also in east Africa, has a population of about 30 million. Influenced by British rule in the colonial period, it adopted Christianity as its major religion and English in addition to Kiswahili as its official language. Since its independence in 1963, Kenya has maintained political stability and established a multiparty democracy. Its economic development, however, has been less stable. The last three decades have been marked by low production, economic stagnation, and high inflation. One of the twenty poorest countries in the world, Kenya had a per capita GDP of $418 in 2003 (World Bank 2005). Since independence, its education system has undergone remarkable expansion; literacy, at 65 percent, is relatively high as a result. Economic stagnation and unemployment of educated people are probable reasons behind Kenyan emigration.

Ghana, known as the Gold Coast during the colonial period, had a population of 22 million in 2002. From the sixteenth to the nineteenth century, it was under the control of several European powers, Britain's in particular. Two cultural results are English as its official language and Christianity as the religion of the majority. After gaining independence in 1957, Ghana endured political instability until 1992, when a relatively stable, democratic government was established. With diverse and rich resources, the country has built its economy primarily on agriculture but is one of the twenty poorest countries in the world with a per capita GDP of $269 in 2003 (World Bank 2005). Nevertheless, like Kenya, Ghana has been expanding its education system since the 1980s. Nine years of schooling are compulsory, the literacy rate is 73 percent, and the system includes public-sponsored tuition from elementary school through college. Economic motives are the major reason for Ghanaian emigration.

Somalia, in eastern Africa, has a population of only 9.1 million, far lower than those of Nigeria, Ethiopia, Kenya, and Ghana. Subject to both British rule and Italian colonization before its independence in 1960, the country saw a civil war in 1991 and was with no central government. Before the war, Somalia's literacy level was 24 percent. There are no current official data for its per capita GDP. Lack of natural resources, extreme political instability, ethnic suppression, and deep impoverishment have generated large waves of refugees to the United States. Certain ethnic groups, such as the Bantu, are victims of a long history of persecution. The civil war forced thousands of Bantus to seek refuge in poverty-stricken refugee camps in Kenya. In 1999, the United States recognized the Somali Bantu as an exiled people in need of protection through resettlement. Somali refugees are one of the largest refugee groups since 1994, when the largest was Russian (Van Lehman and Eno 2003).

Figure 6.1 shows that the average age of African immigrants is very low—76 percent are in the younger group—predicting a large chain migration for the near future. Given their younger ages, African immigrants' marriage rate is relatively high, at 53 percent. Their fertility rate is very high, 34 percent having three or more children. Their educational level is also notable, fewer than 9 percent do not have a high school education. The poverty rate, however, is disproportionately high at 17 percent.

Of these sending countries and regions, then, Jamaica is the more developed and Haiti and sub-Saharan Africa the less developed. It is the African immigrants, however, who have the highest education levels, almost as high as those of native whites and much higher than those of African Americans. The long-term political and economic instability of Haiti propels illegal immigration, but Jamaicans and sub-Saharan Africans usually migrate legally. The political turmoil of Haiti, Ethiopia, and Somalia has created massive scales of political refugees, but U.S. reception has varied notably, favoring those from Ethiopia and Somalia over those from Haiti. Relationships between a home country's conditions and the demographic characteristics of its immigrants are not uniform. Migration patterns are rooted in the geopolitical, economic, and education conditions of sending countries. In addition, the U.S. immigration policy opens different pathways of legal or illegal immigration and shapes the self selection of immigrants.

Wealth Holding Status

The five wealth holding classifications—sufficient, insufficient, asset poor, net-debtor, and paycheck-to-paycheck—of Haitian, Jamaican, and African immigrant groups are compared to those of native whites and African Americans. If a household has net worth to sustain its consumption for twelve months without any income, its wealth holding status is sufficient. If net worth is positive and enough to sustain consumption for three months at the official poverty line but not enough for twelve months, the status is insufficient. A household is asset poor when it has positive net worth but not enough to support the household at the official poverty line for three months. The other two statuses indicate zero or negative net worth. Net-debtor status indicates greater debts than assets or having debts without assets. Paycheck-to-paycheck status indicates no assets and no debts. Based on the SIPP wealth data for 1996 to 1999 and 2001 to 2003, figure 6.2 (table 6.2) shows the proportion in each of the five statuses for each group being examined. This measure reflects group differences at both the net worth level and at the consumption level, which is measured using trimmed annual household income (with 130 percent of the official poverty line as the lower limit and $100,000 as the upper limit). The last column of table 6.2 presents average trimmed an-

Figure 6.2   Wealth Holding Status by Black Group

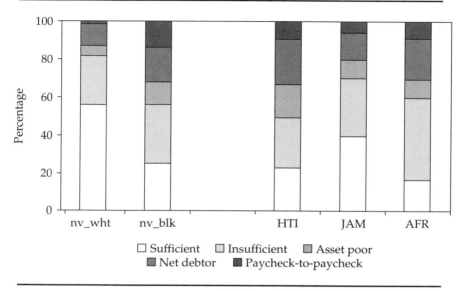

Source: Author's compilation.

nual income to reveal the masked differences by examining only the wealth holding status. The trimmed average annual income is highest for native whites, varies among the black immigrant groups, and is low for African Americans.

Although 56 percent of native whites achieve sufficient wealth holding, only 17 percent of African Americans do. The large trimmed income gap between native whites and African Americans ($53,000 versus $40,000) exacerbates this gap. When sufficient and insufficient statuses are combined, 82 percent of native whites and 56 percent of African Americans live above asset poverty. Compared to native whites, African Americans are substantially more likely to be net-debtors (18 percent versus 11 percent) and living paycheck to paycheck (13 percent versus 1.4 percent).

Among black immigrant groups, Jamaicans fare the best. Approximately 40 percent achieve sufficient status and 70 percent are above the asset poverty line. Their trimmed annual income is $54,000, similar to that of native whites, and their paycheck-to-paycheck rate of 6 percent is the lowest. The next in line are Haitians, with a trimmed annual income of $39,000, 23 percent achieving sufficient status, 50 percent escaping asset poverty, and 9 percent living paycheck to paycheck. Economic insecurity is also severe for African immigrants, only 17 percent achieving

Table 6.2　Wealth Holding Status by Black Group (Percentage)

	Sufficient	Insufficient	Asset Poor	Net Debtor	Paycheck-to-paycheck	Trimmed Annual Income[a]
Native white	0.564	0.257	0.052	0.114	0.014	$52,867
African American	0.256	0.307	0.120	0.184	0.134	$40,330
Haitian	0.233	0.263	0.173	0.239	0.091	$38,637
Jamaican	0.400	0.302	0.098	0.142	0.059	$54,030
African immigrant	0.167	0.432	0.096	0.215	0.089	$47,224

Source: Author's compilation.
[a] Annual income is trimmed at 130% poverty line at the bottom and $100,000 at the top.

sufficient status, 60 percent living above asset poverty, and 9 percent living paycheck to paycheck. Given the high education levels of African immigrants, their wealth attainment is notably low.

Does Africanness matter in wealth attainment? A closer comparison between African Americans and African immigrants reveals that African Americans and immigrants are in a similarly disadvantaged position, though African Americans are slightly worse off than African immigrants. Trimmed annual income is lower for African Americans than for immigrants ($40,000 versus $47,000), which explains why the sufficient status percentage is higher for African Americans than for African immigrants. However, the percentage living above asset poverty is lower for immigrants (56 percent versus 60 percent), as is the paycheck-to-paycheck rate (by 4.5 percentage points). These facts call for a deeper investigation into the structural forces affecting the wealth attainment of African immigrants and African Americans in the United States (see chapter 9).

Distribution of Net Worth, Assets, and Debts

Wealth holding status does not reveal variations in levels of wealth. Comparing wealth distribution among groups, however, offers quantitative details that the wealth holding categories miss. Figure 6.3 draws 99 percentiles of net worth against the cumulative proportion of the population, for each of the groups in comparison. The flat section of the percentile curve is longer for black groups than for native whites. Native whites have the highest net worth at all positions except in the bottom 30 percent of the distribution. The Jamaican curve is located between the native white curve and the curves of other black groups, but is closer to other blacks than to native whites. There is no substantial difference in net worth among Haitian immigrants, African immigrants, and African Americans. This graph conveys an overview of the huge racial gap in wealth, and at the same time, a clear view of the substantial heterogeneity among black groups, especially the better position of Jamaican immigrants.

Examining the central location and the two tails of the net worth distribution can reveal such variations. Because net worth is a household's assets less its debts, examining the distribution of both can further reveal the variations in wealth (see table 6.3). The median net worth for native whites is $72,000, more than ten times the median for African Americans ($6,200). Median net worth is $28,000 for Jamaicans, much lower than for native whites but much higher than for all other black groups. African immigrant median net worth ($6,000) is similar that of their African American counterparts, and Haitian is the lowest at $3,700. At the fifth

Figure 6.3   Percentile Distribution of Net Worth by Black Group

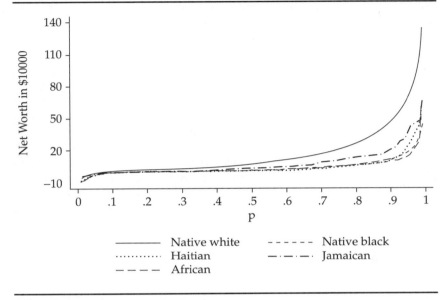

Source: Author's compilation.

percentile, Haitian immigrants stand out as having the highest negative net worth. African immigrants come in a distant second. At the ninety-fifth percentile, native white net worth ($685,000) is 1.8 times that of Jamaicans, the most prosperous black group. Haitian immigrants, African Americans, and African immigrants are lower and in a rank order at their ninety-fifth percentile of net worth. As a result, the spread of net worth distribution is widest for native whites and narrowest for African immigrants.

Between-group differences in assets are similar to but slightly less dramatic than those in net worth. For example, the median for native whites is now about six times of that for African Americans and 50 percent more than that for Jamaicans. This is true at the two ends of the distribution. The between-group disparities in debts are higher at the median than at the ninety-fifth percentile. At the ninety-fifth percentile, the debts of Jamaican and African immigrants almost reach parity with those of native whites. African Americans and Haitians are similarly low at both the median and the ninety-fifth percentile. Because most debts are secured with assets as collateral, the high level of debt among Jamaican and African immigrants suggests that they have greater credit worth than other black groups. At the same time, they are constrained by the housing, lending, and financial market discrimination and are sub-

Table 6.3   Selected Percentiles of Net Worth, Asset, and Debt by Black Group

	Net Worth			Assets			Debts		
	5th	50th	95th	5th	50th	95th	5th	50th	95th
Native white	−11,670	71,886	685,416	1,693	152,786	847,945	0	47,837	262,501
African American	−14,625	6,183	174,963	0	20,000	277,776	0	7,782	157,784
Haitian	−30,701	3,696	233,808	0	12,852	331,918	0	6,773	166,300
Jamaican	−14,161	27,705	373,885	0	108,289	462,069	0	40,500	244,949
African immigrant	−21,931	5,976	133,524	0	19,285	314,725	0	13,500	240,300

Source: Author's compilation.

ject to depreciated values of their assets, leading to their having lower
levels of net worth.

Portfolio

Figure 6.4 depicts net worth, secured debt, and unsecured debt each as a
percentage of native white average total assets. Figure 6.5 depicts them as
a percentage of the group-specific average total assets. The former facilitates between-group comparisons and the latter within-group analysis.

For black groups, the top section of the bar for nonwhite groups (figure 6.4) denotes the gap in total assets between the group and native
whites. The asset gap between native whites and each black group is
large, largest for African Americans and smallest for Jamaicans. Comparing a particular section of the bar (for example, secured debt) across
groups reveals the absolute size differences across groups. For instance,
the secured debt of Jamaican and African immigrants are just moderately
lower than those of native whites, whereas that of African Americans
and Haitians are substantially lower. Levels of debts being both high and
low among African and Caribbean black groups suggest that neither
Africanness nor Caribbeanness is a disadvantage in the credit market.
Because debts are necessary for acquiring major assets (for example, a
mortgage for buying a home), the relatively large secured debt of Jamaicans and African immigrants may hint at future financial security.
Among Haitians and African Americans, secured debts account for a
small percentage of their already small assets, predicting slow wealth accumulation. Unsecured debts, which are acquired for consumption purposes, are similar across groups, but native whites and African immigrants bear slightly more than other groups.

Figure 6.5 focuses on the percentages of net worth, secure debts, and
unsecured debts within groups. Having adequate total net worth is a
sign of financial security. Native whites' net worth accounts for almost 70
percent of total assets, indicating sound financial security. None of the
black groups has as large a share of net worth as native whites. Seemingly comparable shares of net worth for Haitians, Jamaicans, and
African Americans, however, mask their very different asset amounts.

Total equity, measuring the balance between a household's total assets
and its total secured debt, offers another way to look at an immediate financial buffer. Figure 6.6 describes nine portfolio components for each
group as percentages of own total equity: home equity (home in the figure legend), retirement account (ira), bank accounts (intbk and intot),
stocks and mutual funds (stk), business equity (beq), and other equities
(ore). As long as a householder has an adequate amount of total equity, a
smaller percentage of home equity indicates a household's higher capacity and preference for diverse financial investments. On average, native

Figure 6.4   Net Worth and Debts as Percentage of Native Whites' Total Asset by Black Group

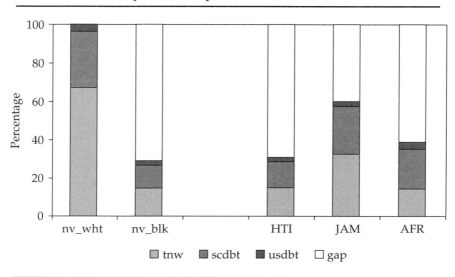

Source: Author's compilation.

Figure 6.5   Net Worth and Debts as Percentage of Total Asset by Black Group

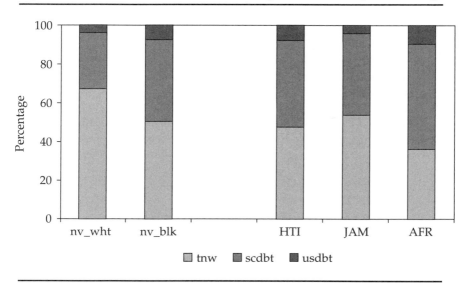

Source: Author's compilation.

whites have about 40 percent of their total equity invested in their homes. African immigrants have a home equity percentage similar to that of native whites. However, because African immigrants have a very low level of total equity, the low percentage of home equity reflects their low homeownership rates. The home equity percentage for Haitian and Jamaican immigrants and African Americans is greater than 50 percent, indicating a less diverse investment portfolio. Retirement accounts weigh more heavily for native whites and African immigrants than other groups. Haitians stand out as being more likely to prefer real estate investment. Business equity is fundamentally different from other components because it is intended for production rather than for consumption. African immigrants appear to favor entrepreneurship and small businesses. Other black groups have a relatively small proportion of business equity.

Home-Related Assets and Debts

A home is the most significant component of wealth. This section examines assets and debts related to the home, including homeownership, negative home equity, and the terms of mortgages. Homeownership differences among black groups are shown in figure 6.7 and table 6.4. When compared to the 70 percent homeownership rate among native whites, all black groups exhibit lower percentages. However, variations among black groups are clear. Jamaican homeownership rates are about 10 percentage points lower than native white, whereas Haitian, African immigrant, and African American rates are about 30 percentage points lower. Age structure explains little of the homeownership for any group. Compared to age structure, marital status and having children explain certain group gaps in homeownership for all groups. Further adjusted to education composition does not further explain the group gaps. Jamaican immigrant homeownership, however, is insensitive to all adjustments conducted here.

Table 6.5 shows odds ratios of homeownership by demographic characteristics. Odds ratios measure the ratio with and without each characteristic. For example, a ratio of 5.05 for the characteristic married white households means that the odds of homeownership are 4.05 times greater for married white households than for unmarried. For native whites, native blacks, and Haitian immigrants, the odds of older households owning a home are greater than those of younger households. The ratio of older to younger households is 2.8 for African Americans, higher than the 2.19 for native whites or 1.33 for Haitians. It is less than 1 for Jamaican and African immigrants, indicating that younger households are more likely than older households in these two groups to own a home. Except among Jamaicans, married households are much more likely to

Table 6.4   Homeownership by Demographic Characteristics and Black Group

	Total	25 to 44	45 to 64	Unmarried	Married	0 Children	1 to 2 Children	3 +	Education < 12	Education ≥ 12
Native white	0.708	0.632	0.790	0.498	0.834	0.643	0.771	0.780	0.485	0.724
African American	0.447	0.338	0.588	0.333	0.669	0.437	0.481	0.380	0.303	0.473
Haitian	0.399	0.370	0.439	0.211	0.602	0.278	0.365	0.551	0.296	0.435
Jamaican	0.612	0.633	0.584	0.579	0.637	0.643	0.613	0.503	0.615	0.611
African immigrant	0.395	0.396	0.391	0.226	0.547	0.147	0.446	0.641	0.115	0.423

Source: Author's compilation.

Figure 6.6.   Portfolio as Percentage of Total Equity by Black Group

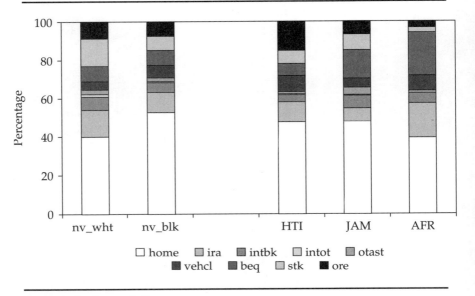

Source: Author's compilation.

own a home. The connection between having children and owning a home is the strongest for Haitian and African immigrants. A larger number of children also increases the odds for Haitians. The reason the number of children does not increase the homeownership much for Jamaicans may be because Jamaicans' better financial situation allows them to purchase a home before having children. Finally, education is most important for African immigrants. For those having a high school degree or above versus those who do not have a degree, the ratio is as high as 5.63, which is much higher than that of native whites (2.79) and African Americans (2.07). Because education is a component of social class, those with higher education are more likely to be middle class, allowing them to cross the color line. Education, however, is not a decisive factor for Jamaicans. Perhaps, as a new model minority group, their ethnic niche provides them opportunities for upward mobility regardless of education.

Another useful way to examine group differences in homeownership is to compare rates after adjusting black group demographics to match those of native whites. Figure 6.7 presents the crude homeownership rates (without adjustments), the rates adjusting for age, marital status and number of children, and education. The homeownership of black groups is not sensitive to age adjustment. After adjusting for marital sta-

Table 6.5   **Odds Ratio of Homeownership by Demographic Characteristics and Black Group**

	45 to 64	Married	0 Children	3 + Children	Education ≥ 12
Native white	2.19	5.05	0.53	1.05	2.79
African American	2.80	4.04	0.84	0.66	2.07
Haitian	1.33	5.66	0.67	2.13	1.83
Jamaican	0.81	1.27	1.14	0.64	0.98
African immigrant	0.98	4.13	0.21	2.22	5.63

Source: Author's compilation.

tus and number of children, African American and Haitian immigrant rates increase but those of African immigrants decrease. Adjustment for education does not significantly affect rates. Overall, the composition in marriage and presence of children explains the homeownership gap among black groups.

A household cannot have home equity without owning a home. Negative home equity (NHE) indicates that the market value of the home is lower than the mortgage or mortgages on the home, a grave financial danger for a household. Figure 6.8 shows that the NHE rates for all black groups are higher than the rate for native whites (see table 6.6 for detail).

Figure 6.7   **Crude and Adjusted Homeownership Rates by Black Group**

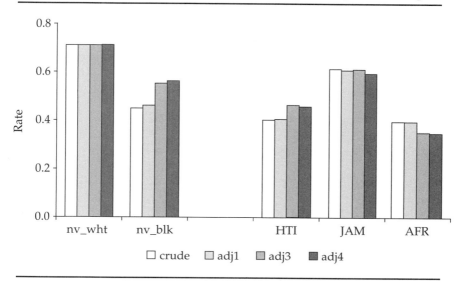

Source: Author's compilation.

Figure 6.8   Crude and Adjusted Negative Home Equity Rates Among Homeowners by Black Group

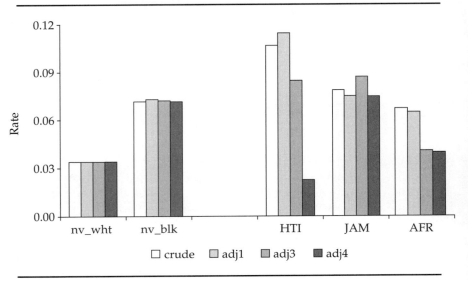

Source: Author's compilation.

Even for Jamaicans, who are better off than all other black groups, the rate is more than 7 percent greater than that for African Americans and African immigrants. Haitians have the highest rate, 10 percent. The rate for African immigrants is a relatively low 5.5 percent. Adjusting for demographic compositions reverses the NHE gap between native whites and Haitian immigrants—the adjusted Haitian rate is the lowest. The African immigrant rate declines significantly after the full adjustment. Adjustments,

Table 6.6   Negative Home Equity Rates by Black Group

	Crude	Adj1[a]	Adj3[b]	Adj4[c]
Native white	0.034	0.034	0.034	0.034
African American	0.072	0.073	0.072	0.072
Haitian	0.106	0.114	0.084	0.022
Jamaican	0.078	0.075	0.087	0.074
African immigrant	0.067	0.064	0.040	0.039

Source: Author's compilation.
[a] Adj1 adjusts for age composition.
[b] Adj3 adjusts for the composition of age, marital status, and number of children.
[c] Adj4 adjusts for the composition of age, marital status, number of children, and education levels.

however, do not change the rates for African Americans and Jamaican immigrants. These mixed Caribbean and African patterns suggest that Africanness versus Caribbeanness is not necessarily an explanation.

A household can have paid off the mortgage on its home or it can have one or more mortgages. Table 6.7 shows that among homeowners, African Americans appear to be better off than native whites, given that 24.6 percent have paid off their mortgages (compared to 20 percent of native whites) and only 6.4 percent have more than one mortgage (compared to 12.6 percent of native whites). Lending institutions sometimes aggressively encourage homeowners to use home equity loans for home improvement, investment in other areas, or payoff of credit card debts. Although having more than one mortgage may reflect middle-class financial strategies, it has been pointed out that such strategies may lead to accruing overwhelming debts that in turn lead to foreclosure. In this sense, the high rate of multiple mortgages among African immigrants (17.7 percent) is not a good sign. Given their low mortgage payoff rate of 9 percent, African immigrant homeowners are financially unstable among groups compared here.

Mortgage characteristics may differ by length of homeownership. Table 6.8 looks more deeply into this possibility. When the sample size under specific length of ownership is less than ten, its statistics are unstable, indicated as n.a. in the table. The left panel shows the proportion of household falling in each length of homeownership. Around 70 percent of all black immigrant homeowners bought their houses within ten years. Small sample sizes in the long-term (twenty or more years) category are found for Haitian and African immigrant homeowners. A small sample size in the medium-length (ten to nineteen years) category is found for African immigrant homeowners.

The native white pattern of more than one mortgage is curvilinear with a higher rate at the medium-length and lower rates at the short- and long-term ownership. This pattern repeats for Jamaican immigrants. Compared with native white new homeowners, new African immigrant homeowners are more likely to take two or more mortgages and their

Table 6.7   Number of Mortgages Among Homeowners by Black Group

	0	1	2 +
Native white	0.200	0.674	0.126
African American	0.246	0.690	0.064
Haitian	0.155	0.770	0.075
Jamaican	0.117	0.794	0.090
African immigrant	0.090	0.732	0.177

Source: Author's compilation.

Table 6.8   Mortgages and NHE Among Homeowners by Years of Ownership and Black Group

	Proportion			2 + Mortgages			Prop. NHE		
	<10	10 ~ 19	20 +	<10	10 ~ 19	20 +	<10	10 ~ 19	20 +
Native white	0.580	0.245	0.175	0.129	0.151	0.080	0.053	0.033	0.017
African American	0.515	0.248	0.236	0.064	0.070	0.055	0.111	0.065	0.048
Haitian	0.701	0.231	0.067	0.064	0.133	n.a.	0.134	0.082	0.000
Jamaican	0.687	0.227	0.085	0.060	0.192	0.059	0.133	0.051	0.284
African immigrant	0.831	0.096	0.073	0.180	n.a.	n.a.	0.100	n.a.	n.a.

Source: Author's compilation.
Note: n.a. indicates cell size < 10.

Haitian and Jamaican counterparts less likely. This mixed pattern suggests that being black might not be the major factor blocking the access to the lending market. The timing of NHE (see the right panel of table 6.8) is more often during the short term than the medium or long term of homeownership. Among new homeowners, the proportions of NHE for black groups more than double the native white rate. Among long-term homeowners, Jamaican immigrants are more likely to have negative home equity. This analysis identifies the timing of financial risk facing black immigrant homeowners.

Do black groups benefit from government programs sponsored by the FHA and VA? Table 6.9 suggests that this is the case. However, relative to other black groups, a smaller percentage of Haitians benefit from these programs. This may have to do with the U.S. policy toward Haitian immigrants, who have not been treated as refugees. Another important aspect of mortgages is the interest rate. It has been documented that African Americans are subject to higher mortgage rates. Do other black groups face the same problem? Table 6.9 shows large variations in mortgage interest rates among black groups. The percentage of having a low rate (under 7.0) is similar for native whites (33.1 percent) and Jamaican immigrants (37.7 percent) and lower for African Americans (25.7 percent), Haitian immigrants (14.9 percent), and African immigrants (19.3 percent). On the other end of the continuum, native whites have the absolute advantage: the percentage having a high rate (greater than or equal to 8.5 percent) is 17.2 percent, much lower than that for any black group. Among black groups, the highest percentages occur among African Americans and Haitian immigrants (31.7 percent and 33.3 percent). This points to the insignificance of Africanness or Caribbeanness.

Other Assets and Debts

Liquid financial assets provide buffer against immediate hardships. Figure 6.9 (table 6.10) examines liquid asset ownership: stocks and mutual

Table 6.9   Program and Interest Rate of First Home Mortgage by Black Group

	FHA/VA	< 7.0	≥ 8.5
Native white	0.200	0.331	0.172
African American	0.452	0.257	0.317
Haitian	0.252	0.149	0.333
Jamaican	0.357	0.377	0.219
African immigrant	0.456	0.193	0.244

Source: Author's compilation.

Figure 6.9   Financial Asset Rates by Black Group

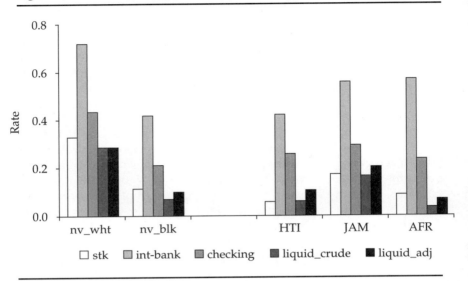

Source: Author's compilation.

funds, interest-earning bank accounts, non-interest-earning bank accounts, and $20,000 or more in financial assets. In liquid assets, native whites have the absolute advantage over any black group. Although 33 percent of native whites own stocks and mutual funds, only 11 percent of African Americans, 6 percent of Haitian and African immigrants, and 17 percent of Jamaican immigrants do. Black group, particularly African American and Haitian, percentages for the interest-earning bank accounts are much lower than native white. African Americans and Haitian and African immigrants are also the most disadvantaged in ownership of non-interest-earning checking accounts. It is for the $20,000 or more in financial assets that African immigrants sink to the bottom, with their ownership rate at 3.1 percent, compared to 28 percent for native whites, 16 percent for Jamaican immigrants, 7 percent for African Americans, and 6 percent for Haitian immigrants. If adjustments are made for demographic composition, the African immigrant rate is still the lowest. Thus, among black groups, Jamaicans are better financially prepared for emergencies and African immigrants the least prepared.

The purpose of retirement accounts is to ensure security in old age. Retirement accounts can also be used as collateral or be liquidated in an emergency, making these accounts quasi-liquid assets. Figure 6.10 (table 6.11) shows that the gaps between whites and black gaps are large in ownership of the two major types of retirement accounts, IRA or Keogh

Table 6.10   Ownership of Liquid Financial Assets by Black Group

	Stock Mutual Fund	Int. Bank Account	Non-Interest Checking[a]	$20,000 or More Combined Liquid Crude	$20,000 or More Combined Liquid Adj4[b]
Native white	0.328	0.720	0.434	0.284	0.284
African American	0.111	0.417	0.209	0.065	0.098
Haitian	0.055	0.418	0.253	0.057	0.101
Jamaican	0.168	0.554	0.290	0.160	0.199
African immigrant	0.082	0.567	0.231	0.031	0.065

Source: Author's compilation.
[a] Among those which have no interest-earning bank accounts.
[b] Adj4 adjusts for age composition, marital status, number of children, and education levels.

and 401(k). Whereas 31 percent of native whites have IRA-Keogh accounts, only 6 to 10 percent of blacks do, with African immigrants at 6 percent. Adjusting for the composition of age and ownership of $20,000 or more in financial assets raises the rate of IRA-Keogh ownership to 11 to 13 percent for all black groups. That after-adjustment gaps are still large suggests different planning strategies and constraints regarding retirement accounts. Most 401(k) plans combine employer and employee contributions. More than 43 percent of native whites own 401(k) accounts, a higher percentage than any black group. Among black groups, about 30 percent of Jamaicans and African immigrants, 24 percent of African Americans, and only 12 percent of Haitians do so. Adjusting for the composition of age and financial assets ownership does not push Jamaican and African immigrant rates up but does for those of African Americans and Haitians. This again suggests that old age support strategies and constraints differ between native whites and black groups.

Life insurance is another way to protect family members in an emergency situation. For workers in the primary labor market, employers provide life insurance. When employers do not, individuals may buy it on their own. Figure 6.11 (table 6.12) shows that the employer-provided life insurance rate is the highest for native whites at 56 percent, higher than for African Americans (45 percent), Haitian immigrants (32 percent), Jamaican immigrants (49 percent), and African immigrants (41 percent). Adjusting for demographic composition does not significantly affect the gaps except for African Americans. African Americans and Jamaican immigrants, however, compensate the deficit in employer-provided life insurance by buying it. The adjusted total life insurance rates

Figure 6.10   Crude and Adjusted Rates of Retirement Accounts by Black Group

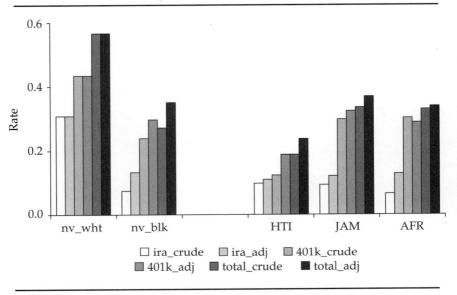

Legend:
□ ira_crude   ▨ ira_adj   ▨ 401k_crude
▨ 401k_adj   ▨ total_crude   ■ total_adj

Source: Author's compilation.

are similar among native whites, African Americans, and Jamaican immigrants, with Haitian and African immigrants lagging.

Consumer debts are an area in which white-black gaps are small (see figure 6.12 and table 6.13). Jamaican immigrants appear to adapt American consumerism quickly and surpass native whites in consumer debt rates (62 percent versus 60 percent). The African American rate is the lowest (48 percent) but is still not substantially lower than that of native

Table 6.11   Crude and Adjusted Rates of Retirement Accounts by Black Group

	Ira/Keo		401k		Total	
	Crude	Adj[a]	Crude	Adj[a]	Crude	Adj[a]
Native white	0.308	0.308	0.434	0.434	0.568	0.568
African American	0.072	0.131	0.239	0.296	0.272	0.351
Haitian	0.095	0.107	0.122	0.186	0.186	0.236
Jamaican	0.092	0.120	0.297	0.323	0.333	0.370
African immigrant	0.062	0.126	0.301	0.287	0.329	0.338

Source: Author's compilation.
[a] Adj adjusts for the composition of age and ownership of $20,000 liquid financial asset.

Figure 6.11   Crude and Adjusted Rates of Life Insurance by Black Group

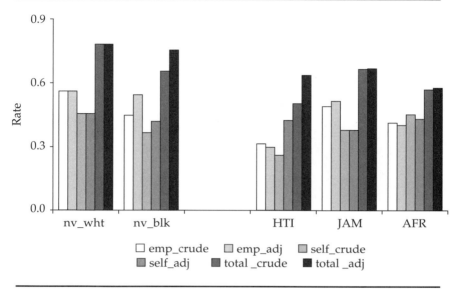

Source: Author's compilation.

whites. After being adjusted for demographic composition, the rates for both Jamaicans and African immigrants are higher than those for native whites and the gap between native whites and African Americans and Haitians is only 1 to 3 percentage points. Little group difference can be found in the average amount of credit card debt. After the very small and very large debts are trimmed, the average credit card debt level is highest for African Americans. With low levels of net worth and liquid financial assets, the white-parity rates and amount of consumer debts place all blacks, native or immigrant, in greater financial instability.

Table 6.12   Crude and Adjusted Rates of Life Insurance by Black Group

	Employer-provided		Self-bought		Total	
	Crude	Adj4[a]	Crude	Adj4[a]	Crude	Adj4[a]
Native white	0.564	0.564	0.457	0.457	0.784	0.784
African American	0.450	0.546	0.366	0.422	0.658	0.755
Haitian	0.317	0.299	0.258	0.424	0.503	0.638
Jamaican	0.491	0.513	0.379	0.378	0.667	0.668
African immigrant	0.410	0.398	0.282	0.274	0.568	0.575

Source: Author's compilation.
[a] Adj4 adjusts for the composition of age, marital status, number of children, and education levels.

Figure 6.12   Crude and Adjusted Rates of Consumer Debts by Black Group

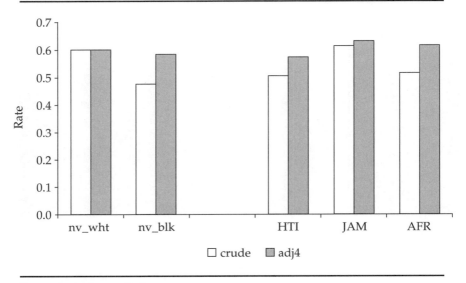

Source: Author's compilation.

It is conventional wisdom that immigrants are more likely than natives to be self-employed. Figure 6.13 (table 6.14) examines ownership of business equity. Like net worth, business equity ranges from negative to positive. Ownership of business equity therefore indicates household members are self-employed or own small businesses. The business equity ownership rate is 15.8 percent for native whites, with African immigrants coming in a close second at 13.1 percent. The rate is particularly low among African Americans (5.4 percent) and Haitian immigrants (3.5 percent) and also low among Jamaican immigrants (8.6 percent), consistent with findings about low self-employment rates among these three

Table 6.13   Crude and Adjusted Consumer Debts by Black Group

	Crude	Adj4[a]	Amount	Trim. Amount
Native white	0.598	0.598	$6,141	$5,658
African American	0.477	0.587	$5,233	$5,068
Haitian	0.508	0.573	$5,551	$5,346
Jamaican	0.616	0.633	$5,268	$5,328
African immigrant	0.517	0.619	$6,243	$6,400

Source: Author's compilation.
[a] Adj4 adjusts for the composition of age, marital status, number of children, and education levels.

Figure 6.13   Crude and Adjusted Rates of Business Ownership by Black Group

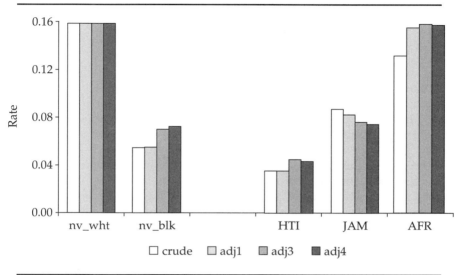

Source: Author's compilation.

groups. However, adjusting for age composition (proxy for experience) boosts the business ownership rate for African immigrants to approach that of native whites. Additional adjustment for the composition of marriage and presence of children (proxy for social capital), increases the business ownership rate for African Americans. Education composition, however, does not appear to influence the group gaps. After the full adjustment, African immigrants are the only ones who match native whites in business ownership. All other black group rates remain very low.

Table 6.14   Business Ownership by Black Group

	Crude	Adj1[a]	Adj3[b]	Adj4[c]
Native white	0.158	0.158	0.158	0.158
African American	0.054	0.055	0.070	0.072
Haitian	0.035	0.035	0.044	0.043
Jamaican	0.086	0.082	0.075	0.074
African immigrant	0.131	0.154	0.157	0.156

Source: Author's compilation.
[a] Adj1 adjusts for age composition.
[b] Adj3 adjusts for the composition of age, marital status, and number of children.
[c] Adj4 adjusts for the composition of age, marital status, number of children, and education levels.

These results suggest that African immigrants are building their entrepreneurship and economic basis but other black groups are not.

The Likelihood of Cross-Border Asset Ownership

The typology of wealth regime classifies countries by their incentive structure attracting emigrants to invest back in their homeland. In chapter 4, figure 4.14 identifies the types of wealth regime in the origin countries of black immigrants examined in this chapter. Haiti and three origin countries of the African immigrant group—Nigeria, Ethiopia, and Somalia—offer the lowest incentive for emigrants to make cross-border investments. The conditions in these countries are least favorable because the very low level of investment environment (a lack of domestic credit market, little protection of property right, and high political instability) precludes any investment incentive. Thus the conditions for home-country investment are absent for immigrants from these countries, just as they are for Colombian and Cuban immigrants (see chapter 4). Kenya and Jamaica offer somewhat more of an incentive because of their medium level of investment environment and medium purchasing capacity of U.S. currency. Low development levels and the heavy obligation emigrants feel toward family members who do not emigrate all promote investment in the home country. These conditions are similar to those for Mexican immigrants (see chapter 4), in large part because the three countries have the same type of wealth regime. Ghana, on the other hand, has a medium investment environment and high purchasing capacity of U.S. currency. Its economic growth is low but stable. All create a stronger incentive for Ghanaian immigrants than for Kenyan and Jamaican immigrants to invest in the home country.

Wealth regime typology provides an understanding of the neccessary conditions under which Caribbean and African immigrants are likely to invest in their homelands. The sufficient condition, however, depends on the self-selection of immigrants. The refugee status of most of Ghana and Kenya immigrants reduces it. Furthermore, despite incentives, the minimal wealth of African immigrants constrains any actual investment activities on their part. The economic immigrant status of Jamaican immigrants, by contrast, increases both likelihood and investment in the homeland. Again, the SIPP does not provide actual data on such investments, but this analysis gives us reason to believe that the level of wealth for Jamaican immigrants may be significantly higher than what the SIPP measure.

Conclusion

Voluntary immigration among blacks occurred over a shorter span than among Latinos and Asians. Jamaicans have the longest immigration history and the demographics (other than race) of many are close to those of native whites. Their favorable reception by American labor markets has also facilitated occupational and employment niches for them. As a result, Jamaicans are economically prosperous relative to other black immigrants. Sub-Sahara Africans have a short history of voluntary emigration, one that did not begin in significant numbers to the United States until 1965. They face racial discrimination and low returns to degrees they earned in Africa, resulting in slower economic attainment.

U.S. refugee policies certainly affect the prospects of refugee immigrants. Those from sub-Saharan African countries such as Somalia and Ethiopia differ sharply from Haitians, for example. The political, economic, and social situations in Africa and Haiti created massive waves of refugees, but U.S. reception of the two groups has been very different, favoring African over Haitian (economic) refugees.

Although black immigrants begin their new lives in the United States with different cultural traditions, migration motives, self-selection, and treatment by the government and labor market, they all face the same formidable barrier of the U.S. racial-ethnic hierarchy, which places blacks at the bottom of the society. Thus, though black immigrants account for only 6 percent of all blacks in the United States, studying black immigrants offers a unique opportunity for understanding interactions among race, nativity, Africanness-Caribbeanness, and refugee status. The color line dominates, but these other factors play into the mix, revealing both similarities and differences.

Several patterns emerge regarding both heterogeneity and homogeneity among black groups. Jamaican immigrants are the best off, but the wealth gap between Jamaican immigrants and native whites remains huge. Variations are large, with African Americans near the bottom. The only area where black immigrants are similar to native whites is consumer debt level. I summarize the major findings for each black group compared with other black groups.

Jamaican immigrants have both more education and legal status. They have achieved greater upward mobility and the highest rates of wealth ownership but show signs of economic vulnerability. Jamaican immigrant long-term homeowners are more likely to have negative home equity, for example.

At the other end of the continuum are Haitian immigrants. With less education and often illegal status, they are blocked from asset building opportunities such as FHA-VA programs, low interest rates on mortgages, employer-provided life insurance, and small business ownership. They are among those with the least net worth, observed homeownership rate, and adjusted retirement account rates.

In some important respects, however, African Americans fare even worse. Notably, their rate of living paycheck to paycheck and their adjusted negative home equity rate are the highest of all black groups. Because of the longer term of homeownership, the percentage of African American homeowners who have paid off their mortgages is also the highest and, interestingly, also higher than that of native whites. However, low homeownership rates and depreciated home values attributable to racial residential segregation means that having paid-off mortgages doesn't necessarily work to the group's advantage.

African immigrants present a perplexing case. Their three outstanding demographic characteristics include youth, high levels of education, and large numbers of children. Although it is expected that wealth is lower at earlier stages of the life cycle, adjusting for age does not change African immigrants' lower wealth attainment. They do not seem to be severely blocked from opportunities, given that they have the highest rate of using FHA-VA programs and owning small businesses. They do, however, have the lowest rates of sufficient wealth holding, observed and adjusted homeownership, and adjusted liquid financial assets. Their likely refugee status, high fertility rates, and African educational degrees may partially explain the puzzling patterns.

Pronounced heterogeneity, then, does exist among black immigrants. At the same time, evidence for a certain level of homogeneity is also strong. The gulf between native whites and the best-off among the black groups—Jamaicans—is much wider than the variations among black groups. Further adding to the depressing picture of black immigrant and black American financial circumstances, consumer debt rates among black groups are catching up to those of native whites. The fragile wealth foundation among black immigrants and Americans makes them vulnerable to financial risk. American spending habits may adversely affect blacks, immigrants and Americans alike, because their wealth levels are already quite low.

═ Chapter 7 ═

Wealth Stratification, Assimilation, and Wealth Attainment

Descriptions of assets and debts in the previous chapters show large gaps in the wealth holding status and wealth components among racial-ethnic groups and immigrant origin-country groups. The conceptual framework developed in chapter 2 provides a rationale for how nativity differences can be subsumed by race-ethnicity and education. Such a structure allows immigration dynamics to create new social forces and transform existing wealth stratification processes. For example, later I note that though rates of return to education may favor racial minorities, postsecondary degrees earned in developing countries may offset this advantage. A strong motivation to improve the life chances of family and children and a home culture that honors having children may boost asset building among immigrants, regardless of their current marital or parenthood status.

The notion of wealth attainment refers to situations in which households have more assets than debts. Wealth attainment is more comprehensive than income attainment and other economic measures. Most households have some income, a substantial proportion do not have greater assets than debts, and some have no assets. Wealth attainment thus encompasses both the probability of an attainment threshold (having more assets than debts) and the amount of wealth above it. Beyond the purely economic, wealth attainment encompasses values, preferences, and lifestyles, all latent dimensions manifested in wealth attainment and the wealth portfolio. For these reasons, wealth attainment is an ideal concept for the study of assimilation. In this chapter, by looking at how it is stratified for both natives and immigrants, I examine the relationships among race, immigration, assimilation, and wealth stratification.

Empirical Models

The integrated framework in chapter 2 develops three ideal-type scenarios arising from a multifactor stratification system (recall figure 2.1). Based on the important roles of racial hierarchy and human capital, I hypothesize a dominance-differentiation system for the stratification of wealth, where race and education are primary factors (dominance) and nativity and immigrant characteristics are secondary factors (differentiation). The change scenario, if tested and confirmed, implies that immigration will eventually transform the existing stratification order and blur color lines. Moreover, the analysis here offers indirect tests regarding two theses of Richard Alba and Victor Nee's new assimilation model, that different immigrant groups assimilate at different paces and that the mainstream is a hybrid of cultures.

Figure 7.1 is an application of the theoretical model in figure 2.1 to wealth attainment in the contemporary immigration era. Starting from a race-education-nativity stratification system, model 1 (M1, see this chapter's appendix for a full discussion of models and methods) specifies that wealth attainment is a function of race-ethnicity, education, and nativity, controlling for household characteristics and the period effects of the years in which the data were collected.

If the coefficients for race, education, and nativity are all significant, then they are all primary factors. If, instead, the coefficient for nativity is insignificant, then nativity is not a primary factor. We move to the right panel of figure 7.1.

The next tasks are to determine whether nativity should be eliminated or retained and whether race and education are interdependent, tasks achieved by examining the interdependence among the three stratification factors in model 2 (M2). If some of the interaction terms for race, education, and nativity are significant, we move to model 3 (M3) for a separate analysis for each of the four racial-ethnic groups. In model 3, we examine the differentiation within racial-ethnic groups by nativity and the interdependence of nativity and education.

Finally, instead of using immigrant status, I use country of origin, age at arrival, and naturalization status in model 4 (M4). Results from M4 can help explain the degree of differentiation by specific immigrant characteristics, particularly by addressing the impact of immigrants' self-selection. Nativity differentiation can also be further examined by allowing different effects of household characteristics by nativity in model 5 (M5).

Models 3, 4, and 5 also test another hypothesis from the integrated framework, namely, immigrants' assimilation through wealth attainment. The new assimilation theory emphasizes the process of assimilation. Results from these models can help gauge the degree to which dif-

Figure 7.1   Testing the Structure of the Race-Education-Nativity Stratification System for Wealth

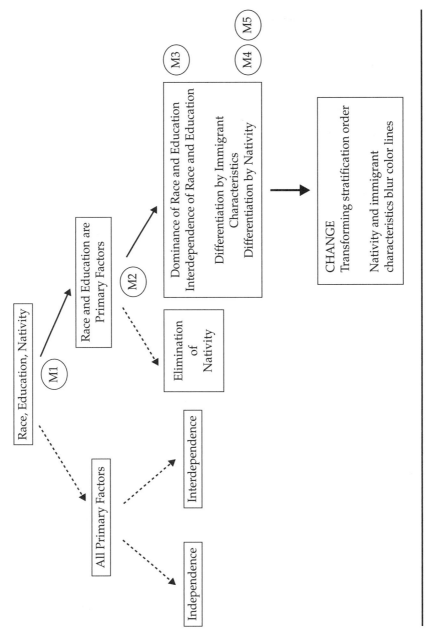

Source: Author's compilation.

ferent immigrant groups assimilate based on their wealth attainment. Wealth attainment may result from different consumption styles, saving motives, and portfolio allocation preferences, which are culturally loaded. High wealth attainment, which commonly provides economic security and benefits for subsequent generations, can facilitate a mainstream that embeds a hybrid of cultures.

Data and Methods

The full description of the methodology is provided in this chapter's appendix. Presented here is a brief version. The empirical work in this chapter makes use of all the available data from the SIPP, including fourteen years of data from ten panels, covering the two-decade period from 1985 to 2003. Households whose race-ethnicity differs from that of the majority of those from the same origin country are excluded. For example, non-Hispanic whites, blacks, and Asians from Mexico are excluded. Because the sample size for African and Caribbean immigrant nationality groups is small, black immigrants are classified as a single group rather than by nationality. Also, Salvadoran and Guatemalan immigrants cannot be identified for all panels and so are included in a larger group of "other" Hispanic immigrants. Similarly, immigrants from Hong Kong and Taiwan cannot be separated from those from mainland China in pre-1996 panels, so in this chapter the Chinese group combines the mainland, Hong Kong, and Taiwan groups.

Table 7.1 shows sample sizes for the four broadly defined racial-ethnic groups—non-Hispanic white, non-Hispanic black, Hispanic, and non-Hispanic Asian (hereafter white, black, Hispanic, and Asian)—and the sample size for ethnicity or nationality groups within each of them. Most range from almost 500 to more than 6,000. Those for Japanese and Polish immigrants are the smallest, at 254 and 162, respectively (see table 7.1).

The dependent variable is net worth, defined as total assets minus total debts. Net worth is a continuous measure of wealth, including negative, zero, and positive values. The notion of wealth attainment considers positive net worth as attaining wealth and negative and zero net worth as attaining none. Wealth attainment thus refers to both the probability and the amount of positive net worth. Such a definition provides an effective solution to the challenge presented by the negative and zero values.

Three stratification factors are race-ethnicity, education, and nativity. Immigrant characteristics are measured by country (region) of origin, non-naturalization status, age at arrival, and place of education. Wealth theory suggests several household characteristics as sources of differences in wealth attainment, including age, types of households, and number of children. The nature of wealth attainment (both probability

Table 7.1   Sample Size of Race-Ethnicity and Nationality Groups

Ethnicity or Nationality	White	Black	Hispanic	Asian
Native white	175,973			
Western European	3,056			
Eastern European	590			
Former Soviet	404			
Polish	162			
Native black		23,562		
Mexican			5,909	
Cuban			781	
Dominican			451	
Puerto Rican			2,452	
Mexican American			6,268	
Cuban American			2,284	
Asian American				1,601
Chinese				1,041
Filipino				912
Japanese				254
Indian				602
Korean				549
Vietnamese				613
Other immigrant	2,004	1,154	2,397	879
Total	182,189	24,716	20,542	6,451

Source: Author's compilation.

and amount) presents a challenge to modeling strategies. An appropriate model is the Tobit model (see the appendix of this chapter for details).

How Wealth Attainment Is Stratified?

Models 1 and 2 (see figure 7.1) are fitted to determine whether, as hypothesized, the stratification system for wealth is a dominance-differentiation system and nativity a secondary stratification factor. The fits of the models are also informative about the strength of the primary factor effects. The analysis of models 1 and 2 is applied to the whole population. The Tobit models estimate the effects of race-ethnicity, education, and nativity on the probability of positive net worth and on the log positive net worth (given positive net worth is achieved), controlling for household characteristics and period effects.

Table 7.2 shows the results for the three stratification factors in model M1 and the additional interaction terms among the three factors in model M2 (the estimates for household characteristics and period effects are not reported in the table). The top panel presents the estimates for the

Table 7.2   Wealth Stratification Factors: Race-Ethnicity, Education, and Nativity

Variable	M1	M2
Effect on positive net worth		
Race-Ethnicity		
Black	−1.962 **	−1.388 **
Hispanic	−1.346 **	−0.983 **
Asian	−0.456 **	−0.285 **
Education		
Years of schooling	0.232 **	0.160 **
Nativity		
Immigrant status	−0.005	0.011
Race × Nativity		
Black × Immigrant status	—	−0.106
Hispanic × Immigrant status	—	−0.156 **
Asian × Immigrant status	—	−0.161 ^
Education × Nativity		
Years of schooling × Immigrant status	—	−0.096 **
Race × Education		
Black × Years of schooling	—	0.109 **
Hispanic × Years of schooling	—	0.049 **
Asian × Years of schooling	—	0.134 **
Effect on probability of positive net worth		
Race-Ethnicity		
Black	−0.037 **	−0.117 **
Hispanic	−0.022 **	−0.083 **
Asian	−0.006 **	−0.024 **
Education	—	
Years of schooling	0.003 **	0.013 **
Nativity		
Immigrant status	0.000	0.001
Race × Nativity		
Black × Immigrant status	—	−0.009
Hispanic × Immigrant status	—	−0.013 **
Asian × Immigrant status	—	−0.014 ^
Education × Nativity		
Years of schooling × Immigrant status	—	−0.008 **
Race × Education		
Black × Years of schooling	—	0.009 **
Hispanic × Years of schooling	—	0.004 **
Asian × Years of schooling	—	0.011 **
Fraction positive net worth	.852	.852
n	233,898	233,898

Source: Author's compilation.
Note: Models 1 and 2 control for household characteristics and period effects.
**p <. 01
*p < .05
^p < .10

amount of positive net worth (conditional on having achieved positive net worth) and the bottom panel those for the probability. The sign and significance level of the effect for an explanatory variable are consistent for both. For example, the effect for being black is significantly negative for both the amount and the probability (-1.962 and -.037, respectively; significant at the .01 level). This is true for all variables included in the model. Therefore, my interpretation will weigh more on the amount of positive net worth than the probability of having it.

The Two Tiers of the Stratification System

To test the hypothesis about the primary versus secondary role of race-ethnicity, education, and nativity, I interpret the sign and statistical significance of the estimates for these factors and leave the interpretation of the magnitude for later. The M1 column shows that—education, nativity, household characteristics, and period effects held constant—all minority statuses have a negative effect when compared with the effect for whites (statistical significance at the .01 level). This joins a large body of racial-ethnic stratification literature supporting the primary role of race-ethnicity in wealth stratification. The coefficient for years of schooling is positive and statistically significant at the .01 level. This finding also supports the long history of human capital and class stratification research holding that education, one dimension of class, is decisive in determining wealth attainment. The estimate for nativity, however, is close to zero and statistically insignificant, providing strong evidence that nativity is not a primary stratification factor.

Model 1 does not provide enough information to answer the question whether nativity is a secondary stratification factor for wealth or should be eliminated. For a factor to be secondary, it should affect primary-factor groups differently and thus differentiate members of primary-factor groups. In this way, a secondary factor stratifies a subpopulation without stratifying the entire population. We examine whether the nativity effect differs by the racial-ethnic groups and by education groups estimated in model 2.

In the M2 column of table 7.2, the interaction terms between race-ethnicity and nativity capture the differential nativity effect. The main effect of nativity is near zero and insignificant, indicating that nativity has no significant effect for whites. The interaction effect of nativity and black status captures the additional effect for being blacks, which is also insignificant. The interaction effect of nativity and Hispanic or Asian status, however, is negative but the significance level is higher for Hispanics (.05) than for Asians (.10). Turning to the interaction between education and nativity, the coefficient is negative and significant. That the main effect of nativity is close to zero and insignificant is adequate support for classifying nativity as a secondary stratification factor.

Model 2 also shows the interdependence between race-ethnicity and education because the race-education interactions are all positive and significant. The education effect is strongest for Asians, followed by blacks and Hispanics. That is, schooling benefits minorities more than whites. Note that even though the education effect differs by race-ethnicity (the race effect by education), race and education remain significant factors in stratifying the population as a whole. This characteristic further supports race and education as the two primary stratification factors that are also interdependent.

The findings from models 1 and 2 regarding the stratification system are strong evidence that race-education-nativity stratification is a dominance-differentiation system. In it, race-ethnicity and education are two primary factors, and their effects on wealth are mutually dependent. Nativity, on the other hand, is a secondary stratification factor because it places immigrant Hispanics below native-born Hispanics and immigrant professionals below native professionals.

Strength of Primary and Secondary Factors

After determining that there is a two-tier stratification, we must further ask how strong the racial-ethnic effect and education effect are, and how strong the nativity effect for particular racial group and educational groups is. To answer these questions, we examine the magnitudes of the estimates.

The interpretation of the magnitude of an effect on log positive net worth is in relative terms. Take the coefficient for being black (-1.962) in model M1 as an example. When controlling for education, nativity, household characteristics, and period effects, blacks' positive net worth is 85.9 percent lower than that of whites.[1] Net worth levels are 74 percent lower for Hispanics and 36.6 percent lower for Asians. In plain terms, if a white household has $100,000 of net worth, in the same year a black household with exactly the same education levels, nativity status, and household characteristics has only $14,100. Corresponding numbers are $26,000 for Hispanics and $63,400 for Asians. Although all minority statuses have strong negative effects, consistent with the wealth stratification literature, the effect of being black is the most pronounced.

In M1, the strength of the racial-ethnic effect on the probability of having positive net worth follows the same pattern as the amount. The interpretation is straightforward: compared with whites, wealth attainment probability is lower by 0.037 for blacks, 0.022 for Hispanics, and 0.006 for Asians. The probability for the entire population is 0.852, but only 0.815 for blacks (0.852 minus 0.037), 0.83 for Hispanics, and 0.846 for Asians. All minorities, particularly blacks and Hispanics, are less likely to have positive net worth. This disadvantage for minorities is compounded with their disadvantage in the amount, constituting the foundation of racial-ethnic stratification of wealth attainment.

Concerning the effect of education in M1, a one year increase in schooling brings about 23 percent increase in net worth, holding race, nativity, household characteristics, and the year of data collection constant. On average, being a college rather than a high school graduate (four more years of schooling) increases net worth by 153 percent. The percentage increase is not linear in regard to the increase in the years of schooling. The eight-year increase from eighth grade to college graduation raises net worth by 540 percent. Although college education is difficult to access for many working-class individuals, it is nearly impossible for laborers with very low levels of education. In this way, education stratifies wealth. Having an additional year of schooling increases the probability of having positive net worth by 0.003. This effect on the probability again compounds the effect on amount reinforcing the primary role of education in wealth attainment.

Model M2 introduces the interaction between race-ethnicity and nativity (see column M2 of table 7.2). To grasp this potential differential, I calculate the specific effect for immigrants versus natives within racial groups and present a graphic view in figure 7.2. The minority effect appears to be more negative for immigrants than for natives. But only Hispanic immigrants have significantly less net worth than their native counterparts. The differences for whites and Asians are essentially nonexistent. How strong is nativity's effect for Hispanics? The combination of the main effect and the corresponding interaction effect: $(.011 - .156) = -.145$ on the log of positive net worth. This can be translated as that immigrant Hispanics have 13.5 percent less net worth than native Hispanics, all else being constant. The nativity effect also differs by educational levels because the interaction term between nativity and education is negative, indicating that the return to education is lower for immigrants than for natives. From model M2, the differential effect of education by nativity is significantly negative (-.096). This does not offset the main effect of 0.16, so immigrants' returns to education is positive but much lower than native-born counterparts. Nativity thus differentiates wealth within either racial-ethnic groups or within education groups.

The interdependence between race and education is another important finding. The wealth returns to education are higher for minorities. Figure 7.3 shows that the education effect is the largest for Asians, followed by blacks, then Hispanics, and the least for whites.

Under this dominance-differentiation system, a closer and more effi-

Figure 7.2   Differential Effects of Race-Ethnicity on Positive Net Worth

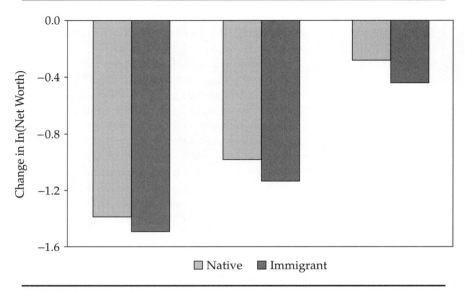

Source: Author's compilation.

Figure 7.3   Differential Effects of Education on Positive Net Worth

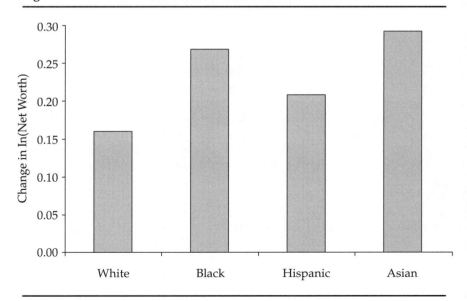

Source: Author's compilation.

cient investigation into the differentiation by nativity is to use model M3 for each of the four racial-ethnic groups.[2]

Differentiation

Models M3 and M4 are designed to evaluate the differentiation with racial-ethnic groups, and both are applied to each of the four groups. M3 specifies how nativity differentiates wealth of members within racial-ethnic groups by education. M4 replaces the indicator of nativity with country of origin, naturalization, and place of education. The results of these models are presented in tables 7.3 and 7.4.

Nativity differentiates racial-specific distributions of wealth through the interaction between education and nativity. Returns to education may depend on the country in which the highest degree was granted. Some immigrants received their highest postsecondary education in the United States and others did so in their home countries. Among whites, western European degrees may be considered somewhat comparable with U.S. degrees, but U.S. employers are unfamiliar with degrees from the former Soviet Union and other eastern European countries and don't see these degrees' applicability to the U.S. economy. Table 7.3 and figure 7.4 show a significant negative interaction effect (-.06) for white immi-

Table 7.3   Differentiation by Nativity (M3)

Variable	White	Black	Hispanic	Asian
Effect on positive net worth				
Nativity				
Immigrant status	−0.026	−0.024	−0.254 **	−0.180 *
Education				
Years of schooling	0.167 **	0.237 **	0.203 **	0.231 **
Education × Nativity				
Years of schooling × Immigrant status	−0.060 **	−0.098 **	−0.120 **	−0.022
Effect on probability of positive net worth				
Nativity				
Immigrant status	−0.002	−0.003	−0.028 **	−0.014 *
Education				
Years of schooling	0.012 **	0.029 **	0.023 **	0.018 **
Education × Nativity				
Years of schooling × Immigrant status	−0.004 **	−0.012 **	−0.013 **	−0.002
Fraction positive net worth	0.885	0.701	0.740	0.859
n	182,189	24,716	20,542	6,451

Source: Author's compilation.
Note: Model 3 controls for household characteristics and period effects.
** $p < .01$
* $p < .05$
^ $p < .10$

Table 7.4   Differentiation by Immigrant Characteristics (M4)

Variable	Effect on Positive Net Worth	Effect on Probability of Positive Net Worth
White		
Western European	0.523 **	0.038 **
Eastern European	0.167	0.012
Former Soviet	−0.937 **	−0.067 **
Polish	0.108	0.008
Other white immigrant	−0.031	−0.002
Age at arrival	−0.028 **	−0.002 **
Non-naturalized	−0.437 **	−0.031 **
Education	0.165 **	0.012 **
Education received at home country	−0.218 ^	−0.016 ^
Black		
Black immigrant	0.550 **	0.067 **
Age at arrival	−0.014	−0.002
Non-naturalized	−0.644 **	−0.078 **
Education	0.229 **	0.028 **
Education received at home country	0.104	0.013
Hispanic		
Mexican	0.355 **	0.040 **
Cuban	0.355 **	0.040 **
Dominican	−2.327 **	−0.264 **
Other Hispanic immigrant	−0.219 *	−0.025 *
Puerto Rican	−1.423 **	−0.161 **
Age at arrival	−0.032 **	−0.004 **
Non-naturalized	−0.514 **	−0.058 **
Education	0.134 **	0.015 **
Education received at home country	−0.031	−0.003
Asian		
Chinese	0.654 **	0.051 **
Filipino	0.056	0.004
Japanese	0.630 **	0.049 **
Indian	−0.033	−0.003
Korean	−0.174	−0.014
Vietnamese	−0.049	−0.004
Other Asian immigrant	−0.191	−0.015
Age at arrival	−0.038 **	−0.003 **
Non-naturalized	−0.616 **	−0.048 **
Education	0.194 **	0.015 **
Education received at home country	0.094	0.007

Source: Author's compilation.
Note: Model 4 controls for household characteristics and period effects.
** $p < .01$
* $p < .05$
^ $p < .10$

Figure 7.4   Differential Effect of Education on Amount of Positive Net Worth, by Nativity

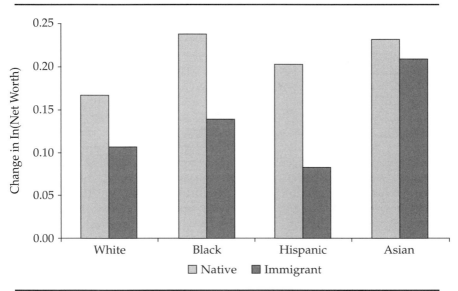

Source: Author's compilation.

grants, which may reflect difficulty in transferring education brought from eastern European countries. The same reasoning may explain why the discount rates for black and Hispanic immigrants are higher than those for white immigrants, given that the economies and educational systems of countries in the Caribbean Basin, Africa, and Latin America are less developed.

Asian immigrant education, however, is not discounted (the coefficient is small and insignificant). This result suggests that the demand for skilled workers and the characteristics of the educational system of sending countries must be taken into account. Many Asian immigrants, particularly those from the Philippines and India, earned degrees in their home countries. The 1965 immigration law established the employment-based preference policy, drawing professionals from the Philippines and India. An upward-spiral feedback process thus began with new developments in sending countries' educational systems, such as adopting a substantive American curriculum and making knowledge applicable to the American economy. As a result, these countries sent increasing numbers of professionals to the United States to meet increasing demand resulting from rapid technological development and the aging population in the United States. These professionals are admitted to industries with substantial shortages of highly skilled workers, such as the health and computer industries. Despite the fact that most Asian sending nations are developing countries, the market demanded fields of specialty, and the characteristics of the educational systems in these countries may do away with the potential discount.

Table 7.4 shows the heterogeneity among immigrants within racial-ethnic groups. This heterogeneity is primarily given rise by different countries of origin. The indicator of origin country captures, first, that country's characteristics and U.S.-relations, as well as the scale and functioning of ethnic networks, all of which contribute to immigrant self-selection, and, second, the reception by U.S. policy and society. Heterogeneity is also increased by arrival cohorts, captured by age at arrival together with age and year when data were collected. During the adaptation process after arrival, some immigrants obtained naturalized U.S. citizenship, an explicit action of assimilation. The large inflow of professional immigrants, some of whom received their highest degree in the home country and came to work directly in the American labor market, warrant a close look at the return on immigrant foreign degrees.

Overall, table 7.4 seems to indicate that nativity (immigrant status) and immigrant characteristics (immigrant country of origin, age at arrival, and naturalization) contribute to a more dispersed within-group wealth distribution, with both the lower and higher ends expanded. The difference between citizens and noncitizens widens the within-racial wealth distribution. With the exception of blacks, older age at arrival expands the lower end of within-racial wealth distribution. The expansion of the upper end differs. Among whites, immigration expands both ends because western Europeans have a higher probability and amount of positive net worth whereas former Soviet immigrant status is negatively associated with wealth attainment. Among blacks, the immigration expands the upper end because black immigrant status is positively associated with wealth attainment. Among Hispanics, both ends are expanded because Mexican and Cuban immigrants fare better than native-born Hispanics (except Puerto Ricans) and Dominican and other Hispanic immigrants fare worse (see figure 7.5). The Asian distribution has a greater expansion at the top than at the bottom because no specific immigrant group is significantly worse off than native-born Asian and because Chinese and Japanese immigrants are faring better than Asian Americans (see figure 7.6).

Thus far, the empirical evidence provided by the analysis based on models 1 through 4 supports the hypothesis that wealth stratification is a dominance-differentiation system in which race and education are primary factors and nativity a secondary one. Both race and education exert strong effects on the placement of blacks and Hispanics and the less educated at the lower tail of the wealth distribution. It is within the racial-ethnic groups that nativity and immigrant characteristics differentiate wealth of racial group members in systematic but different ways. The ex-

Figure 7.5   Effects of Latino and Puerto Rican Origin on Amount of Positive Net Worth Compared with Native-Born Latinos

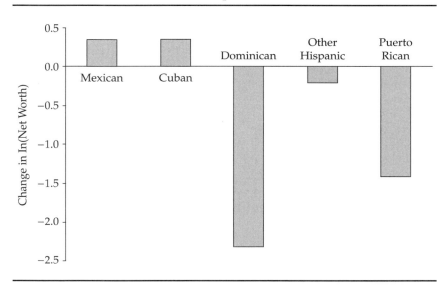

Source: Author's compilation.
Note: Puerto Ricans are excluded from the basis of comparison (native-born Latinos). Puerto Ricans, who are U.S. citizens, are separated from other native-born Latinos and compared with Latino immigrant groups because many Puerto Ricans experienced migration.

Figure 7.6   Effects of Asian Origin on Amount of Positive Net Worth Compared with Native-Born Asians

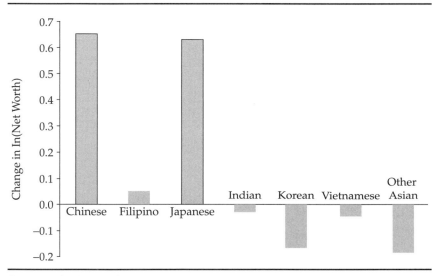

Source: Author's compilation.
Note: Bars without a border indicate insignificant effects.

panded lower end of the white distribution and the upper end of the Asian distribution contribute to the blurring divide between whites and Asian. Similarly, the expanded within distribution of blacks and Hispanics makes those racial divides less obvious. The replenishment of diverse immigration in the decades ahead will continue this differentiation and its long-term impact on transforming the race-education-nativity stratification system for wealth.

Assimilation Through Wealth Attainment

Wealth attainment by the immigrant generation itself offers a lens to view intragenerational assimilation. Such assimilation is facilitated or constrained by the stratification order in the United States and enabled by immigrants' wealth accumulation behavior.

Intragenerational Wealth Attainment and Assimilation

Assimilation theory considers multidimensional assimilation beyond rather than within the immigrant generation (Gordon 1964; Portes and Zhou 1993; Alba and Nee 2003). Socioeconomic assimilation, a form of structural assimilation, however, has been examined both across generations and within that of immigrants. The incomes of earlier European white immigrants caught up to those of their native-born counterparts within a decade or so (Chiswick 1978). My earlier research shows that, with the same conditions in race-ethnicity, education, household characteristics, and number of productive adult years in the United States, immigrant wealth catches up to native wealth within two decades (Hao 2004). Immigrant nationality groups, however, experience various degrees to which their wealth attainment is similar to the mainstream. The previous chapters documented the vast heterogeneity of origin countries for immigrants within racial-ethnic categories. Immigrants differ among themselves in three other ways. They arrive at different ages, and older age at arrival is a disadvantage. Some are naturalized and others are not. Naturalization captures two things: the length of U.S. residence (because immigrants must live in the United States at least five years before applying for naturalization) and assimilation (because naturalized citizens are more likely to be committed to a permanent stay and to adopt American values). Some immigrants received their highest degree in the United States and others did so in their home countries, which may result in different rates of return to education. Model 4 allows these variations in determining wealth attainment. Table 7.4 reports results from model 4.

Although the SIPP identifies country of origin for western European immigrants, given their relative homogeneity and small group sizes, they are grouped as one region. Most SIPP panels do not identify country of origin for eastern European immigrants (except for those from countries of the former Soviet Union) or black immigrants. Regional identifications are thus also used to indicate these two groups. For the two racial-ethnic groups with the largest percentage of immigrants, Hispanics and Asians, I identify nine countries of origin, including Mexico, Cuba, the Dominican Republic, China (including Hong Kong and Taiwan), the Philippines, Japan, India, Korea, and Vietnam.

The heterogeneity of same-race immigrant groups is evident for whites, Hispanics, and Asians. The small sample sizes of origin-country black groups prevent identifying their specific effects. Compared with native-born whites, western European immigrants exhibit a greater probability of wealth attainment. The probability of their having positive net worth is .038 higher than native whites, meaning that, on average, 92 percent have positive net worth. Correspondingly, their amount of positive net worth is about 69 percent higher than that of native whites. Although Polish or other eastern European immigrants are similar to native whites, former Soviet immigrants exhibit a smaller probability (by .067) and amount of positive net worth (by 61 percent). Compared with African Americans, black immigrants from Caribbean Basin and the African continent show an edge in probability of attaining positive net worth from a mean of .701 to .768, and an increase in the amount of positive net worth by 73.3 percent.

Identifying more origin-country groups among Hispanics and Asians allows specific comparisons for more groups than is possible with immigrant whites. Table 7.4 shows ample heterogeneity among Hispanic immigrant groups, with two groups faring better and two faring worse than native-born Hispanics who are not Puerto Ricans. The edge is almost identical for both Mexican and Cuban immigrants: an increase of .04 in probability of having positive net worth and a 42.6 percent increase in amount. Although the higher attainment for Cuban immigrants is expected, given the extensive literature, the finding that Mexican immigrants have a similar edge is new. Note again that these comparisons are made based on having the same education level, age, and household characteristics. As detailed in chapter 4, the unique features of Mexican immigrants lie in their very low education and high likelihood of illegal status, both of which are impediments to wealth accumulation.

For Dominican immigrants, the probability of positive net worth is reduced by 0.264, down to .476, compared to .74 for native-born Hispanics. The amount is reduced by 90.3 percent. Dominican immigrant education levels are actually not as low as those of Mexican immigrants, and the comparison was against native-born Hispanics with similar education levels. Moreover, most Dominicans are black, whereas most non–Puerto

Rican Hispanics are not black. It makes more sense to compare Dominicans to Puerto Ricans. Table 7.4 indeed shows the disadvantage among Puerto Ricans, yet the Dominican disadvantage is much deeper.

None of the six origin-country Asian groups fares worse than Asian Americans, holding education, age, and household type constant. The Chinese and Japanese are two groups that surpass Asian Americans, with the probability of positive net worth among them about .05 higher and the amount 92 percent greater. Here, the Chinese group includes those from Hong Kong and Taiwan, whose wealth profiles are the highest of all native and immigrant groups. Thus Hong Kong and Taiwan Chinese wealth substantially contributes to the edge for the Chinese found in table 7.4. Contemporary immigrants from Japan, an economic superpower, are likely to bring in capital to settle in America. Korean immigrants are also likely to do so but are engaged more heavily in small businesses. Instead of having an edge, the sign of the Korean coefficient is negative, and the magnitude is larger than the coefficients for other capital-poor groups such as Filipinos, Indians, and Vietnamese. These important differences are hidden in the group comparisons because most surveys do not collect information on capital brought in by immigrants.

These results provide evidence that the wealth different immigrant groups acquire goes in different directions and at different speeds. Given the minor difference in wealth between Asians and whites, that of Asians can be a sign of assimilation to the mainstream. Assuming the same education and demographic conditions, western European, Chinese, and Japanese immigrants follow the footsteps of earlier European immigrants—able to surpass mainstream wealth attainment within the immigrant generation. Polish, eastern European (except for former Soviet), Filipino, Indian, Korean, and Vietnamese immigrants all have the potential to reach parity with the mainstream. Similarly, assuming the same socioeconomic conditions, Mexican and Cuban immigrants have the potential to surpass native-born Hispanics. This edge, however, does not offset the gap between Hispanics and whites documented in table 7.2. Thus, though Mexicans and Cubans are upwardly mobile, their speed of assimilation in wealth attainment is slower because they are lower in the racial-ethnic hierarchy. Black immigrants, likewise, are upwardly mobile and exhibit the potential to surpass African Americans. Again, this edge does not offset the black-white wealth gap observed in table 7.2, suggesting that black immigrants' speed of assimilation in terms of wealth attainment is relatively slow. In contrast to such upwardly mobile groups, Dominican and other Hispanic immigrants, such as those from Colombia, El Salvador, and Guatemala, show signs of downward mobility. Assuming the same education levels and demographic conditions, wealth attainment for these two groups is lower than that of native-born Hispanics.

Readers should keep in mind that these analytic patterns are not what we directly observed in chapters 4, 5, and 6. With observed patterns, we always wonder how much the group gaps result from education and demographic conditions. The analysis presented here is a scientific way to tease out these confounding education and demographic conditions. Such a separation helps determine the potential for upward mobility and downward mobility. More generally, such a study of wealth attainment enhances our understanding of immigrants' assimilation.

Immigrants' Specific Wealth Behavior

Why do immigrants assimilate so differently? Although I emphasize the facilitating and constraining role of the race and education primary stratification factors, I recognize the role that human agency plays in the accumulation of wealth along a household's life cycle. Wealth theory identifies the areas in which individual households may behave differently, leading to different wealth outcomes. A few highlights of the theoretical rationales for why immigrants' wealth and natives' wealth differ include that immigrants are self-selected, positively or negatively, with different motivations for migration; they may encounter differential treatment in the racial-ethnic hierarchy; and they may bring in the norms and cultures that continue to govern their economic goals and means. These rationales lead to a focus on the potential differential effects of age and age squared (capturing the nonlinear life cycle patterns shaped by earning, consuming, and saving behaviors), number of children and its squared term (capturing the potential non-linear effect of the motivation for enhancing children's life chances), and marriage and parenthood (capturing the values on family and the high expectation of having children). Driven by these rationales, in this section I empirically investigate the differential effect of the above-mentioned factors related to wealth behavior on wealth attainment of immigrants versus natives.

Results from model 1 about the effect of demographic characteristics, such as age, household type, and number of children show their prominent role in wealth attainment (see table 7.5). These characteristics are proxies for household earning, consuming, saving, and portfolio allocating behaviors, all of which factor in wealth accumulation. Both the percentage increase in positive net worth and the probability of attaining positive net worth are higher if the household head is older, has more education, is married with children, and has a small number of children. Wealth attainment is lower if the household head is younger, is female, lives alone, or has a large number of children. Net worth increases with age at a decelerating rate, peaking at age sixty-six, which is beyond the age limit of our population.[3] Married couples with children have higher positive net worth (13.4 percent) than married households without chil-

Table 7.5   Effect of Demographic Characteristics on Wealth Attainment (M1)

Variable	M1
Effect on positive net worth	
Age	0.2245 **
Age-squared	−0.0017 **
Married with children	0.1256 **
Female headed	−1.6279 **
Single man	−1.1245 **
Single woman	−1.4257 **
Other household type	−0.7198 **
Number of children	0.0577 **
Number of children squared	−0.0222 **
Rural residence	−0.0452 **
Effect on probability of positive net worth	
Age	0.0189 **
Age-squared	−0.0001 **
Married with children	0.0106 **
Female headed	−0.1368 **
Single man	−0.0945 **
Single woman	−0.1198 **
Other household type	−0.0605 **
Number of children	0.0049 **
Number of children squared	−0.0019 **
Rural residence	−0.0038 **

Source: Author's compilation.
Note: Other coefficients of model 1 are shown in table 7.2. Model 1 controls for period effects for fourteen years.
** $p < .01$

dren. In contrast, female-headed households have 80.4 percent less positive net worth than married couples without children. Single women have lower positive net worth than single men. In all types of households with children (married, female-headed, and other types), net worth increases with number of children at a decelerating rate and reaches the maximum at 1.3 children, meaning that household wealth is less if there are two or more children.

Immigration theory and assimilation theory suggest that immigrants' wealth accumulation behaviors can be quite different from those of natives, as explained in chapter 2. The assumption of no differences in the effects of household characteristics is relaxed in a separate analysis for each of the four racial-ethnic groups. Estimates for the differential effects of demographics are from model 5, which includes interaction terms between nativity and various demographic characteristics (see table 7.6).

Table 7.6   Specific Immigrant Wealth Behavior (M5)

Variable	White	Black	Hispanic	Asian
Effect on positive net worth				
Age	0.24916 **	0.13354 **	0.19820 **	0.19994 **
Age × immigrant	−0.00178	0.07781	−0.08249 *	0.07336
Age-squared	−0.00189 **	−0.00070 **	−0.00154 **	−0.00146 *
Age-squared × immigrant	−0.00004	−0.00097	0.00091 *	−0.00113
Married with children	0.05213	0.25502 *	0.23222 *	0.97869 **
Married with children × immigrant	−0.33941 **	−0.37117	−0.21811 *	−0.82489 **
Number of children	0.07927 **	0.05311	−0.07010	−0.44429 *
Number of children × immigrant	0.25903 **	0.20020	0.18999 *	0.43379 *
Number of children squared	−0.02013 **	−0.04475 **	−0.00282	0.01662
Number of children squared × immigrant	−0.05284 **	−0.03031	−0.01257	−0.03479
Effect on probability of positive net worth				
Age	0.01788 **	0.01613 **	0.02204 **	0.01544 **
Age × immigrant	−0.00013	0.00940	−0.00917 *	0.00567 *
Age-squared	−0.00014 **	−0.00009 **	−0.00017 **	−0.00011 **
Age-squared × immigrant	0.00000	−0.00012	0.00010 *	−0.00009 *
Married with children	0.00374	0.03081 *	0.02582 *	0.07559 *
Married with children × immigrant	−0.02436 **	−0.04484	−0.02425 *	−0.06371 *
Number of children	0.00569 **	0.00642	−0.00779	−0.03432
Number of children × immigrant	0.01859 **	0.02419	0.02113 *	0.03350 *
Number of children squared	−0.00144 **	−0.00541 **	−0.00031	0.00128
Number of children squared × immigrant	−0.00379 **	−0.00366	−0.00140	−0.00269

Source: Author's compilation.
Note: Model 5 controls for education, interaction between education and nativity, and period effects.
** $p < .01$
* $p < .05$

The life cycle hypothesis posits that households save and invest in assets along the life cycle up until retirement, then spend the wealth afterward. The study population is aged twenty-five to sixty-four, and we therefore expect that the age profile increase with a deceleration for all racial-ethnic groups. This is in fact the case, but we are reminded of the differential growth rates of wealth by race-ethnicity, ranking from whites, Asians, Hispanics, and blacks. Within racial-ethnic groups, one would expect that the saving rate (through the age effect) would be higher for immigrants than for natives, given the strong economic moti-

Figure 7.7   Nativity Difference in Wealth Profile Among Hispanics

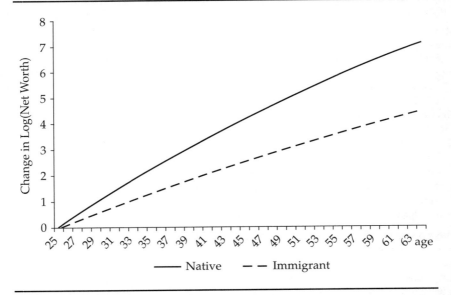

Source: Author's compilation.

vation among most immigrants. That is, the interaction effect of age and immigrant status should be positive. Contrary to my expectation, the estimates are negative and statistically significant for Hispanics, though insignificant for whites, blacks, and Asians. The predicted age profiles of wealth by nativity for Hispanics are shown in figure 7.7. The age effects are changes in the log of positive net worth. The age profile for immigrants is flatter than that for natives.

The null finding about the differential saving rate for non-Hispanic groups may be a result of failing to account for the fact that over half of immigrants start to accumulate wealth later than natives because they arrive in the United States after age twenty-five. In other words, the expected stronger age effect for these immigrants is trumped by the late start of wealth accumulation. But how do we explain the slower wealth accumulation rate of Hispanic immigrants, who are likely to arrive at younger ages? The flatter wealth profile for Hispanic immigrants over their native-born counterparts is likely to capture a substantial proportion of Hispanic immigrants who have experienced a long process of illegal-to-legal transition that pushes the start of wealth accumulation to a later age. Moreover, as discussed in chapter 4 regarding the likelihood of investing in the homeland, both the type of the wealth regime and the obligation to support extended family and kin increase the likelihood that immigrants from Mexico, El Salvador, and Guatemala may own assets in the home country, which is missed in the SIPP data used here.

Compared with married households without children, the enhancing effect of being married with children disappears altogether for immigrants. In particular, married parenthood has a negative effect for white and black immigrants, and no effect for Hispanic and Asian immigrants. These findings do not seem to fit the prediction of motivated immigrant commitment to improving the future of the family and their children.

The effect of the number of children differs radically across racial-ethnic groups and between immigrants and natives within them. For whites, net worth increases with number of children with a deceleration; such an effect is stronger for immigrants than for natives. Having more children actually harms the net worth of blacks, regardless of nativity. Number of children does not matter for native-born Hispanics, but increases net worth for their immigrant counterparts. Last, it has a negative effect for Asian Americans but none for Asian immigrants.

On the surface, these findings suggest that the motivation for securing their children's future is lower for immigrants than for natives. This prediction is based on the normative, stage-sensitive saving behavior of natives. A native-born person does not start saving for a child's future until a child is born or even a few years later. Economic immigrants, in contrast, make the decision to migrate based on strong motivations to improve not only their own life chances, but also those of their children. This motivation to save and build assets is not necessarily enhanced by marriage or the birth of a child, but instead has been constantly high since migration. For immigrants, therefore, neither marriage nor the presence of children would seem to have any strong enhancing effect. If this conjecture is correct, black and Asian immigrants are more highly motivated economically than white and Hispanic immigrants (as evidenced by the negative interaction effect of married households with and without children). The lower net worth among Asian immigrant married households with children suggests that Asian parents are investing in their children.

Conclusion

In the context of immigration today, wealth stratification by race and education is complicated by the continuous flow of immigrants entering and adapting to American society. Empirical evidence supports four conclusions. First, race and education are primary factors and nativity is a secondary factor in wealth stratification. That is, though both race and education stratify the wealth of the entire population, nativity does not. Second, race and education are interdependent. In other words, the race effect attenuates as the education level increases, and the education effect favors racial-ethnic minorities. Third, nativity differentiates same-race household wealth because of the heterogeneity of same-race immigrants, including factors such as their origin countries, age at arrival, naturalization, and place of education. Fourth, immigrant wealth accumulation behaviors do not completely mirror those of their native counterparts. The age profile of immigrant Hispanics is significantly flatter than their native-born counterparts'. Marriage and parenthood do not necessarily enhance wealth for immigrants, but do for natives. As a whole, these findings suggest that contemporary immigration may play a key role in transforming the existing stratification order. The nonwhiteness and bimodal education of immigrants do not reinforce the stratification order by race and education. Rather, immigrant characteristics expand both tails of the wealth distribution for each racial-ethnic group. I conclude that, in the long run, contemporary immigration will help racial minorities transcend color lines.

This conclusion is consistent with immigrants' assimilation through wealth attainment. Within the immigrant generation, some groups show greater potential for achieving both positive net worth and more net worth but others are far behind. This asynchronicity attests to the differential pace of wealth assimilation. At the same time, the wealth accumulation of high achieving immigrant groups not only represents their economic prosperity but also embodies their culturally loaded lifestyle. Because this lifestyle is not separable from economic prosperity, such groups are likely to be accepted and respected by the mainstream, accelerating their eventual integration.

Appendix: Models and Methods

This appendix provides a full description of the methodology used in the chapter and justifications for it—including the equation expressions of the empirical models used to test the hypothesized stratification system for wealth, the data and sample used for analysis, the measurement of the dependent variable and the key independent variables, and the statistical modeling strategy.

Empirical Models

Let y_{it} denote net worth for household I i in year t, R_{it} a set of three dummy variables representing four racial-ethnic groups with non-Hispanic whites as the reference, E_{it} a continuous measure of years of schooling, N_{it} an indicator for immigrant status, and X_{it} a vector of household characteristics, including types of households defined by marital status, presence of children, and living arrangement, the linear and quadratic forms of the head's age and the number of children, and period effects of years when the data were collected. The baseline model, model 1 (M1), can be expressed as:

$$y_{it} = \beta_0 + \beta_1 R_{it} + \beta_2 E_{it} + \beta_3 N_{it} + \beta_4 X_{it} + \varepsilon_{it} \tag{7.1}$$

I use the statistical significance of coefficients to determine whether race, education and nativity are or are not all primary factors. Although a more restricted criterion involves the magnitude of the effect, given the different measurement levels (some are continuous, others are categorical) and the arbitrary criterion on the standardized magnitude for a primary factor, I use the significance without referring to the magnitude. Specifically, if β_1, β_2, and β_3 are all significant, race, education and nativity are all primary factors. If, instead, β_3 is insignificant, then nativity is not a primary factor (as we will later see is indeed the empirical result). We move to the right panel of figure 7.1.

The next task is to determine whether nativity can be eliminated or retained and whether race and education are interdependent by examining the interdependence among the three stratification factors in model 2 (M2).

$$y_{it} = \beta_0 + \beta_1 R_{it} + \beta_2 E_{it} + \beta_3 N_{it} + \beta_4 X_{it} + \beta_5 R_{it} \cdot E_{it}$$
$$+ \beta_6 R_{it} \cdot N_{it} + \beta_7 E_{it} \cdot N_{it} + \varepsilon_{it} \tag{7.2}$$

If some of the interaction terms are significant (as found in the empirical analysis), we move to model 3 (M3) for separate analysis for each of the four racial-ethnic groups, a design for the dominance-differentiation stratification system (the effect of the primary factor of race-ethnicity dominates the effect of the secondary factor of nativity, which differentiates wealth within racial groups). For $j = 1, \ldots, 4$ racial-ethnic groups, model 3 is specified as:

$$y_{jit} = \delta_{j0} + \delta_{j1} E_{jit} + \delta_{j2} N_{jit} + \delta_{j3} X_{jit} + \delta_{j4} E_{jit} \cdot N_{jit} + \delta_{j5} X_{jit} \cdot N_{jit} + v_{jit}. \tag{7.3}$$

Note that all terms for variables on the right hand side are implicit interaction terms with race-ethnicity. For example, E_{jit} is implicitly $R_{it} \cdot E_{it}$ for race j. The same is true for all other terms. Similarly, the two-way interaction is implicit a three-way interaction: $E_{jit} \cdot N_{jit}$ is implicitly $R_{it} \cdot E_{it} \cdot N_{it}$. In such a setup, we examine the differentiation within racial-ethnic groups by nativity and the interdependence between nativity and education and other household characteristics.

Next, I substitute nativity (a dummy variable for immigrant status) with country of origin, age at arrival (capturing the arrival cohort when age is included), and naturalization status, denoted by Z_{jit}. Model 4 (M4) is specified as:

$$y_{jit} = \delta_{j0} + \delta_{j1}E_{jit} + \delta_{j2}Z_{jit} + \delta_{j3}X_{jit} + \delta_{j4}E_{jit} \cdot N_{jit} + v_{jit}. \qquad (7.4)$$

Results from M4 can inform the degree of differentiation by specific immigrant characteristics, particularly addressing the impact of immigrants' self-selection.

Finally, I allow the household characteristics to vary by nativity:

$$y_{jit} = \delta_{j0} + \delta_{j1}E_{jit} + \delta_{j2}Z_{jit} + \delta_{j3}X_{jit} + \delta_{j4}E_{jit} \cdot N_{jit} + \delta_{j5}X_{jit} \cdot N_{jit} + v_{jit} \qquad (7.5)$$

Results from M5 may reveal the differences in wealth accumulation behaviors between immigrants and natives, such as age profiles and the role of marriage and parenthood in wealth accumulation.

Data

The empirical work in this chapter makes use of all the available data from ten panels of the SIPP, including eighteen cross-sections of data, covering the two decades from 1984 to 2003. Four of the panels have multiple waves of wealth data: two waves each for the 1984, 1985, and 1986 panels, three waves for the 2001 panel, and four for the 1996 panel. Households change quite frequently as a result of marriage, divorce, re-marriage, and children leaving home so that over the years during a panel, some older households are dissolved and some new ones are established. The stacked data include 139,214 unique households, of which 60.1 percent were observed once, 18.5 percent twice, 4.6 percent three times, and 16.8 percent four times. Households observed more than once had the same head at each observation. These multiple observations show substantial annual changes in household net worth, accounting for 16 percent of the total variations. These changes are associated with changes in head's age, household type, number of children, and period effect (such as economic cycle) in a particular year.

The stacked data provide three advantages. First, they increase variations and reduce the random variability of wealth measures. The distribution of net worth is more unequal but also more stable over time than income distribution. Using all years rather than just one per panel increases the observations of net worth by roughly thirteen times, thereby increasing observed between- and within-group variations. Using this data may minimize the random variability in net worth because the random measurement errors in one year may be canceled out by those in another. The second advantage is that using multiple years of wealth data helps to disentangle the effects of period (year), head's age, and head's age at arrival in the United States, which a cross-section of data could not do because of collinearity among the three variables.[4] For this analysis, it is important to isolate period effects (the condition of the year's economy, labor, stock, and housing markets) from age effects (which capture earning, consuming, and saving variations along the life course), and from age-at-arrival effects (older age at arrival gives immigrants less time to accumulate wealth). Finally, the stacked data provide an opportunity to explore differences among specific immigrant nationality groups with adequate subsample sizes, which are critical for precise estimates. Note that this chapter's analysis cannot specify immigrant groups such as Salvadoran, Guatemalan, Haitian, Jamaican, or Hong Kong–Taiwan because the pre-1996 SIPP panels do not collect as many countries of origin as the 1996 and 2001 panels. Because data on the nationality of black immigrants are not available in most of the panels, black immigrants are classified as a single group rather than by nationality. An adequate sample size ranging from almost 500 to more than 6,000 can be found for all immigrant groups except Japanese and Polish, whose sample sizes are 254 and 162, respectively.

Measurement

The dependent variable is net worth, defined as total assets minus total debts. Net worth is a continuous measure of wealth, which in previous chapters was categorized into five wealth holding statuses. Some households have more assets than debt, resulting in positive net worth and putting them into sufficient, insufficient, and asset poor wealth holding categories (see chapter 3 for definitions). Some have neither assets nor debts, resulting in zero net worth, the paycheck-to-paycheck situation. Still others have more debt than assets, resulting in negative net worth and placing them in the net debtor category. The five categories can be collapsed to three of negative, zero, and positive net worth. See table 7A.1 for the distribution of negative, zero, and positive net worth by race-ethnicity, nativity, and immigrant nationality.

Zero and negative net worth present a challenge to researchers with interests in economic attainment. Substantively, attainment has a positive connotation. It is hard to regard negative or zero net worth as an economic accomplishment. In addition, because zero net worth is the worst situation, the continuum from negative to zero to positive does not correspond to the trend of well-being. The notion of wealth attainment considers positive net worth as attaining wealth and negative and zero net worth as attaining no wealth. It is measured by a censored continuous variable which replaces the dollar value of negative net worth with zero. Here, the value of zero indicates that households have not attained positive net worth. The

Table 7A.1   Negative, Zero, and Positive Net Worth

Group	Negative	Zero	Positive
Total	0.112	0.362	0.852
Race-ethnicity			
White	0.100	0.014	0.886
Black	0.165	0.140	0.695
Hispanic	0.158	0.100	0.742
Asian	0.105	0.031	0.863
Native			
White	0.100	0.014	0.886
Black	0.164	0.143	0.693
Hispanic	0.160	0.099	0.741
Asian	0.125	0.022	0.853
Immigrant			
White	0.082	0.027	0.891
Black	0.185	0.084	0.731
Hispanic	0.156	0.101	0.743
Asian	0.099	0.035	0.867
Immigrant nationality			
Western European	0.061	0.009	0.930
Eastern European	0.089	0.022	0.890
Former Soviet	0.096	0.106	0.798
Polish	0.122	0.032	0.846
Other white immigrant	0.105	0.035	0.859
Black immigrant	0.185	0.084	0.731
Mexican	0.141	0.091	0.767
Cuban	0.103	0.070	0.827
Dominican	0.192	0.368	0.440
Other Hispanic immigrant	0.200	0.086	0.714
Chinese	0.061	0.031	0.909
Filipino	0.095	0.024	0.880
Japanese	0.072	0.022	0.906
Indian	0.119	0.016	0.865
Korean	0.143	0.022	0.836
Vietnamese	0.106	0.056	0.838
Other Asian immigrant	0.107	0.062	0.831
Native ethnicity			
Native white	0.100	0.014	0.886
Native black	0.164	0.143	0.693
Puerto Rican	0.174	0.217	0.610
Mexican American	0.158	0.057	0.785
Cuban American	0.151	0.090	0.759
Asian American	0.125	0.022	0.853

Source: Author's compilation.

conceptualization of wealth attainment, which is both the probability of having positive net worth and the amount of wealth obtained among households with positive net worth, provides an effective solution to the challenge presented by the entire range of net worth values.

Three stratification factors are race-ethnicity (measured by a set of dummy variables for non-Hispanic black, Hispanic, and Asian with non-Hispanic white as the reference), education (a continuous variable for the completed years of schooling), and nativity (an indicator of foreign born). Immigrant characteristics are measured with country (region) of origin, non-naturalization status, age at arrival, and place of education (U.S. versus foreign postsecondary degrees). When both age and age at arrival are specified in the model, arrival cohorts are effectively being controlled. I chose not to directly measure arrival cohorts because the combination of age and age at arrival can give an estimate of productive years in the United States under the life cycle hypothesis.

Differences in wealth attainment are also influenced by household characteristics, including age, age-squared, types of households, and number of children. Because chapters 4 through 6 detail the comparisons between immigrant and native groups within broadly defined racial-ethnic groups, the purpose of table 7A.2 is to show a brief overview of these distributions using a larger sample than that in chapters 4 through 6.

Statistical Modeling Strategy

The nature of wealth attainment (both probability and amount) also presents a challenge to modeling strategies. First, with information on both its probability and size, a logit or probit model examining only the probability of attainment is inefficient because it disregards the size of positive net worth. Second, if we use a multiple regression model, the large subsample having no attainment will violate regression assumptions about linearity and normality. Third, simply using the subsample of households with positive net worth for an analysis of the size of wealth attainment would also be inappropriate because the reasons why some households do not attain positive net worth are determined by the same set of covariates, race-ethnicity, and household characteristics. For example, a young single man may spend all his earnings as he does not have strong economic motivation to buy a house or build other assets, resulting in his having zero net worth. A husband and father may lose his job and go into debt to support his family, resulting in his household's having negative net worth. The same set of covariates can determine the propensity of a household for achieving positive net worth while simultaneously determining the amount of positive net worth. Failing to consider this propensity will cause bias in estimates for the size of wealth attainment.

Table 7A.2 Household Characteristics of Race-Ethnicity and Nationality Groups

	Age	Ed.	Children	Metro. residence	Married w/o	Married w/	Female-headed	Single Man	Single Woman	Other HH Type	Age at Arrival	Non-natural.	Foreign Ed.
Total	43.34	13.49	1.06	0.79	0.19	0.41	0.11	0.11	0.09	0.09	—	—	—
Race-ethnicity													
White	43.78	13.86	0.98	0.76	0.22	0.41	0.08	0.11	0.10	0.08	—	—	—
Black	42.55	12.68	1.21	0.83	0.09	0.26	0.29	0.12	0.12	0.11	—	—	—
Hispanic	41.03	10.97	1.55	0.89	0.09	0.47	0.17	0.08	0.06	0.13	—	—	—
Asian	41.94	14.68	1.29	0.95	0.13	0.55	0.06	0.09	0.05	0.11	—	—	—
Immigrant nationality													
Western European	46.81	13.83	0.99	0.90	0.22	0.42	0.09	0.10	0.10	0.08	23.56	0.42	0.24
Eastern European	45.24	13.94	0.94	0.95	0.20	0.46	0.06	0.12	0.09	0.07	27.09	0.44	0.25
Former Soviet	45.64	15.00	1.07	0.98	0.23	0.46	0.07	0.07	0.08	0.08	32.00	0.53	0.45
Polish	42.03	14.86	1.05	0.89	0.26	0.43	0.03	0.13	0.03	0.13	25.23	0.45	0.31
Black immigrant	41.86	12.63	1.28	0.97	0.09	0.35	0.19	0.12	0.10	0.13	25.38	0.51	0.11
Mexican	40.03	8.55	2.05	0.89	0.06	0.60	0.12	0.05	0.02	0.14	22.42	0.75	0.03
Cuban	47.33	12.16	0.87	0.91	0.16	0.42	0.11	0.11	0.08	0.11	24.71	0.46	0.13
Dominican	41.69	11.08	1.55	0.99	0.06	0.26	0.42	0.05	0.06	0.15	24.95	0.59	0.09
Chinese	42.41	14.93	1.20	0.96	0.11	0.60	0.04	0.09	0.07	0.09	27.16	0.43	0.24
Filipino	44.87	14.92	1.26	0.95	0.14	0.55	0.08	0.05	0.06	0.11	27.34	0.30	0.57
Japanese	42.12	15.33	0.88	0.95	0.14	0.41	0.07	0.14	0.13	0.10	26.21	0.70	0.42
Indian	39.05	16.79	1.33	0.94	0.14	0.69	0.01	0.05	0.02	0.10	26.62	0.62	0.51
Korean	42.39	14.74	1.24	0.98	0.18	0.59	0.06	0.04	0.05	0.08	26.63	0.48	0.33
Vietnamese	42.75	12.87	1.52	0.98	0.08	0.56	0.09	0.08	0.02	0.18	27.00	0.32	0.14
Native ethnicity													
Native white	43.73	13.85	0.97	0.75	0.22	0.41	0.08	0.11	0.10	0.08	—	—	—
Native black	42.59	12.68	1.21	0.83	0.09	0.25	0.30	0.12	0.12	0.11	—	—	—
Puerto Rican	41.81	11.68	1.31	0.95	0.09	0.33	0.26	0.10	0.11	0.10	—	—	—
Mexican American	41.11	11.81	1.49	0.84	0.11	0.45	0.17	0.09	0.06	0.12	—	—	—
Cuban American	40.55	12.92	1.16	0.88	0.12	0.34	0.20	0.12	0.08	0.14	—	—	—
Asian American	41.07	14.63	1.12	0.93	0.16	0.45	0.08	0.13	0.06	0.11	—	—	—

An appropriate model to handle both the probability and size of wealth attainment is the Tobit model, a hybrid of probit analysis and multiple regression analysis. It considers the reasons that some households have positive net worth and that, once the threshold of wealth attainment is reached, the amount of positive net worth differs. Like other regression models, the Tobit model assumes that the errors of the model follow a normal distribution (a symmetric bell curve.)

The estimates directly provided by the Tobit model are not sufficient for interpretation in terms of the probability and size of wealth attainment. The decomposition technique proposed by John McDonald and Robert Moffitt (1980) provides two sets of coefficients for the probability of attaining positive net worth and the size of positive net worth, two important questions in the analysis of wealth attainment. Using the results from model 1, table 7A.3 illustrates the relationship between the coefficients obtained from the Tobit estimation and the decomposition of the two effects evaluated at the observed proportion of households that have positive net worth. This proportion can be expressed as the cumulative standardized normal distribution (Fz), its corresponding density (fz), and the corresponding value of the standardized normal variable (z).

Table 7A.3   **An Illustration of Marginal Effects at the Observed Censoring Rate: Decomposition of Tobit Coefficients**

Variable	Tobit Coefficient	Positive Net Worth	Probability of Positive Net Worth
Black	−2.278	−1.962	−0.037
Hispanic	−1.539	−1.346	−0.022
Asian	−0.510	−0.456	−0.006
Observed proportion positive net worth	0.852		
Standard deviation of the error term	4.257		
Factor for effect on positive net worth	0.644		
Factor for effect on probability	0.054		

Source: Author's compilation.
Note: Let z be a value of the random variable for the cumulative probability Fz of the standardized normal distribution, fz is the corresponding density function, and σ is the standard error of the error term in the tobit model. According to McDonald and Moffitt (1980), the factor for the effect on positive net worth is $1 - z\dfrac{fz}{Fz} - \dfrac{fz^2}{Fz^2}$ and the factor for the effect on the probability of having positive net worth is $\dfrac{fz}{\sigma}$. In this case, from the data we get $Fz = 0.852$ and from the estimation we get $\sigma = 4.257$. Given these, we obtain $z = 1.047$ and $fz = .231$, then we calculate factor1=0.644 and factor2=0.054. The resulting decomposed effects are obtained by multiplying the respective factor with the tobit coefficient.

Figure 7A.1   Distribution of Positive Net Worth, Raw Scale

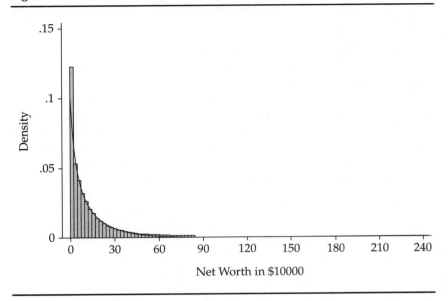

Source: Author's compilation.

The decomposition factor for the amount of positive net worth involves a nonlinear combination of z, fz and Fz, as well as the estimated standard error of the model error term, evaluated at the observed proportion of households that have positive net worth (about 85 percent) (see table 7A.3 for details.)

To check whether positive net worth follows a normal distribution, I examine the histogram of positive net worth. The SIPP did not collect data for very wealthy households, so the wealth distribution excludes the top 0.5 percent of the population (see details in appendix). Even excluding the top 0.5 percent, the positive net worth distribution has a very long, thin upper tail, as shown in figures 7A.1 and 7A.2. The overwhelming majority of households (more than 95 percent) fall below $500,000, but the right tail stretches to over a million dollars. This distribution is far from a normal distribution, violating the distributional assumption of the Tobit model. The few data points with very high values may be influential in the estimates, which then will not reflect the true relationships for the majority of households.

This analysis uses a log transformation for positive net worth and retains the value of zero for the group having either zero or negative net worth.[5] Log transformation is the most commonly used technique to

Figure 7A.2   Distribution of Positive Net Worth, Log Scale

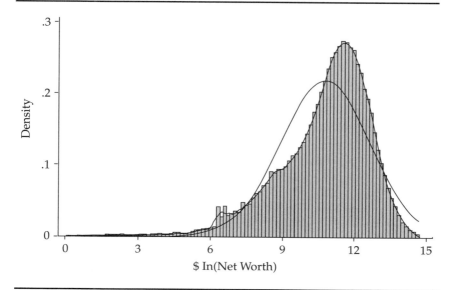

Source: Author's compilation.

transform a right-skewed distribution to one that is closer to a normal curve. Figure 7A.2 shows the density function of log positive net worth. Although the original right-skewed distribution is slightly overcorrected, it is now much closer to a normal curve (imposed on the graph) than figure 7A.1. In addition, log transformation is better than other transformations that address right skewness, such as squared root transformation, because of its mathematical tractability and meaningful coefficient interpretations. The estimated parameter for an explanatory variable is approximately the percentage change in positive net worth brought about by a unit change in the explanatory variable. The percentage change interpretation is preferred to the metric interpretation because a metric change at the higher tail of the conditional distribution of positive net worth means much less than the same metric change at the lower tail of the conditional distribution. For example, an increase of a thousand dollars means a lot to a family with $10,000 net worth but it would be a trivial increase for a family with a million dollars net worth. In contrast, the same percentage change at the higher and lower tails measures the impact in relative terms, keeping in mind though that the metric amount differs dramatically.

= Chapter 8 =

Contextual Conditions of Wealth Attainment

R ace and education are, as we saw in chapter 7, the primary factors in the wealth stratification system; nativity and immigrant characteristics are secondary factors. The theoretical framework developed in chapter 2 indicates that the process of asset building and wealth accumulation is shaped not only by the nationwide racial hierarchy and education and by immigrant nationality group characteristics, but also by a household's contextual conditions. Local economy and labor market conditions, such as the unemployment rate, offer economic opportunities but impose constraints on residents' financial standing and property ownership as well. Residential segregation in metropolitan areas favors some groups at the expense of others. The nativity of the local population may change the degree of local labor market competition, particularly among workers with low skills, thus benefiting some groups and harming others. In addition, a large foreign-born population in a metropolitan area increases the local population's racial and ethnic diversity, which in turn adds complications to the dynamics of racial residential segregation. This chapter addresses how these contextual factors operate in addition to the stratification factors and household characteristics examined in chapter 7.

Wealth attainment is defined as positive net worth. Three sets of contextual factors for wealth attainment include the local economy and labor market, captured by the state unemployment rate, residential segregation, captured by black-white and Hispanic-white segregation across neighborhoods within metropolitan areas, and nativity composition, captured by the foreign-born percentage of the metropolitan area population. Because state labor market conditions affect the statewide population, residential segregation and nativity composition are salient features of metropolitan areas, I analyze the effects of local labor market conditions using the whole population and the effects of residential segregation and nativity composition using the metropolitan population.

The analyses pay special attention to the expected different effects of residential segregation and nativity composition for different groups. To this end, I analyze a pooled sample consisting of four broadly defined racial-ethnic groups and then analyze each. My focus is on identifying the similarities and differences in the effects of contextual variables in determining wealth attainment among racial-ethnic groups and then looking at the effects of these same variables by nativity within race-ethnicity groups.

Three Contextual Conditions

To better explain variations in wealth attainment, this chapter considers the roles of the local labor market conditions, residential segregation, and nativity composition. An essential indicator of local labor market conditions is the minimum wage rate. Employment opportunities directly affect earnings, which in turn affect consumption and saving during the process of wealth accumulation. Periods of unemployment force households to liquidate wealth to maintain their customary level of consumption, which then affects their current amount of wealth. As a result of job loss, households often accrue consumer debt, postpone mortgage payments, and lose homes to foreclosure (Warren and Tyagi 2003).

Residential segregation institutionalizes multiple forms of discrimination against minorities in the labor, housing, and lending markets, exacerbating the slow process of minority wealth attainment. Changes in racial and educational compositions induced by flows of immigrants intensify labor market competition among low-skilled workers, affecting their wealth attainment by creating winners and losers.

Local Labor Market Conditions

The ups and downs of local labor market conditions directly impact earning and indirectly change the amount of net worth in households. These conditions vary across time and states. In the United States, the unemployment rate was higher (7.1 percent) between 1984 and 1986 and lower (4.4 percent) between 1997 and 2001 (U.S. Bureau of Labor Statistics 2007). During the same periods, variations in unemployment rates across states were large, with higher rates in some states, such as Mississippi and Louisiana, and lower rates in others, such as Connecticut, Maryland, and Minnesota. A higher unemployment rate means that workers face greater risks of job loss and long-term unemployment. To maintain their lifestyle, affected workers usually either liquidate their previously accumulated wealth or borrow money (most often via consumer debts), ending up with lower net worth.

Using the 1984 to 2002 SIPP data, the first column of table 8.1 shows the unemployment rate facing members of broadly defined racial-ethnic groups, immigrant nationality groups, and native racial-ethnic groups.[1] Unemployment rates for Hispanics and Asians are higher than they are for whites and blacks. In looking more closely at the distribution, it is clear that Mexican immigrants generally live in states with relatively higher unemployment rates (6.11 percent) than the states housing many other immigrant groups. Compared to all minority groups, native whites more often live in states with low unemployment rates.

Residential Segregation

Although unemployment rates capture variations in local labor market conditions, they do not necessarily overlap with social conditions, in which economic inequality is deeply rooted. An important social condition in the United States is residential racial segregation, largely an urban and suburban phenomenon. Addressing the black-white divide and the urban poor, Massey and Denton (1993) argue that residential segregation has played an important role in exacerbating and ultimately amplifying the social stratification process. Residential segregation acts as the institutional apparatus that supports other processes that go beyond institutional racial discrimination in the labor market. In addition, segregation propagates its effects through racially blind practices that adversely affect everyone, regardless of race in primarily minority communities. These constitute spillover effects for those not the target of segregation.

The mechanism produces white communities with better public services and black communities with inferior ones. The existence and isolation of these two types of communities within a metropolitan area are the primary sources of segregation's costs. One of these is that segregation limits life opportunities for blacks. These limitations occur through spatial mismatch, a situation in which low-skilled workers are concentrated in one location (usually in the central city or inner-ring suburbs) but many of the job opportunities they are qualified for are offered elsewhere (Wilson 1996). Economists have shown that mismatch results in spatially concentrated, low-skilled workers earning less than they would if they lived closer to more available low-skilled jobs (Bound and Hotzer 1993). Among those who commute for the sake of affordable housing, transportation costs can be higher than half of the total household expenses (Center for Housing Policy 2006). Blacks' confinement to segregated communities reduces their income, increases their transportation costs, and makes it more difficult for them to save and build assets.

Furthermore, their confinement to segregated neighborhoods systematically reduces their access to investment opportunities. Our data show that the middle class invests the largest share of its wealth in housing equity, which amounts to 43 percent of white assets and 63 percent of black

Table 8.1   Contextual Conditions for Race-Ethnicity and Nationality Groups

Group	Nationwide		MSA Sample	
	Unemployment	Black-White D	Hispanic-White D	Percentage Foreign Born
Total	5.63	68.26	48.28	14.85
Race-ethnicity				
White	5.58	68.17	47.25	13.17
Black	5.63	70.73	47.82	13.81
Hispanic	5.96	66.90	53.82	23.52
Asian	5.94	66.68	51.48	22.04
Immigrant nationality				
Western European	5.95	71.17	53.27	19.19
Eastern European	5.74	77.01	58.51	21.82
Former Soviet	5.87	73.50	57.32	24.21
Polish	5.81	69.99	55.88	21.51
Black immigrant	5.60	75.18	56.53	27.33
Mexican	6.15	64.39	54.17	24.09
Cuban	5.43	73.21	50.66	37.96
Dominican	5.91	78.75	62.89	29.23
Chinese	6.00	69.24	54.05	24.79
Filipino	6.07	66.38	51.38	24.02
Japanese	6.12	66.49	51.32	22.49
Indian	5.68	73.43	55.94	21.19
Korean	5.83	69.19	55.06	21.84
Vietnamese	5.99	65.40	49.42	21.20
Native ethnicity				
Native white	5.57	68.00	46.91	12.79
Native black	5.63	70.44	47.24	12.90
Puerto Rican	5.66	75.12	58.88	22.05
Mexican American	6.00	61.12	51.32	20.33
Cuban American	5.95	67.56	50.45	19.80
Asian American	5.95	61.41	47.67	20.97

Source: Author's compilation.
Note: D denotes dissimilarity index.

assets. Confined to less-desired neighborhoods, blacks see a much lower average rate of return to their housing investments than whites do. Because credit worthiness depends on wealth, lower home values for blacks mean that they are less able to get credit on favorable terms than otherwise equally qualified whites are. Segregation raises the costs of asset building for blacks but lowers them for whites. Among these higher costs are real estate industry practices such as redlining and higher mortgage rates. Blacks and Hispanics are turned down for home financing more often than statistically similar whites (Myers and Chan 1995; Schill and Wachter 1994). As a result, blacks suffer the cumulative loss because of denial of mortgages and higher mortgage interest rates. The current generation of blacks, for example, carries a loss of $24 billion (see Oliver and Shapiro 1995, 64, 150–1).

Residential segregation as an institution protects some groups at the expense of others. Over the history of black-white segregation, the main motivation has been to safeguard the economic advantages and perceived psychological comfort of whites (Massey and Denton 1993). White antipathy towards blacks often leads to concentrated poverty and oppositional culture among blacks, which in turn fuel white antipathy, creating a vicious cycle. As white prejudice causes housing discrimination, bank disinvestment, isolation from social networks, and white flight, demonstrating that racism is a major cause of segregation. However, segregation propagates its overt effect through purportedly color-blind mechanisms, which include low housing values, poor public services, business flight, and few job opportunities. These negative mechanisms hurt all other minority groups living in the affected community. Although racial segregation is not the only factor, regardless of the target race, it can be a major cause of systematic economic disadvantage for all minorities. Moderately to highly segregated black and Hispanic neighborhoods are almost always markedly poor, more so than most of the majority white neighborhoods in the same metro region. Racial segregation is thus the main source of poverty for inhabitants of minority neighborhoods. Evidence from the 2000 census suggests that for ethnic minorities, segregation is associated with living in poorer and lower-status neighborhoods than those of whites at similar income levels (Lewis Mumford Center 2002, 2003). Because wealth attainment reflects cumulative economic disadvantages, racial segregation can affect wealth attainment more than it affects income.

Hispanics are another large, disadvantaged, minority group. When compared to the long history of black-white segregation, Hispanic-white segregation is a relatively new phenomenon. It largely coincides with class segregation, given that there has been little segregation of middle- and upper-class Hispanics. White-to-black discrimination causes segregation across class lines, but the degree to which discrimination causes Hispanic-white segregation may be less extreme. It is also less clear whether the negative consequences of Hispanic-white segregation spill over to other racial-ethnic groups living in predominantly Hispanic neighborhoods.

Racial-ethnic diversity, primarily brought about by immigration, further complicates the dynamics of residential segregation. During the 1980s, black and Hispanic segregation trends went in opposite directions: the first declined and the second increased. Increasing racial diversity contributed to these trends (Frey and Farley 1996: Krivo and Kaufman 1999). John Iceland (2004) finds that increased diversity from 1980 to 2000 is associated with decreases in black-white segregation and increases in Hispanic and Asian. Hispanic segregation is rising in MSAs with a growing Hispanic population, suggesting increased ethnic concentration brought on by large influxes of Latino immigrants (Lewis Mumford Center 2002).

William Frey and Reynolds Farley (1996) examine the redistribution dynamics within metropolitan areas that saw racial diversity increase between 1980 and 1990. Racial diversity may influence real estate marketing, creating less segregated neighborhoods because white residents stay (Santiago 1991). As a result, black segregation is likely to decline in multiracial metropolitan areas. The rapid growth of Hispanic immigrants, however, is likely to increase Hispanic segregation to some degree because of voluntary clustering. Hispanic immigrant settlement is part of segregation dynamics. The white-to-black population succession in a community is now a black-to-Hispanic succession. The growing penetration of the most disadvantaged newcomer Hispanics into what were once mostly black residential areas in the western United States has created tensions and conflicts (Johnson and Oliver 1989; McDonnell 1994). Thus, the growth and continued metropolitan concentration of immigrant populations, especially Hispanics, give rise to changing residential segregation patterns within these areas.

Although Asian immigration is also on the rise, Asian immigrants are residentially divided, with the highly skilled concentrated in affluent suburban neighborhoods and the less-skilled concentrated in coethnic urban neighborhoods (Logan, Alba, and Zhang 2002). Because of the relatively small size of the Asian immigrant group and its heterogeneous modes of concentration, the Asian impact on the larger picture of segregation is probably small.

In sum, residential segregation, particularly black-white segregation, is the cumulative result of multiple forms of institutional discrimination. The consequences of residential segregation are fundamentally distinct between whites and minorities, being positive for the former and negative for the latter. Moreover, the negative effect may spill over to other minority groups beyond the target. With the resurgence of immigration, the U.S. population has become more racially and ethnically diverse, a factor that interacts with residential segregation in a complicated way. Thus, a large percentage of foreign-born residents may present opportunities for some groups and constraints for others.

To measure segregation, I use the index of dissimilarity commonly used in the literature. The index at the MSA level captures the aggregate situation, showing whether the two groups are distributed evenly in the census tracts within metropolitan areas. Technically, it indicates the total percentage of the two groups that would have to move to achieve an even distribution across census tracts.[2] The dissimilarity index (D) ranges from 0 to 100. Higher values indicate a greater degree of segregation. For example, a black-white index of 85 means that 85 percent of the blacks (or whites) would have to move to achieve zero segregation. According to calculations by the Lewis Mumford Center, the black-white index in 2000 was the highest (85) for Detroit, Michigan, and second highest (84) for Gary, Indiana. New York and Chicago fell toward the high end (82 and 81 respectively), Los Angeles in the middle (68),and Santa Cruz, California, at the bottom (27). Aggregated on a national level, Hispanic-white segregation was lower than black-white. The higher Hispanic-white were found in New York (67), Los Angeles (63), Chicago (62), Santa Cruz (57) and Houston (56),and the lower were found in Seattle (31) and San Jose (19). Using the identification for the MSA of residence, the SIPP household data were merged with the black-white and Hispanic-white dissimilarity indexes created by the Lewis Mumford Center. The 1980 indexes were merged with the 1984 to 1990 data, the 1990 indexes were merged with the 1991 to 1999 data and the 2000 indexes were merged with the 2001 to 2003 data. This allows for the maintenance of a clear temporal order—previous segregation affects wealth attainment measured in later years.

The second column of table 8.1 shows the average degree of black-white segregation in areas where various racial-ethnic and nationality groups live. More blacks than any other broad racial minority live in highly black-white segregated MSAs. Variations are greater across nationality groups and native racial-ethnic groups than across broad racial-ethnic groups. European immigrants, particularly eastern European, tend to live in high black-white segregation areas, as do Dominicans and Puerto Ricans. For example, more than 70 percent of Dominicans, nearly 50 percent of Puerto Ricans, and more than 25 percent of eastern Europeans live in New York City. By contrast, Mexicans, both foreign-born and native-born, are most likely to live in areas with low black-white segregation. Mexicans are likely to live in Texas and California and to settle in cities of various sizes. The lower black-white segregation in these regions and smaller cities explains why Mexicans do not face high black-white segregation.

Moving to column 3 of table 8.1, the Hispanic group experiences the highest Hispanic-white segregation (53.82) among the four racial-ethnic groups. All immigrant nationality groups are more likely than native groups to live in highly Hispanic-white segregated areas. Dominicans are the most likely to live in such areas and Vietnamese immigrants the least likely. Vietnamese refugee settlement areas assigned by the government are usually mid-size or small cities with low racial segregation. Although some Vietnamese resettled in ethnic communities in large cities, many new Vietnamese communities have been developed so that, on average, Vietnamese immigrants do not live in highly Hispanic-white segregated areas. Other Hispanic groups also live in areas with relatively higher levels of Hispanic-white segregation. Cubans are an exception because more than half of Cuban immigrants live in Miami, which became increasingly ethnically diverse and less segregated between 1980 and 2000. Over those two decades, the Hispanic-white segregation index for Miami declined, from 53.0 in 1980, to 50.8 in 1990, to 44.1 in 2000 (Lewis Mumford Center 2002). The Hispanic divide among native ethnic groups is clear: Hispanic Americans, particularly Puerto Ricans, face high Hispanic-white segregation, whereas Asian American groups live in relatively low Hispanic-white segregated areas.

Aggregate experiences of residential racial segregation are divided more sharply by racial-ethnic lines among natives than they are among immigrants. This reflects the fact that immigrants as a whole tend to live in areas of high residential racial segregation. In particular, Dominicans and eastern Europeans tend to live in areas with both high black-white and Hispanic-white segregation. One possible explanation for immigrants' high exposure to segregation is that immigration gateway cities attract many immigrants, and gateway cities are thus more racially segregated. Another possible explanation is that the increasing racial and ethnic diversity induced by immigrant inflows may have gradually changed the nature of racial segregation, making neighborhoods more diverse, which may ultimately reduce the negative consequences of the segregation. The analysis in this chapter pays special attention to how black-white and Hispanic-white segregation affect racial-ethnic groups and the nativity groups within them differently.

Immigration-Induced Labor Market Competition

Changes in population composition influence people's life chances. The rapidly growing Hispanic and Asian populations, largely formed through immigration, have important implications not only for immigrants but also for the native born. The inflow of low-skilled immigrant labor is insensitive to economic cycles because chain migration perpetuates even during economic recessions in the United States (Massey, Durand, and Malone 2002). As discussed in chapter 2, the immigrant status of a household complicates the existing racial and ethnic hierarchies, affecting immigrants' wealth accumulation. By changing the racial and educational compositions of the supply side of the labor market, immigration can affect both immigrants' and natives' wealth attainment beyond the household level.

One public concern regarding immigration is that growing numbers of less-educated immigrants will compete for jobs with less-educated native-born workers, particularly native-born blacks. In a comprehensive study on the demographic and economic impacts of immigration, the National Research Council concludes that immigration has only a small adverse effect on the wage and employment opportunities of competing native groups (Smith and Edmonston 1997). Other empirical literature in sociology and economics generally agrees that there are adverse effects but disagrees about the size of those effects for particular groups of workers (Hamermesh and Bean 1998).

In sociology, some research finds that immigration composition substantially reduces the relative wages of Latinos and Asians and increases wage inequality (McCall 2000, 2001). Studies on illegal immigrants in a single labor market or specialized occupation find a substantial displacement effect (Huddle, Corwin, and MacDonald 1985; Martin 1986). Some studies, however, reveal small negative displacement and wage effects on native-born blacks (Hamermesh and Bean 1998) or little overall displacement effects (Muller and Espenshade 1985). In one economic study (Altonji and Card 1991), immigration is found to have a small negative effect on the employment and wages of native-born minorities and less-skilled workers but a large effect on earlier immigrants' wages. Other studies show the effect on native-born workers to be substantial (Borjas, Freeman, and Katz 1996). Elaine Reardon (1998) finds that recent immigrants replace less-skilled native-born workers of all races and the displacement effect is small.

The sociological literature suggests that three main factors determine labor market outcomes: job characteristics proposed by segmented labor market theory, worker characteristics according to status attainment theory, and job-worker matching processes explicated by ethnic queue and job search theory. Together with human capital and signaling theories, these theories explain the impact of immigration on the labor market, earnings, and wealth accumulation.

The secondary labor market, as opposed to the primary, offers jobs with low wages, poor working conditions, harsh and arbitrary rule enforcement, and little opportunity to advance, thus confining the already disadvantaged to the secondary sector. Traditionally, teenagers, women, and poor urban minorities were captives in the secondary labor market. However, women's labor force participation and career development during the past four decades have opened the primary sector to women. The wider availability of college education prolongs youth's schooling so that teens are less likely to have long-term jobs. Changing labor force compositions together with industrial restructuring, technological advancement, and postindustrialization, have influenced the evolution of the secondary labor market. At the same time, service sector expansion has further increased the demand for low-skilled workers. In response to the demand for low-skilled workers, families in source countries often send an initial immigrant to the United States. Once started, immigration perpetuates because immigrant communities and networks sustain chain migration regardless of economic cycles, creating a continuous supply of low-skilled workers (Massey et al. 1993).

This evolution of the secondary labor market has two implications. According to the microeconomic model (Smith and Edmonston 1997), if low-skilled immigrants are substitutes for low-skilled native and earlier immigrant workers, an influx of low-skilled immigrants will increase the supply of low-skilled labor and drive down wages. Because newcomers are usually willing to take any jobs available, even those with very low wages, they may displace existing secondary workers. However, if less-educated immigrants take jobs that even low-skilled native and earlier immigrant workers will not take, there will be no wage effect or displacement effect and therefore no influence on wealth attainment.

The displacement of low-skilled black workers by immigrants is a central theme in labor market research, but more research is needed to clarify the differential effects among racial-ethnic groups. There are two reasons displacement may have a weak effect on black workers. Unions' collective bargaining and encouraging of self-worth discourage black workers who previously worked in higher-paying blue-collar positions from taking secondary market jobs. Moreover, blacks cannot find jobs in inner-city areas. The mismatch theory (Wilson 1987) attributes the joblessness of inner city residents to the limited availability of low-skilled jobs in inner-city markets. Thus, black workers, either former blue-collar workers or the urban poor, are not likely to work in the secondary market and thus are not displaced by immigrants. In contrast, Hispanic workers, many of who arrived in the United States during and after the economic restructuring of the 1970s, work in the secondary labor market in the South and West (Moore and Pinderhughes 1993; Morales and Bonilla 1993). The continuous settlement of new Hispanic immigrants in the Sunbelt exacerbates the displacement effect on low-skilled Hispanic workers, either native or foreign born. The impact of immigration on Asians is another story. Low-skilled Asian workers mainly arrived after the passage of the 1965 immigration law. Well-established ethnic economies in Asian immigrant communities have protected low-skilled Asian workers from the larger-scale labor dynamics in the secondary labor market (Portes and Rumbaut 1996). These lines of reasoning suggest that large inflows of immigrants, particularly recent immigrants, are most likely to displace Hispanic workers and slow down their wealth attainment.

Nativity composition is measured by the percentage of residents in MSA who are foreign born. The Lewis Mumford Center provides 1990 and 2000 data on two types of percentage foreign born in MSAs, one for all immigrants and the other for recent immigrants. Because of the high correlation between the proportion of immigrants and the proportion of recent immigrants, the majority of whom are low-educated Hispanics, the analysis here uses the overall percentage. The 1990 percentages of foreign-born residents are high in Miami (45.1 percent), Los Angeles (32.7 percent), and New York (26.8 percent). Cincinnati and Albany are two that had low percentages in 1990 (1.8 percent and 0.9 percent respectively.) In 2000, the percentages were higher: 50.9 percent for Miami, 36.2 percent for Los Angeles, 33.7 percent for New York, 2.6 percent for Cincinnati, and 1.7 percent for Albany. Using the identifier of the MSA of residence in the SIPP, I merge the 1984 to 1995 SIPP data with the percentages of foreign-born residents from the 1990 Lewis Mumford Center data and the 1996 to 2002 SIPP data with those from the 2000 data.

The fourth column of table 8.1 shows the group distribution of nativity composition. Whites and blacks are less likely to be exposed to a large presence of foreign-born residents. Hispanics and Asians are naturally more likely to live in metropolitan areas with large percentages of foreign-born residents because they themselves contribute to this larger percentage. Examining nationality groups shows that Cubans and Dominicans in particular live in MSAs with high proportions of foreign-born residents. The concentration of Cuban immigrants in Miami and Dominicans in New York City explains this pattern.

Overall, what are the differences in the context of the place where racial-ethnic and nationality groups live? That blacks live in high black-white segregated areas is well known. I find a new pattern that applies to Hispanics and Asians, the two fastest-growing groups. They live in areas with higher unemployment rates, higher Hispanic-white segregation, and higher proportions of foreign-born residents than average. Among immigrant nationality groups, Mexicans and Dominicans exhibit very different patterns from one another and from other groups. Mexicans tend to live in areas with high unemployment rates, low black-white segregation, low Hispanic-white segregation, and low proportions of foreign-born residents. Their scattered settlement pattern and their economic niche in agriculture, household services, and day labor may be the reason. By contrast, Dominicans live in areas with high black-white segregation, high Hispanic-white segregation, and high proportions of foreign-born residents, but with average unemployment rates. Dominican high concentration in New York City may be the reason for their context of high segregation and high immigrant presence context. These settlement choices and the resulting contextual conditions can profoundly impact the divergence of wealth attainment between the two groups.

Effects of Contextual Conditions on Wealth Attainment

The effects of the three types of contextual conditions on wealth attainment can be fairly assessed only among households with the same characteristics, for example, those at the same life cycle stage, of the same household type, with the same number of children, and with the same level of education. To this end, I build on the chapter 7 models that consider the full array of race-education-nativity stratification factors and household characteristics and now include measures of the three types of contextual conditions. The dependent variable is the log of positive net worth, censored at zero net worth (excluding zero and negative net worth). An appropriate model for both the probability and amount of wealth attainment is Tobit analysis (discussed in chapter 7). To assess local labor market conditions, I use unemployment rates, which vary across states and years. For residential segregation, I use black-white and Hispanic-white dissimilarity indexes, which vary across MSAs and decades. The 1980 segregation indexes are used to explain wealth variations in 1984 to 1990. Similarly, the 1990 segregation indexes are for wealth in 1991 to 1999, and the 2000 segregation indexes are for wealth from 2001 to 2003. For immigration-induced labor market competition, I use the percentage of foreign-born residents, which varies across MSAs and decades. Again this variable is measured in a census preceding the years when wealth is measured. This data handling is to keep a clear temporal order between contextual variables and the outcome variable.

Based on the previous discussion about the potential economic consequences of contextual conditions, one would expect that the unemployment rate would affect the entire population in a similar way—that higher unemployment rates would reduce the probability and size of wealth attainment. In addition, residential segregation and nativity composition should have differential or even opposite effects for different groups. The following analyses allow estimations of these differential effects. Because residential segregation occurs where population is dense, such as in metropolitan areas, and because immigrants are more likely to settle in metropolitan than in rural areas, the MSA population is the study population for estimating racial residential segregation effects. By using a set of dummy variables indicating each year (minus 1), all models take into account that the price of housing, stocks and other wealth components that may change over the years.

A Naïve Model of Contextual Effects

Before focusing on the analysis for the metropolitan population, I ask whether the context (here measured only by state unemployment) has different effects for the whole population vs. the metropolitan population. Model M1a adds the state unemployment rate to model M1 in chapter 7, which includes race-ethnicity, life cycle stage, education level, household type, number of children, and period effects. Results for the national and the metropolitan sample in table 8.2 show that, all else being equal, a 1 percent increase in the unemployment rate is associated

Table 8.2   Contextual Conditions and Wealth Attainment, a Pooled Analysis (M1a and M1b)

Variable	M1a Nationwide sample	M1b Metropolitan sample	
Effect on positive net worth			
Local economy and labor market			
State unemployment (%)	−0.0376 **	−0.0422 **	−0.0464 **
Segregation			
Black-white segregation (D 10%)	—	—	0.0245 **
Hispanic-white segregation (D 10%)	—	—	−0.0102
Immigration			
Percentage foreign born (10%)	—	—	0.0188 *
Effect on probability of positive net worth			
Local economy and labor market			
State unemployment (%)	−0.0032 **	−0.0036 **	−0.0040 **
Segregation			
Black-white segregation (D 10%)	—	—	0.0021 **
Hispanic-white segregation (D 10%)	—	—	−0.0009
Immigration			
Percentage foreign born (10%)	—	—	0.0016 *
Fraction positive net worth	0.852	0.847	0.847
n	233,898	134,845	134,845

Source: Author's compilation.
Note: The models control for all variables specified in Model 1 (M1) of Chapter 7, including race–ethnicity, household characteristics and period effects.
** $p < .01$
* $p < .05$

with a 3.7 percent[3] decrease in positive net worth for the national population and a 4.2 percent decrease for the metropolitan population. The associated decreases in the probability of wealth attainment for the national and metropolitan populations are −.0032 and −.0036, respectively. Thus, the effect of the unemployment rate is quite similar for the national and metropolitan populations.

Using the unemployment rate improves the explanatory power of the model.[4] The effects of all the variables in the original M1 model, however, remain unchanged. This suggests that local economic and labor market conditions operate independently of household-level variables, which is also true for the segregation measures and nativity composition added in further model specifications. The independence is important because my data show that the contextual variables are not a function of the measured household characteristics included in the model, and thus that those household-level variables can be treated as exogenous in the model.

To evaluate the effects of residential segregation and nativity composition on wealth attainment, I use the metropolitan population. Model M1b further adds racial residential segregation measures and nativity composition to M1a in table 8.2.[5] Model M1b restricts the effects of the contextual variables to be the same for the four race-ethnicity groups. When the contextual effects are restricted to be constant for all racial-ethnic groups, black-white segregation has a positive, statistically significant effect. Increasing the black-white dissimilarity index by 10 percentage points raises the amount of household wealth roughly by 2 percent and the probability of wealth attainment by .0021. As segregation theory postulates, this positive effect can be a combination of a positive effect for whites and a negative effect for minority groups. In the same model, Hispanic-white segregation has no significant effect on wealth attainment for all racial-ethnic groups. Nativity composition, however, increases the amount of positive net worth by 2 percent. Again, these findings could be a result of a combination of a positive effect for some groups and negative effect for other groups.

Differential Effects by Race-Ethnicity

Do contextual conditions differently affect racial-ethnic groups? Building on model M3, which separately analyzes each race-ethnicity group in chapter 7, model M3a adds the contextual variables. The separate analysis allows differential effects for all variables by race-ethnicity, including contextual variables. Table 8.3 shows the results. The state unemployment effect captures formal but not informal labor market conditions and therefore captures wealth attainment differently across racial-ethnic groups. For whites, the effect of the unemployment rate on the amount of positive net worth (−.0750) is stronger than it is for the population at large (−.0464 in M1b table 8.1). Local labor market conditions, however, have quite a different impact on minority wealth attainment. The negative effect is weaker and only marginally significant for blacks. A possible reason is that the employment rate among black men is low (Western 2002) and a large proportion of black households are female-headed; thus these households often are not in the primary labor market. In addition, segregated black areas have relatively high unemployment rates. In these areas, segregation may play a far more important role than local labor market conditions. It is surprising to find that the unemployment rate has a positive effect on wealth attainment for Hispanics. A possible reason is that many Hispanic workers, particularly immigrants, are in the secondary or the informal labor market, which may be inversely related to the primary market. Given the high proportion of Hispanics, who are foreign born, and the different types of work done by immigrant versus native Hispanics, the positive effect of the unemployment rate

Table 8.3   Contextual Conditions and Wealth Attainment, a Separate
Analysis (M3a)

Variable	White	Black	Hispanic	Asian
Effect on positive net worth				
State unemployment (%)	−0.0750 **	−0.0377 ^	0.0775 **	0.0381
Black-white segregation (D 10%)	0.1270 **	−0.1023 **	−0.1563 **	−0.0645
Hispanic-white segregation (D 10%)	0.0193 *	−0.1277 **	−0.2471 **	−0.0069
Percentage foreign born (10%)	0.0330 **	0.0058	0.0222	0.0178
Effect on probability of positive net worth				
State unemployment (%)	−0.0052 **	−0.0046 ^	0.0087 **	0.0029
Black-white segregation (D 10%)	0.0088 **	−0.0125 **	−0.0176 **	−0.0049
Hispanic-white segregation (D 10%)	0.0013 *	−0.0156 **	−0.0278 **	−0.0005
Percentage foreign born (10%)	0.0023 **	0.0007	0.0025	0.0013
Fraction positive net worth	0.890	0.687	0.734	0.863
n	97,976	16,099	15,582	5,188

Source: Author's compilation.
Note: The estimates are based on the metropolitan sample. The model adds the presented variables to model M3 of chapter 7, including education, the interaction between education and immigrant status, household characteristics and period effects.
** $p < .01$
* $p < .05$
^ $p < .10$

should not necessarily be a big surprise. Among Asians, the unemployment rate does not influence wealth attainment. A possible reason is that jobs done by the well educated are relatively stable and the ethnic community protects the less educated.

Metropolitan contexts of residential segregation and nativity composition shape wealth attainment differently by race-ethnicity and nativity. Figure 8.1 visualizes the contrasting effect across the four racial-ethnic groups based on table 8.3 and against the pattern for the total metropolitan population from table 8.2. Black-white segregation has a large positive effect for whites, a large negative effect for blacks, an even larger negative effect for Hispanics, and no significant effect for Asians. These varying effects drive a small positive effect for the total population. The exact coefficients in table 8.3 show that an increase of 10 percentage points in black-white segregation raises average positive net worth of whites by about 13 percent and their probability of wealth attainment by .0088. The effect of residential segregation for blacks is as hypothesized: an increase of 10 percentage points in the black-white dissimilarity index causes a drop in positive net worth by about 10 percent and the probability of wealth attainment by −.0125. The estimated negative effect of black-white segregation is stronger for Hispanics: an increase of 10 percentage points in the black-white dissimilarity index reduces the size of wealth by about 16 percent and the probability of wealth attainment by .0176. These findings provide strong evidence to support that black-white segregation benefits whites and harms blacks. It is a new finding that the detrimental effect of black-white segregation spills over to Hispanics to an even greater degree. This excessive negative externality may be related to the fact that more than 50 percent of Hispanics are immigrants, some of them illegal, who tend to cluster in low-rent, black-concentrated areas. The lack of effect of black-white segregation for Asians is as expected. About 75 percent of the Asian population are immigrants. Professional Asian immigrants are likely to live in suburbs, whereas Asian labor immigrants are likely to live in co-ethnic communities, both of which shield Asians from the spillover of the detrimental impact black-white segregation has for minorities.

In figure 8.1, a similar pattern of opposite effects is found for Hispanic-white segregation. The effect for whites remains positive but much smaller. The detrimental effect is now the strongest for Hispanics, the target group. This strong detrimental effect of Hispanic-white segregation has not been documented in previous literature. A few possible reasons for the segregation effect include the significant resurgence of low-skilled Hispanic immigration, black-to-Hispanic neighborhood transitions, and analyzing the phenomenon of wealth attainment rather than income or earnings. There is also a strong spillover detrimental effect for blacks and the magnitude is smaller than that for the target group of Hispanics. This negative externality was not documented in the literature but is along the direction of recent neighborhood transitions. As Latino immigrants move into black neighborhoods, black-white segregation declines but Hispanic-white segregation rises. The demographic transitions of these neighborhoods do not involve whites and thus remain poor in resources and short on opportunities. The significant spillover effect of Hispanic-white segregation for nontarget black residents is a new finding with profound implications for theory and policy. Theoretically, racial residential segregation theory needs to move beyond the target-focus perspective to a more inclusive view that theorizes the process of spillover. Correspondingly, policies aiming to reduce the social isolation and victimization of blacks must consider not only black-white segregation but also Hispanic-white segregation, both of which victimize blacks. Asians remain unaffected by Hispanic-white or black-white segregation. This may have to do with the two areas where Asians usually settle: middle-class white suburbs and Asian communities in central cities. Asian communities often have strong economic bases that help buffer the impact of segregation.

The literature to date has documented the serious consequences of black-white segregation for blacks without a parallel analysis of its impact on whites or on other minority groups. The impact of Hispanic-

Figure 8.1   Effects of Racial Residential Segregation and Immigrant Share, by Race-Ethnicity

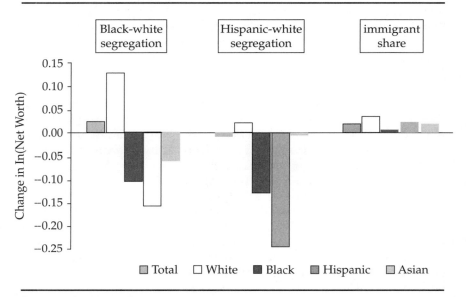

Source: Author's compilation.
Note: Bars without a border indicate insignificant effects.

white segregation has also been understudied. My analysis shows the importance of extending the focus on black segregation to Hispanic segregation, distinguishing between the dominant group and the subordinate group, and distinguishing between target and nontarget minority groups. My findings about the harm of Hispanic-white segregation for Hispanics and the spillover effects of both black-white and Hispanic-white segregation on the wealth attainment of nontarget minority groups provide strong evidence for this analytic approach.

The last set of bars in figure 8.1 depicts the effect of immigrant share. The effect is mildly positive and significant for whites, and is somewhat greater than that for the total population. However, no effect of immigrant share is detected for any racial minority groups. The nativity differential effect of immigrant share may obscure what we observed in Figure 8.1 for each racial-ethnic group as a whole.

Differential Effects by Nativity and Race-Ethnicity

The next analysis allows that contextual conditions have differential effects by nativity. Figures 8.2, 8.3, and 8.4 present results from this analysis based on the coefficients in table 8.4. The black-white segregation effect differs markedly between native whites and immigrant whites. Whereas native whites benefit from black-white segregation, immigrant whites do not: combining the main effect and interaction effect yields a nonsignificant, close-to-zero effect (.1344 − .1365). Immigrant whites are not part of the U.S. black-white segregation history, and the analysis shows that living in highly segregated areas does not benefit immigrant whites as it does for native whites.

Figure 8.2 shows that the detrimental effect of black-white segregation is significant for African Americans but insignificant for immigrant blacks from African or Caribbean countries. This finding is consistent with the previous finding that immigrant blacks have fewer black-white work relationship problems and develop economic niches (Waters 1999; Waldinger 1996). It also suggests, however, that black immigrants may face less discrimination in housing and lending markets so that their net worth is not significantly affected by black-white segregation, which is different from what Mary Waters found (1999). Black-white segregation is more detrimental for native-born Hispanics (−.2132) than for immigrant Hispanics (−.2132 + .1505 = −.0627). Perhaps Hispanic immigrants

Figure 8.2   Effects of Black-White Racial Residential Segregation, by Nativity and Race-Ethnicity

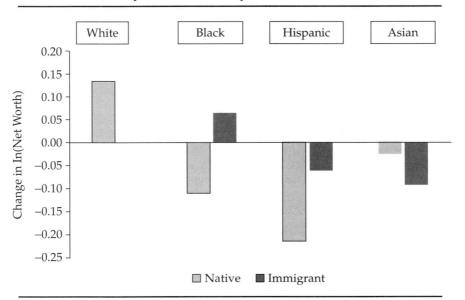

Source: Author's compilation.
Note: Bars without a border indicate insignificant effects.

Figure 8.3   Effects of Hispanic-White Residential Segregation, by Nativity and Race-Ethnicity

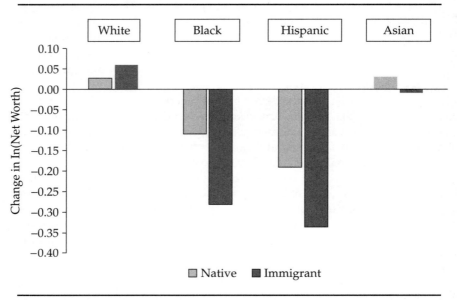

Source: Author's compilation.
Note: Bars without a border indicate insignificant effects.

are less affected because some have moved into working-class black communities with established public services.

Regarding Hispanic-white segregation, the nativity differential occurs only among Hispanics (see figure 8.3). Among whites, Hispanic-white segregation benefits native whites, but the effect becomes small and insignificant. A spillover of the negative effect of Hispanic-white segregation is significant for native-born blacks but not significant for immigrant blacks. The analysis reveals a very different effect of Hispanic-white segregation for immigrant versus native-born Hispanics. The negative effect of Hispanic-white segregation is much stronger for Hispanic immigrants than for Hispanic Americans. An increase of 10 percent in the Hispanic-white dissimilarity index decreases Hispanic Americans' positive net worth by 17.6 percent and Hispanic immigrants' by 28.7 percent. Understandably, new, overcrowded Hispanic communities may have limited economic opportunities and public services.

Nativity composition also has differential effects for immigrants and natives (see figure 8.4). The effect of nativity composition is positive for native whites (.0515) but negative for immigrant whites (.0515 −.2688 = −.2173) (about 19.5 percent reduction in net worth due to an increase of

Table 8.4   Differential Contextual Conditions by Nativity on Wealth Attainment, a Separate Analysis (M3b)

Variable	White	Black	Hispanic	Asian
Effect on positive net worth				
Main effect				
Black-white segregation (D 10%)	0.1344 **	−0.1107 **	−0.2132 **	−0.0251
Hispanic-white segregation (D 10%)	0.0151 ^	−0.1107 **	−0.1932 **	0.0321
Share of foreign born (10%)	0.0515 **	−0.0210	0.0524	0.0599
Interactive effect				
Black-white segregation (D 10%)	−0.1365 **	0.1763	0.1505 **	−0.0677
Hispanic-white segregation (D 10%)	0.0456	−0.1720	−0.1447 *	−0.0463
Percentage foreign born × immigrant	−0.2688 **	0.1918 *	−0.0728	−0.0478
Effect on probability of positive net worth				
Main effect				
Black-white segregation (D 10%)	0.0094 **	−0.0136 **	−0.0240 **	−0.0019
Hispanic-white segregation (D 10%)	0.0010 ^	−0.0136 **	−0.0218 **	0.0024
Share of foreign born (10%)	0.0036 **	−0.0026	0.0059	0.0045
Interactive effect				
Black-white segregation (D 10%)	−0.0095 **	0.0216	0.0170 **	−0.0051
Hispanic-white segregation (D 10%)	0.0032	−0.0211	−0.0163 *	−0.0035
Percentage foreign born × immigrant	−0.0187 **	0.0235 *	−0.0082	−0.0036
Fraction positive net worth	0.890	0.687	0.734	0.863
n	97,976	16,099	15,582	5,188

Source: Author's compilation.
Note: The estimates are based on the metropolitan sample. The model adds the presented variables to model M3 of chapter 7, including education, the interaction between education and immigrant status, household characteristics and period effects.
** $p < .01$
* $p < .05$
^ $p < .10$

10 percentage point increase in immigrant share). For native whites, a large immigrant presence is an advantage. For immigrant whites, a large presence of immigrants constrains wealth attainment opportunities.

The analysis, however, detects that higher proportions of foreign-born residents have a positive effect for immigrant blacks but no effect for African Americans. The labor market composition hypothesis is thus not supported for African Americans. How immigrant blacks find a niche in areas with high immigrant concentrations is a topic for future research. The analysis does not detect a significant impact of immigrant share on either native or immigrant Hispanics' wealth attainment. Similarly, the immigrant share does not impact Asians, whether native-born or immigrant.

Figure 8.4   Effects of Percentage Foreign Born, by Nativity and Race-Ethnicity

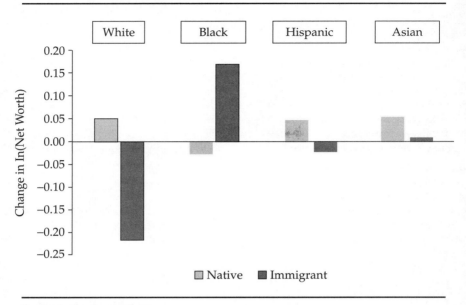

Source: Author's compilation.
Note: Bars without a border indicate insignificant effects.

Conclusion

This chapter examines contextual conditions under which immigrant and native households accumulate their wealth. Chapter 7 demonstrated that though race-ethnicity is the primary factor in wealth stratification, nativity, and nationality within racial-ethnic groups further stratify wealth. The driving forces of racial-ethnic stratification and nativity-nationality stratification are structural. This chapter investigated the contextual conditions created by the distribution of race and immigrants. Theory regarding the racial-ethnic stratification of wealth emphasizes racial residential segregation, which combines multiple forms of discrimination and creates differential social contexts in which households accumulate their wealth.

Immigrant settlement patterns may change the dynamics of residential segregation. Large inflows of Latino immigrants make it inevitable that new immigrants cluster in previously settled Latino communities as well as black communities because these areas are generally the most affordable. Moving into established Latino communities increases Hispanic-white segregation, whereas entering black communities changes black-white segregation to both black-white and Hispanic-white segregation. These community dynamics may modify the nature of Hispanic-white segregation and the spillover effect of black-white segregation.

Asian immigrants, however, exhibit two different patterns of settlement. With their stable income from professional jobs, which place them on the middle-class route to wealth accumulation, highly educated Asians are likely to settle in suburban areas. Like their Latino counterparts, less-educated Asians cluster in ethnic communities. However, unlike Latino communities, many Asian communities have strong economic institutions and voluntary organizations, which shield newcomers from the harsh barriers to asset building often encountered in ethnically segregated areas. Black immigrants, a more slowly growing immigrant group, have a bimodal, high-low educational distribution. The better educated are expected to face the same strong structural constraints from residential segregation as the less educated because black-white segregation affects both lower- and middle-class blacks.

The continuous, large influx of low-skilled immigrant workers during the last three decades contributes to changes in contextual conditions. This influx has intensified competition among similarly low-skilled workers. Competition, however, is likely to be confined to the immigrant population because native-born, low-skilled workers often have jobs in the primary labor market, have jobs with union protection, or live in inner-city areas that have little demand for consumer services provided by low-skilled immigrant workers. Therefore, low-skilled immigrant workers are generally not substitutes for native-born workers. Instead, newer immigrants compete with earlier immigrants. The analysis here shows that white immigrants living in high immigrant areas, many of whom are from eastern Europe, face this competition.

Settlement patterns and the low-skilled labor supply created by immigration primarily affect metropolitan areas, changing contextual conditions in those areas. These conditions are measured by black-white segregation, Hispanic-white segregation, and proportion foreign born. A valid evaluation of the impact of settlement patterns and the low-skilled labor supply on wealth attainment must be undertaken under the same local economic and labor market conditions. The impact of each of these contextual variables should also be examined among households comparable in characteristics such as life cycle stage, race-ethnicity and nationality, education level, marital status, and number of children.

Several findings emerge. First, the analysis provides strong evidence to defy the assumption that residential racial segregation has a uniform impact on the population as a whole. Rather, residential segregation has markedly differential effects by both race-ethnicity and nativity. Native whites, but not immigrant whites, are the only beneficiaries of black-white segregation. African Americans, but not black immigrants, are the target of black-white segregation. Hispanic Americans, but not Hispanic immigrants, suffer from the spillover of black-white segregation. Hispanics are the target of Hispanic-white segregation and all blacks suffer from the spillover of Hispanic-white segregation. From a social welfare perspective, residential segregation is highly unfair and inefficient because native whites reap benefits at the expense of immigrant whites and minorities. Residential segregation affects not only the target groups (blacks suffering from black-white segregation and Hispanics suffering from Hispanic-white segregation) but also spills over to nontarget groups (all blacks suffer from Hispanic-white segregation and all Hispanics suffer from black-white segregation). Keep in mind that these results are obtained controlling for education level, household type, number of children, and period effects.

The harmful effects of Hispanic-white segregation for both Hispanics and blacks raise a red flag about the nature of Hispanic-white segregation. Most segregation scholars focus their attention on black-white segregation and generally take Hispanic-white segregation as a type of economic constraint rather than as social prejudice and discrimination. However, this analysis reveals the hampered wealth attainment of all Hispanics and blacks because of Hispanic-white segregation, suggesting that Hispanic-white segregation has a more serious impact than previously thought. Whether Hispanic-white segregation is a result of voluntary Hispanic clustering or not, the substantial negative effect of segregation on wealth attainment may foster multiple forms of discrimination.

Nativity composition also has differential impacts on wealth attainment by race-ethnicity and nativity. In the literature, it is highly correlated with the proportion of foreign-born Hispanics, is often used to capture the impact of immigration. Here, I assess the impact of immigration by controlling for residential segregation, both black-white and Hispanic-white, as well as the local labor market conditions. Controlling for Hispanic-white segregation is particularly important because Hispanic-white segregation is higher in areas with a high proportion of foreign-born residents. A large immigrant presence benefits native whites and immigrant blacks but harms white immigrants. The positive effect for native whites is consistent with economic theory regarding immigration (Smith and Edmonston 1997). The theoretical basis for the negative effect of nativity composition is the assumption that there is labor market competition among low-skilled workers who have little union protection. African American workers are more likely to be protected by unions, and the civil rights movement has sensitized the quality of the job. Most scholars agree that immigration's impact on black workers should be small to nonexistent (Hamermesh and Bean 1998). A similar but weaker argument can be made for Hispanic Americans.

Finally, Asian Americans and Asian immigrants appear to have been affected the least by these racial and ethic conflicts and competitions. Although many Asian Americans have assimilated to the white middle class, they do not reap any benefits from residential segregation, perhaps because they themselves are a minority. Asian immigrants with low levels of education should be affected by residential segregation and compete for so-called immigrant-type jobs. The fact that they seem to be protected, I reason, is because of their ethnic communities and the social structures and institutions that facilitate Asian immigrant asset building (Light 1972; Zhou and Bankston 1998).

= Chapter 9 =

Looking Ahead:
Immigration, Stratification,
and Assimilation

Douglas Massey and his colleagues (2002) predict that chain-migration from Latin America will continue for generations. It will persist from Asia and Africa. Uninterrupted streams of immigrants who are for the most part neither white nor highly skilled perpetuate a first generation that requires rethinking of two broad issues—the impact of immigration on American society and the assimilation of the first-generation immigrants. The mass population movement of immigrants introduces the factor of nativity into the American wealth stratification system. Nativity will transform this system by changing the ways that immigrants assimilate economically and culturally by accumulating wealth. The transformation goes hand in hand with the transformation of racial residential segregation. Settlement patterns of contemporary immigrants have reshaped both the landscape of racial residential segregation and the consequences of such segregation for various racial groups. The large presence of first-generation immigrants suggests a rethinking of the century-old practice of focusing on second and higher generation assimilation. It is imperative to pay equal attention to the first generation. Ultimately, the role of immigration should be evaluated not only by examining the assimilation of immigrants but also by examining the impact of immigration on the native-born population and society as a whole.

This conclusion places the key findings from the book within the larger picture created by immigration, stratification, and assimilation. Immigrants and natives alike are constrained by the American racial hierarchy. Nativity, however, differentiates members within racial-ethnic groups and, in the long run, contributes to the weakening of racial-ethnic inequality. This two-tiered process justifies reconceptualizing social stratification, a process that can take a number of factors into account. Results concerning the contextual effects help us understand how immigration-induced changes in society affect immigrants and natives. At the same time, findings about the differences and similarities in wealth between immigrants and natives demand that we rethink assimilation. By examining nonwhite first-generation immigrant assimilation, this book underscores a distinction between the role of race-ethnicity and nativity in shaping the path either toward or away from the American mainstream.

Immigration and Racial Ethnic Stratification

The stratification literature stresses three factors—race-ethnicity, class, and gender. This book argues that when the immigrant population is substantial, nativity and nationality of those immigrants are new factors that bear on social stratification. When multiple stratification factors are present, it is important to consider and distinguish all of the possible ideal-type scenarios. This book develops three. When all stratification factors are competing, each remains influential and the system persists. When one factor becomes indecisive, it loses its influence and the system is reduced. When the primary factors dominate the secondary, the secondary differentiate the population and, in the long term, transform the stratification order.

The observed patterns show that in wealth stratification race is the primary factor dominating nativity (chapter 3), as they reveal wide racial-ethnic gaps and narrow nativity gaps. The small nativity gaps in age profiles of net worth within racial-ethnic groups further testify to the dominant role of race-ethnicity over nativity. Immigrants' country of origin, age at arrival, and naturalization, can be more important than nativity in social stratification. Differences by country of origin are indeed sharper than differences by nativity. However, racial-ethnic stratification remains primary. After all, most origin-country groups are clustered within the same racial-ethnic groups. Only two origin-country groups cross color lines: immigrants from Hong Kong–Taiwan surpass native whites (and all other native groups) and Cuban immigrants have the advantage in many wealth measures over Korean and Vietnamese immigrants. This is scant evidence to support that immigrant characteristics could contest the importance of race-ethnicity.

Evidence from chapter 7 indicates that the two-tiered system of race-ethnicity and nativity also withstands multivariate analysis. Racial-ethnic gaps in both the probability and the size of having positive net worth remain substantial after education, nativity, and household characteristics are taken into account. The results not only confirm a wide black-white gap, but also reveal one between Hispanics and whites. In addition, because Asian educational attainment is high, the white-Asian gap becomes wider after education levels are held constant. These findings show that the influence of racial-ethnic stratification on wealth gaps is powerful for blacks as well for Hispanics and Asians. Nativity, on the other hand, has no significant effect for the whole population.

Results from the separate analyses for each racial-ethnic group show how nativity operates as a secondary factor in the two-tiered system. First, the effect of education on wealth attainment differs by nativity. Immigrants' education brings them lower returns. These differential effects work against immigrants' odds of wealth attainment compared with their native racial counterparts. Second, country of origin further differentiates members of racial ethnic groups. All else being equal, Mexican, Cuban, Chinese, and Japanese immigrants exhibit significant advantages over their native-born racial counterparts, whereas Dominican immigrants face significant disadvantages compared with native-born Hispanics. Third, later age at arrival and not being naturalized have negative effects on wealth attainment.

Together, these descriptive and multivariate analyses provide the first evidence to support a two-tiered stratification system where race-ethnicity is the primary factor and nativity is the secondary for wealth stratification. A theoretical implication is therefore that revisiting the existing thinking about social stratification is called for. The single-factor theorizing tradition needs to be extended to multiple factors, taking into account their interdependence and relative importance. When the population is changing because of immigration, new stratification factors may be created and some existing factors may become less important or even cease to be significant. In the current era of high immigration, nativity, country of origin, and other immigrant characteristics have emerged to differentiate the population. These phenomena lead to the proposed two-tiered stratification system of race-ethnicity and nativity. Although this volume provides evidence to support the new idea, much more theorizing and empirical testing for different phenomena (such as wealth versus income) and in different historical periods (such as contemporary versus historical immigration eras) are needed to further develop the idea. It is my hope that this book will initiate a comprehensive rethinking of and research on social stratification.

Immigration and Social Context

Immigration also creates new structural forces, particularly immigrant settlement patterns and low-skilled labor supplies. Through these forces, immigration changes social contexts with respect to racial residential segregation and local labor market competition. To a certain extent, wealth attainment is determined by the household's social context, because social context determines opportunities and constraints.

The dynamics of immigrant settlement depend on three conditions:

residential patterns of the host society, settlement patterns of earlier im-migrants from a specific country, and the volume of new inflows of im-migrants from the same country. Residential segregation between blacks and whites is a social problem with long historical roots that involves multiple forms of racial oppression and discrimination (Massey and Denton 1993). Residential segregation between Hispanics and whites is also long-standing, but the literature usually treats it as a class rather than a racial-ethnic matter (Frey and Farley 1996). Because Latino immi-grants make up such a large group, their settlement patterns contribute to the changing dynamics of racial residential segregation. Two processes are thus initiated and maintained by Latino immigration: the clustering of immigrant settlement, which raises the level of white-Hispanic segre-gation, and the movement of Latino immigrants into black communities, which reduces the level of black-white segregation. Given the large inflows of Latino immigrants, their settlement patterns could play a pro-found role in reshaping current black-white and Hispanic-white residen-tial segregation and alter the consequences of racial residential segrega-tion for natives and immigrants.

The continuous, large influx of low-skilled immigrant workers over the last three decades has increased the supply of low-skilled labor in lo-cal markets. Previous research has not reached consensus about the ef-fects of this increase. There are two possibilities. The large labor supply may either push the native labor force to leave the local area or displace native and earlier immigrant workers of similar skills in the same local-ity, but it is difficult to address these two possibilities simultaneously (McCall 2000, 2001; Hamermesh and Bean 1998; Altonji and Card 1991). Competition for low-skilled jobs is, however, likely to be confined to the immigrant population either because native-born, low-skilled workers in the primary labor market often have union protection, or because they live in inner cities with little demand for consumer services provided by low-skilled immigrant workers. Low-skilled immigrant workers would therefore probably not substitute for their native-born counterparts. They would instead compete among themselves or with those who had arrived earlier. This is likely among Hispanic immigrants, among whom the numbers of low-skilled workers is large.

The analyses in chapter 8 suggest the need to revise the evaluation of the consequences of racial residential segregation that does not stress the potentially different effects for whites and minorities. Evidence here calls attention to differential effects for different racial-ethnic nativity groups. The results show that black segregation benefits native whites but vic-timizes African Americans. This finding captures the power structure embedded in black-white segregation. That white and black immigrants are not affected by black segregation suggests that they may not live in segregated neighborhoods, thereby avoiding the segregation effects. Being foreign born is a disadvantage in the sense that immigrant languages, cultural practices, and social values are not easily accepted by local natives. Immigrant whites, many of whom now come from former Soviet countries, who do not live in segregated white neighborhoods do not reap benefits from the white-black power structure. Given their small inflows, black immigrants may cluster in small neighborhoods, thereby avoiding the existing segregated black neighborhood. Moreover, the contextual analyses in chapter 8 reveal that the effects of black-white residential segregation spill over to Hispanic Americans, but not to Hispanic and Asian immigrants and Asian Americans.

One important finding is that Hispanic-white residential segregation negatively affects the wealth attainment of not only Hispanics but also blacks, regardless of nativity. The size of this negative effect is at least as strong as the effect of black segregation. It suggests that Hispanic segregation may in fact be an issue of racial-ethnic discrimination. New theorizing is needed to address this dimension. Does the critical mass of a minority group constitute a new threat to whites? Or does Latino heritage become a target of nationalism and anti-immigration sentiment? Because Hispanic segregation is a natural consequence of large inflows of immigrants and clustering settlement patterns, more theoretical and empirical investigation into the causes and consequences of Hispanic segregation is needed.

Results regarding the impact of nativity on the wealth attainment of racial-ethnic nativity groups provide an updated evaluation of the competing labor market argument. When black and Hispanic segregation are controlled, having a large percentage of local residents who are immigrants benefits native whites but not immigrant whites. High percentages of immigrant residents correspond to high percentages of Latino low-skilled immigrants, who, according to economic theory, are not in competition with native whites. Although earlier white immigrants are now well established, recent white immigrants, particularly those from less developed former Soviet countries, may compete for low-paying jobs such as those in hotels and restaurants. African Americans are not affected by a large presence of the foreign born, but black immigrants actually benefit from it. The mechanism leading to this result requires further investigation.

Assimilation and Wealth Attainment

Today's continuously growing nonwhite immigrant population is unprecedented in American history. The fact that most do not speak English, combined with their diverse cultures and different religions, may make many native-born Americans uncomfortable. Middle-class attainment by first generation nonwhite immigrants may significantly ease these concerns. Therefore, information about whether first-generation immigrants can achieve middle-class status is essential for immigration policy makers concerned with the treatment of illegal immigrants and programs for temporary workers. For nonwhite immigrants, the success of intragenerational assimilation is decisive in intergenerational assimilation for nonwhite immigrants because middle-class status can be transmitted across generations. When first-generation nonwhite immigrants do not attain middle-class status, the assimilation of subsequent generations is compromised.

Assimilation theory was first developed during a historical period of low immigration (Warner and Scrole 1945; Gordon 1964) and addressed the successive higher generations of European white immigrants who arrived around the turn of the twentieth century. Significant developments of assimilation theory are found in the ideas of cultural pluralism (Schiller, Basch, and Blanc-Szanton 1995), segmented assimilation (Portes and Zhou 1993), and the new assimilation theory (Alba and Nee 2003). In these theories, even though the nonwhiteness of contemporary immigrants is addressed, the focus on intergenerational assimilation remains.

The assimilation of nonwhite higher generations is inevitably shaped by racial-ethnic stratification, making achieving middle-class status by the first generation more important than it was for previous white generations. As shown in this volume, sufficient wealth holding offers economic security in times of crisis, sustains a comfortable living standard, enables investments in children's education, and can be passed on to the next generation through inheritances. If the first generation manages to attain sufficient wealth, the prospects for the next generation's assimilation are high. Thus, an understanding of tomorrow's assimilation requires an understanding of today's first generations' assimilation.

In their far-reaching study on the wealth of blacks and of whites (1995), Oliver and Shapiro suggest the need to include wealth in any analysis of economic well-being. Analyses in this volume provide strong evidence for the need to use wealth as a vehicle to study first generation assimilation. My findings also support this suggestion but particularly emphasize three unique immigrant characteristics—a lack of inheritance, freedom from the burden of U.S. racist history, and self-selection. Because wealth is accumulative whereas income fluctuates over time, wealth can capture the process by which the three characteristics of the first generation play a role in its assimilation. Wealth then can validly gauge stages of immigrant assimilation.

Researchers are often concerned with the reliability of wealth measures. In survey data, the very rich are underrepresented and wealth components of the very rich (annuities and trusts, for example) are rarely included in survey data. This book does not look at the top 0.5 percentile of the net worth distribution (more than $2.32 million constant dollars in 2000). By focusing on the lower 99.5 percent of the wealth distribution, these analyses focus on the wealth level of middle class.

The two-tiered stratification system of race-ethnicity and nativity offers a useful way to look into the assimilation process of immigrants. As explained, nativity and immigrant characteristics differentiate specific racial-ethnic groups. Where color lines highlight the racial-ethnic divides, country lines underscore distinctions between natives and immigrants as well as among immigrants with respect to self-selection, motivation, networks, cultural roots, host society reception, and specific experience in the United States. Positive selection, high motivation, a strong work ethic, a forward-looking perspective, high value on the family, and high expectation for children inject energy into wealth accumulation behaviors. Healthily functioning communities with a strong ethnic economy can sustain and reinforce these immigrant advantages and shield minority racial immigrants from outside discrimination. Favorable reception from the U.S. government and the labor, housing, and credit markets provide opportunities for upward mobility. Under all these circumstances, racial minority immigrants can gradually overcome the racial barrier, transcend the color line, and advance toward the American mainstream. This upward mobility can take place within the first generation and indeed has among immigrants from Hong Kong and Taiwan. It is happening among those from China, India, Japan, the Philippines, and Cuba. It is taking small steps among those from Korea, Vietnam, Mexico, and Jamaica. This volume, however, does not offer sweeping optimism. Observed and analytical results show a stagnation of wealth among Salvadoran, Guatemalan, Haitian, and African immigrants and a downward path for Dominican immigrants.

The findings illuminate how first-generation immigrants succeed, progress, struggle, or fail to assimilate. Hispanics appear near the bottom of the racial-ethnic hierarchy. Correspondingly, they have been depicted as low achievers and as a source of decline in recent immigrants' quality (Borjas 1999). Findings from the analyses of particular components of wealth (see chapter 4) show that all Latino immigrants have a lower rate of retirement accounts ownership than their native-born counterparts and native whites. This implies insecurity in old age and questionable prospects for passing wealth to the next generation.

Consistent with previous research, Cuban immigrants are found to surpass native-born Hispanics in many aspects of wealth. One new finding on Mexican immigrants, however, contradicts the previous literature. Mexicans, by far the largest immigrant group, have wealth indicators that rank unexpectedly high. Despite their very low education levels and frequent illegal status, some 25 percent of Mexican immigrant households are able to accumulate sufficient wealth to support their households in the United States for one year without additional income. Although 25 percent is not high when compared to the more than 50 percent of native whites and 33 percent of Hispanic Americans, it is double the rate of Dominican immigrants and higher than that for Salvadoran and Guatemalan immigrants, all of whom have higher education levels. Mexican immigrants achieve relatively high rates on other wealth indicators, such as homeownership, and usually avoid second mortgages or high mortgage interest rates. These facts stand in striking contrast to the high poverty rate of Mexican immigrants, which is the second highest among the six Latino immigrant groups examined. If only income or poverty is considered, Mexican immigrant progress toward upward mobility is not observed.

The findings from multivariate analyses in chapter 7 regarding Mexican immigrants may be even more impressive. When education, age, marital status, number of children, and year of data collection are controlled, Mexican immigrants achieve significantly higher net worth than Hispanic Americans. Their edge is similar to that of Cuban immigrants. This finding may capture high motivation, strong effort, network support, positive reception by the American labor market, and other unobserved characteristics of Mexican immigrants and their environments, all of which appear to promote mobility and enhance wealth.

Mexican immigrants are a showcase for explaining the paradox why a lack of inheritance is important in constraining African American wealth accumulation but is not for many immigrants. Low-educated Mexican immigrants appear to be self-selected positively on motivation and work ethic. This, however, is not the full answer. The large demand for the kind of low-paying work most Mexican immigrants undertake, their favorable treatment by the labor market, and the employment-related information channels their networks and communities provide all contribute to an opportunity structure that helps explain how they can overcome the lack of inheritance.

At the same time, the typology of wealth regime developed in this volume predicts that Mexican immigrants are likely to make cross-border investment in Mexico in part because of the relatively stable investment environment and the purchasing capacity of U.S. currency relative to the peso. Much anecdotal evidence suggests that it is not uncommon for Mexican immigrants to own a home, a shop, a piece of land, and livestock purchased with their U.S. earned dollars. As a result, survey-based data on Mexican immigrants' wealth may be underestimated.

These findings about Mexican immigrants are encouraging, but they are offset by low wealth levels. Three obstacles hinder the assimilation of Mexican immigrants: low education levels, high fertility, and a preponderance of illegal status. It will take enormous efforts to surmount these obstacles. Moreover, their low socioeconomic status and low U.S. wealth predict low academic achievement and slow assimilation for the second generation and beyond.

Wide variations in wealth indicators are found among Latino immigrant groups. Salvadoran and Guatemalan immigrants are struggling with low rates of sufficient wealth holding, homeownership, and liquid financial resources. Even after demographic characteristics and education are controlled, the Dominican immigrant disadvantage remains large. A lack of inheritance is not the only reason these groups make little progress in assimilation. Many Salvadoran and Guatemalan immigrants came to the United States primarily to escape wars and turmoil, making their self-selection different from that of economic immigrants. The reception and inadequate networks do not enhance their upward mobility.

Considered a model minority, Asians are recognized as hard working and successful, but are a diverse group and face a different type of discrimination (Kim and Lewis 1994). The exceptionally superior wealth attainment of those from Hong Kong and Taiwan may be based on factors such as capital brought with them, high levels of education, and the success of their ethnic economies. The majority of Asian immigrant groups, including mainland Chinese, Filipino, Indian, and Japanese, are near parity with their native-born counterparts. Surprisingly, in spite of their high education levels and entrepreneurship, Korean immigrants fare less well. Unlike Chinese, Japanese, and Indian entrepreneurs, who serve mainly co-ethnics in enclaves, Korean small businesses often serve disadvantaged minority neighborhoods. This different business strategy may leave Koreans more vulnerable to racial ethnic conflicts. It may also require a longer time to establish businesses without a co-ethnic community base.

Also labeled a model minority, Jamaican immigrants are the best-off among blacks, achieving greater upward mobility than other black immigrants and African Americans. However, the wealth gap between Jamaican immigrants and native whites is large. Although Jamaicans are relatively highly educated and usually have legal immigrant status, they show signs of economic vulnerability. For example, Jamaican homeowners are more likely to have negative home equity. Thus, though upwardly mobile, Jamaicans are often in a fragile financial situation, which endangers opportunities for their next generation.

It is expected that African immigrants' high education levels counteract the negative effects of race on their wealth accumulation. However, the African immigrant wealth level is low across the board—sufficient wealth holding, homeownership, and liquid financial assets. Their foreign degrees and refugee status may explain this seeming illogic. That first-generation African immigrants are not upwardly mobile hinders the next generation in moving toward assimilation.

Wealth analyses provide evidence that intragenerational assimilation is possible for some but not all nonwhite immigrant groups, which has implications for policy makers aiming for a better integrated society. The wealth of immigrants from Hong Kong and Taiwan surpasses that of native whites and provides extra resources for the second and subsequent generations to overcome racial barriers to upward mobility and assimilation. Many other Asian immigrant groups approach parity with Asian Americans. Their second generations may have a rougher upward path than the second Hong Kong and Taiwan generation. Korean immigrant difficulties in assimilating suggest that policies addressing racial-ethnic conflicts in promoting small businesses could help Koreans establish economic security.

Evidence shows that Mexican immigrants have made progress in assimilating and have the potential to move even further. The intragenerational assimilation of Mexican immigrants—given their low education levels, large numbers of children, and likelihood of illegal status—becomes key to the successful integration of the next generation. Policies on the treatment of illegal immigrants and regulation of informal labor markets could help Mexican immigrants to assimilate more quickly.

The financial situation of black immigrants is fragile, even for model groups such as Jamaican immigrants. For the first-generation, high educational attainment is not enough to ensure assimilation. The progress black immigrants make in wealth accumulation can be easily negated by hardships and their vulnerability raises a serious challenge for policy makers. Policy addressing the barriers of upward mobility that the ever-increasing black immigrant population faces will have important implications for race relations in the United States.

The prospect of immigrants' upward mobility and assimilation also has important implications for natives. As assimilation theorists have abandoned the idea that white Anglo Saxon Protestants are the American mainstream, theories have become more inclusive and diverse. This trend will continue (Alba and Nee 2003). If a substantial proportion of an expanding first generation moves upward into the mainstream, race-ethnicity will become less of a factor in individual life chances and social inequalities. That is, race-ethnicity could become secondary rather than primary, leaving human capital as the most decisive factor. An important aspect of immigration is thus its potential to eventually weaken racial-ethnic stratification and enhance the well-being of the American population as a whole.

By simultaneously considering color lines and country lines, this volume demonstrates the broad impact of racial-ethnic stratification, which will ultimately be weakened by the effects of nativity and nationality. Wealth not only expresses the striking disparities among racial-ethnic groups, it also reveals gaps among nationality groups. It is thus a useful tool in studying stratification and assimilation. Immigration changes American society through its impact on racial-ethnic stratification, social mobility, and social inequality. More research is needed at the micro and the macro levels to fully describe and test immigration's effects. At the micro level, following the same households over time with particular attention to their wealth trajectories could capture immigration's impact on the wealth mobility of both immigrants and natives. At the macro level, following the wealth inequalities of specific countries over time could reveal the societal-level effects of immigration. Ultimately, the best tests of the causal impact of immigration on host societies will be analyses of macro-to-micro and micro-to-macro transitions that link immigration, household wealth mobility, and changing societal wealth inequality. I hope this volume will prove the starting point for such research.

= Appendix =

Survey of Income and Program Participation

The book's analyses draw data from a national survey—the Survey of Income and Program Participation (SIPP)—which includes ten panels and covers 1984 through 2003. This section provides justifications for using the SIPP and develops adjustments in order to improve the data and make it suitable for the analyses in this book.

SIPP Data

The survey design of the SIPP is a continuous series of national panels, with sample size ranging from approximately 11,000 to 35,000 interviewed households. The duration of each panel ranges from thirty to forty-eight months. The SIPP sample is a multistage-stratified sample of the U.S. civilian noninstitutionalized population. The 1984 panel was introduced in October 1983. For 1985 to 1993, a panel was introduced each year in February, which covers thirty to forty months. A forty-eight-month panel was introduced in April 1996 and a thirty-six-month panel was introduced in February 2001. The SIPP collects monthly data every four months (a wave) by interviewing the original sampled adults and other individuals with whom they reside. The SIPP includes core questions asked in each wave and topical modules of specific topics asked in only certain waves. This book uses data from core questions on labor force participation and income and data from three topical modules: migration history, assets and liabilities, and education history.

The migration history module asks whether each person in the household was born in the United States, and if born abroad, the country of birth and the year of arrival in the United States. The education history model collects information about respondent's highest level of school completed or degree received, fields of study, and dates and places of receipt of high school and postsecondary degrees or diplomas. The assets and liabilities module asks about the ownership and amount of assets and debts. Components of assets include residential home, vehicles, savings and checking accounts, stocks, mutual funds, bonds, real estate, business assets, and retirement accounts. Components of debts include mortgage, secured debts (such as home equity loans, car loans, and debts on stocks and mutual funds) and unsecured debts (such as credit cards and medical bills).

The assets and liabilities module is included in ten of the twelve total SIPP panels (the 1988 and 1989 panels did not contain such a module). Five of the ten panels collected data on assets and liabilities for more than one wave (the 1984, 1985, 1986, 1996, and 2001 panels). Together, these ten panels provide eighteen cross-sections of data on assets and debts for fourteen years (1984, 1985, 1987, 1988, 1991, 1993, 1995, 1996 through 1999, and 2001 through 2003) because some panel years overlap.

Quality of Wealth Data

The availability of wealth, migration, and educational history data, together with its large sample sizes of pooled multiple panels and waves, make the SIPP the prime candidate for a study of immigrants' wealth because no other national survey includes all of these attributes. However, the quality of the SIPP wealth data must be considered and compared with the wealth data provided by the Survey of Consumer Finances (SCF). The SCF is considered the most reliable survey data regarding the wealth distribution of the U.S. population. However, it lacks the migration and education history information necessary for studying immigrant wealth. In addition, its sample size is too small (fewer than 4,000 households) to allow studying small groups. The primary SIPP goal is to provide information needed for government program applications, including welfare programs, social security, Medicare, and Medicaid. It therefore pays less attention to the very wealthy and as a result the very rich are underrepresented. In addition, for confidentiality reasons, the SIPP topcodes components of assets. For example, the topcodes in the 1996 panel include $25,000 for saving bonds, $5,000 for own checking account, $375,000 for total equity value of properties, and $72,500 for total amount of joint interest-earning accounts. This topcoding, together with the undersampling of the very wealthy, leads to two limitations in the SIPP wealth data: the distributions of net worth and assets are incomplete, without an appropriate upper tail, and some components of assets relevant to the wealthy are left out, resulting in a smaller amount of total assets, overestimated shares of the middle portions, and underestimated shares of the upper portions. The two limitations have raised concerns over the use of the SIPP net worth and asset data in research without some form of adjustment, even thought the SIPP debt data are largely not affected.

The Social Security Administration (SSA), a primary user of SIPP, recently published a report, prepared by John Czajka, Jonathan Jacobson, and Scott Cody of Mathematica Policy Research (2003), comparing the SIPP and the SCF with respect to survey estimates of wealth data. Using family units, which align with the "primary economic unit" in the SCF, their analysis uses the 1998 SCF and wave 9 of the 1996 SIPP panel, which has a reference period covering late 1998 and early 1999. Table A.1 summarizes the estimated SIPP aggregates as the percentage of those of the SCF for all families and for all families excluding those with $2 million or more net worth. Among assets for all families (see column 2), home and 401(k) and thrift accounts almost match those in the SCF. The percentages for IRA-Keogh, stocks and mutual funds, and bank accounts are 55 to 63 percent of those in the SCF, and the percentage for business equity is merely 17 percent of that in the SCF. Because of the underestimates of asset components surveyed in the SIPP and a lack of components relevant to the rich, such as pension accounts, annuities, and trusts, the SIPP total assets amounts to only 55 percent of that in the SCF. Net worth is defined as total assets minus total debts. Even though the debts

Table A1   The SIPP Estimated Aggregate as Percentage of SCF: 1998 to 1999

Type	All Families	Without Wealthy Families (Net Worth < $2 Million)
Net worth	50	75
Assets	55	80
Home	91	100
Vehicles	76	82
Bank accounts	63	79
Stocks and mutual funds	59	84
401(K) and thrift	99	100
IRA/Keogh	55	76
Other real estate	41	74
Business equity	17	50
Other financial assets	71	100
Debts	90	101
Home mortgage	95	—
Vehicle loans	100	—
Other secured debts	100	—
Mortgage on rental property	42	—
Margin and broker accounts	30	—
Credit card and store debt	100	—
Loan from financial inst.	73	—

Source: Author's compilation, Czajka, Jacobson, and Cody 2003.

data in the SIPP are excellent, accounting for 90 percent of that in the SCF, net worth is hampered by the low amount of total assets such that the net worth in the SIPP is only 50 percent of that in the SCF. Excluding the very wealthy (those with $2 million or more net worth) greatly improves these percentages, particularly the quality of IRA-Keogh, stocks and mutual funds, and bank accounts. The one component that remains poor is business equity (50 percent). John Czajka and his colleagues' decomposition analysis shows that the SIPP wealth data fail to measure the assets of the very wealthy by underestimating the assets of the wealthy (accounting for 72 percent of the difference) and not measuring all assets (accounting for 13 percent). Their results support excluding the very wealthy when using the SIPP net worth and asset data.

Excluding the very wealthy, however, does not raise the percentile distribution to the SCF percentiles. We must keep in mind that the percentile distribution of net worth and assets is systematically lower in the SIPP than in the SCF. Table A.2 shows a set of selected percentiles in the SCF as the benchmark and the corresponding percentiles in the SIPP. For instance, the SCF tenth percentile of net worth is corresponding to the SIPP fifteenth percentile. Other examples for net worth are twenty-fifth versus thirty-first, fiftieth versus fifty-eighth, seventy-fifth versus eighty-first, ninetieth versus ninety-fourth, and ninety-fifth versus ninety-eighth. The assets distribution has smaller gaps up to the median and then remains similar to net worth above the median. In contrast, the SIPP debt distribution is in close agreement with the SCF debt distribution.

Four other findings from the SSA report are worth noting. First, SIPP ownership rates for checking and savings account, IRA and Keogh accounts, real estate other than the home, and other financial assets lag behind SCF rates. Second, the SIPP tracks the SCF in the growth of aggregate assets by type. Between 1993 and 1999, SIPP assets grew by 39 percent and SCF assets grew by 43 percent. The growth for financial as-

Table A2   **Corresponding SIPP and SCF Percentiles of Net Worth, Assets, and Debts, 1998**

Benchmark	Net Worth	Assets	Debts
SCF Percentile		SIPP Percentile	
10	15	13	10
20	26	24	20
25	31	29	25
50	58	56	50
75	81	81	75
90	94	94	90
95	98	98	95

Source: Author's compilation, Czajka, Jacobson, and Cody 2003.

sets was 81 percent for the SIPP and 78 percent for the SCF, and for property assets it was 25 percent for the SIPP and 24 percent for the SCF. Third, the distribution of assets was similar in 1992 between the SIPP and the SCF but the gap increased between 1992 and 1998. Over this period, the distribution of debts remained in close agreement between the SIPP and the SCF. Fourth, the SIPP shows stronger differentials than the SCF in median net worth by age, race, and income below 400 percent of poverty. For assets and debts, the differentials are very similar between the two surveys. These findings raise both concerns and confidence in this book's use of SIPP wealth data. Caution should be taken in analyses using data on IRA and Keogh accounts, real estate other than the home, and other financial assets. Confidence is strengthened when using multiple panels of the SIPP covering two decades because the time trends are very much in agreement with those in the SCF and when using the SIPP to study group differentials and wealth stratification because the group differentials in the SIPP are at least as strong as those in the SCF.

The SSA recommends two remedies. The first is reweighting the SIPP sample according to the SCF income distribution because the SIPP underrepresents the high-income households and it also slightly underrepresents the low-income households. The second is recoding based on econometric models to adjust the SIPP distributions of types of assets to more closely resemble the distributions in the SCF. The SSA report provides the reweighting factors and the recoding parameters for the year of 1998 only. These are not applicable to SIPP wealth data in other years.

Adjustments to Improve Data

Although the SSA's findings and recommendations are important, they are not entirely appropriate for the analyses required in this volume, for two reasons. If the SSA reweighting strategy is strictly followed, this study, which uses SIPP wealth data in multiple years would require reweighting factors constructed from the SCF for these years. Because the SCF surveys occur less frequently than the SIPP surveys and do not correspond to the years covered by the SIPP, reweighting factors for all the SIPP years cannot be constructed. Second, the SSA-recommended recoding strategy relies on important stratification variables such as race-ethnicity, education, age, household type, and income level. That is, the recoded asset variables are constructed with the coefficients for these grouping variables and other household characteristics estimated from the SCF, the value of the observed grouping variables and household characteristics in the SIPP, and random error terms generated from residuals of the same model using the SIPP. This strategy creates a more accurate wealth distribution of the whole population at the expense of losing power in detecting the grouping effects on wealth distribution. Because one of the primary objectives is to detect these grouping effects, this book does not adopt the recoding strategy. Instead, it will improve the quality of the wealth data in the SIPP by using a modified reweighting strategy, excluding the very wealthy households, and avoiding using asset components that are poorly measured.

First, the SFC is not the only source of income distribution weights. The Current Population Survey (CPS) also provides income distribution data that can be used to reweight the SIPP. There are three advantages in using the CPS income distribution. Its March Annual Demographic Supplement is the official source of estimates of income and poverty in the United States. Next, its annual data is available for all the SIPP years. Finally, it is fairly close to the SCF income distribution for 1998, according to the SSA report. My investigation of the differences in household income distribution between the SIPP and the CPS from 1984 to 2002 finds that the SIPP underrepresent both the upper and lower ends of the CPS income distribution. For the top quintile, the SIPP population counts on average only 17 percent, with a range from 15 percent to 18 percent. In particular, for the top 5 percent of the CPS income distribution, the SIPP population counts only 2 to 4 percent, and 3 percent on average. For the bottom quintile, the SIPP population counts 18 to 19 percent. As a result, for the middle 60 percent, the SIPP population counts 63 to 65 percent. Because income and wealth are highly correlated, these results support a reweighting strategy using the CPS income distribution to correct the underrepresentation of the two tails in the SIPP.[1]

Second, this volume excludes the very wealthy households. Given the potentially different wealth distributions of the SIPP in multiple years, a relative cut-off (the ninety-nine and a half percentile of net worth) is used.

Third, this book will focus on more reliable components of wealth, such as own home, interest-earning assets besides bank accounts, and all debt components, and it will avoid using poorly measured asset components such as real estate other than the home. Because business equity is an important topic among immigrants, a brief discussion on small business is included.

Tables A.3 and A.4 summarize the impact of the first two remedies on the quality of the SIPP wealth data. The first remedy is to reweight the SIPP net worth and assets data using the CPS income distribution. Comparisons are made between the CPS and the SCF reweightings. Table A3 presents the original SIPP, SCF-reweighted SIPP, and CPS-reweighted SIPP as proportion of the 1988 SCF for selected percentiles of net worth, total assets, and total debts. The SIPP data are from wave 9 of SIPP panel 1996 (late 1998 and early 1999) and the SCF data are from the SSA report. As documented in the SSA report, the percentiles of net worth in the original SIPP using the SIPP-provided sampling weights are severely underestimated for the lower and upper tails (column 1). For example, the twenty-fifth percentile is 30 percent of that of SCF and the ninety-ninth percentile is 32 percent of that in SCF. The median, seventy-fifth, ninetieth, and ninety-fifth percentiles are about two-thirds of those in SCF. Using the SCF reweighting factor provided by SSA, the SIPP percentiles improve by 3 to 8 percent (column 2). The CPS-reweighted results are very similar to the SCF-reweighted results, with a greater improvement up to the fiftieth percentile and a slightly smaller improvement for the upper tail (column 3). Columns 4 through 6 show that a similar pattern for assets as for net worth. The last three columns are for total debts. The original SIPP percentiles are slightly greater than those in SCF except for the ninety-ninth percentile. The two reweighting methods produce even greater gaps, suggesting no need for reweighting for debt data. These results suggest that CPS-reweighting is as effective as SCF-reweighting.

The second remedy is to exclude the very wealthy households. The analysis carried out in this volume excluded the top 0.5 percent of households. In order to compare the relative distribution of SIPP against the published SCF statistics (where the ninety-ninth and a half percentile is not available) we examine the wealth distribution up to the ninety-ninth percentile here. The percentiles for the total population will remain in the subpopulation, that is, the subpopulation will represent the lower 99 percent of the distribution rather than the full distribution. Table A.4 compares the aggregate shares of net worth, total assets, and total debts between SIPP and SCF for the year 2001. The SIPP data are from wave 3 of SIPP panel 2001 (late 2001 and early 2002). The SCF data are calculated based on the latest report on the 2001 SCF by Arthur Kennickell (2003). The table shows the results for the subpopulation without households with net worth above the ninety-ninth percentile. A general pattern for the total population from the SCF data is that one-third of the total net worth owned by households below the ninetieth percentile, one-third owned by households between the ninetieth and the ninety-ninth percentile, and one-third owned by households above the ninety-ninth percentile. By excluding the households above the ninety-ninth percentile, roughly one-half of the shares are owned by those below the ninetieth percentile and another half are owned by the ninetieth to the ninety-ninth percentile group, which is shown in the first column. The ninetieth to the ninety-ninth percentile group owns about 37 percent of the total net worth. Neither SCF-reweighting nor CPS-reweighting improves the under share for the ninety-fifth to the ninety-ninth percentile group in net worth. It does not improve the under share problem in total assets either.

In sum, the results from tables A.3 and A.4 confirm the effectiveness of our remedies. First, the CPS-reweighting strategy here is effective in correcting the bottom and top tail distribution of net worth and total assets. The degree of correction is similar to the SCF-reweighting strategy. The

Table A3 SIPP as Proportion of SCF, Selected Percentiles, 1998

Percentile	Net Worth			Asset			Debt		
	Original SIPP	SCF-rew. SIPP	CPS-rew. SIPP	Original SIPP	SCF-rew. SIPP	CPS-rew. SIPP	Original SIPP	CF-rew. SIPP	CPS-rew. SIPP
10	—[a]	—[a]	—[a]	0.38	0.36	0.43	—[a]	—[a]	—[a]
25	0.30	0.33	0.35	0.57	0.60	0.65	—[a]	—[a]	—[a]
50	0.58	0.63	0.65	0.80	0.85	0.87	1.05	1.18	1.22
75	0.66	0.72	0.71	0.75	0.81	0.81	1.04	1.13	1.14
90	0.66	0.74	0.72	0.69	0.78	0.76	1.04	1.11	1.10
95	0.58	0.65	0.64	0.62	0.71	0.68	1.04	1.15	1.14
99	0.32	0.36	0.34	0.59	0.69	0.65	0.83	0.90	0.89

Source: Author's compilation; Czajka, Jacobson, and Cody 2003.
[a] The SCF percentile is zero.

Table A4   Aggregate Shares of Net Worth Excluding Top 1 Percent of Households, 2001

Percentile groups	Net Worth				Assets				Debts			
	SCF	Original SIPP	SCF-rew. SIPP	CPS-rew. SIPP	SCF	Original SIPP	SCF-rew. SIPP	CPS-rew. SIPP	SCF	Original SIPP	SCF-rew. SIPP	CPS-rew. SIPP
0–50	4.1	2.4	2.5	2.8	7.9	11.8	11.0	11.7	27.6	35.3	33.0	34.2
50–90	40.7	50.7	49.4	50.3	42.3	49.8	49.0	49.6	51.0	47.6	47.9	47.7
90–95	18.0	19.2	19.3	19.1	16.6	16.3	16.6	16.4	9.2	9.2	9.8	9.5
95–99	37.2	27.8	28.8	27.8	33.2	22.1	23.4	22.4	12.3	7.9	9.3	8.6

Source: Author's compilation; Kennickell 2003.

results also confirm that it is not necessary to reweight the debt data. Second, excluding the top tail of the net worth distribution is effective to further overcome the underestimation of the very wealthy.

Analytic Sample

The study population in this book is restricted to households headed by those aged twenty-five to sixty-four years old. Households headed by individuals younger than twenty-five are excluded because they are less likely to start accumulating wealth. Elderly households are excluded because elderly immigrants may have a very different portfolio from elderly natives. Elderly immigrants are less likely to have social security and more likely to receive Supplemental Security Income (SSI) than do natives (Hu 1998; Hao and Kawano 2001). Thus elderly households deserve a separate study focusing on life-time employment, private and

Table A5   Selected Percentiles of Net Worth, Assets and Debts Among Households with Heads Aged Twenty-Five to Sixty-Four, 2001

	Net Worth			Assets		
Percentile	Original SIPP	SCF-rew. SIPP	CPS-rew. SIPP	Original SIPP	SCF-rew. SIPP	CPS-rew. SIPP
Households						
10	−4,000	−3,400	−3.450	2,600	2,500	2,750
25	3,350	3,800	4,354	15,775	16,500	18,620
50	49,374	54,500	56,500	120,000	128,600	132,520
75	171,354	192,100	192,750	272,104	299,762	300,800
90	402,668	459,550	449,170	530,911	611,609	594,360
95	638,352	751,300	715,375	801,541	926,903	893,775
99	1,536,420	1,816,268	1,717,519	1,752,208	2,130,161	2,026,225
Native households						
10	−3,721	−3,090	−3,092	3,145	3,100	3,600
25	4,650	5,162	5,404	20,854	22,854	25,800
50	55,650	61,400	63,050	128,650	136,850	140,550
75	181,925	203,354	203,300	281,200	309,499	309,922
90	418,707	479,899	468,570	546,425	632,372	611,400
95	659,939	777,062	734,444	823,986	943,228	914,118
Immigrant households						
10	−4,082	−3,410	−3,600	600	600	750
25	750	1,000	1,100	5,356	5,504	5,902
50	17,850	20,804	22,008	59,000	66,120	70,000
75	113,425	130,316	132,625	214,400	238,637	242,275
90	295,750	355,404	347,362	462,625	523,708	523,150
95	485,354	583,318	568,450	680,355	779,675	759,470

Source: Author's compilation.

Table A6   Household Samples in SIPP, 1984 to 2001 Panels

Panel	Wave (year)	Total Sample	Study Sample Total	Native	Immigrant
1984	3 (1984)	19,997	7,394	6,903	491
	7 (1985)	16,078	7,720	7,195	525
1985	3 (1985)	13,799	7,993	7,489	504
	7 (1987)	11,000	7,284	6,800	484
1986	4 (1987)	11,423	7,453	6,898	555
	7 (1988)	10,932	7,262	6,732	530
1987	7 (1988)	11,465	7,639	7,226	413
1990	4 (1991)	22,058	14,766	13,288	1,478
1991	7 (1993)	13,732	7,516	6,845	671
1992	4 (1993)	19,628	13,205	11,994	1,211
1993	7 (1995)	18,963	12,484	11,316	1,168
1996	3 (1996)	33,853	23,763	21,325	2,438
	6 (1997)	30,745	21,321	19,159	2,162
	9 (1998)	29,000	19,949	17,938	2,011
	12 (1999)	28,215	19,321	17,427	1,894
2001	3 (2001)	27,330	18,975	16,730	2,245
	6 (2002)	26,521	17,951	15,841	2,110
	9 (2003)	25,401	17,118	15,140	1,978
Total		370,140	239,114	216,246	22,868

Source: Author's calculation.
Note: To total sample includes households with heads whose age ranges 0 to 93. The study sample is defined as households headed by twenty-five to sixty-four year olds, are members of white, black, Hispanic, or Asian, and having valid data on immigrant status. The study sample also excludes the top 0.5 percent in the net worth distribution in each wave among the twenty-five to sixty-four year olds. The reduction in size from the full sample to the study sample is due to the definition and the fact that wealth data were collected in waves different from the wave when the migration history questions were asked (therefore considerable missing information on immigrant status). The study sample in 1984 is particularly small because the migration history was asked in Wave 8 when only three out of four rotation groups of the sample were interviewed and a larger attrition occurred in this late wave than earlier waves.

employer-provided pensions, social security, social insurance, and welfare programs.

Because the study population differs from the total population, it is necessary to examine how these aforementioned adjustments improve the wealth distribution of the study population and whether the improvements differ between native and immigrant households. Table A.5 presents selected percentiles of net worth, assets, and debts among households with heads aged twenty-five to sixty-four in 2001. Results in table A.5 show that the percentile distribution for the study population is similar to that for the total population. The CPS-reweighting does a better job than the SCF-reweighting in correcting underestimation up to the seventy-fifth percentile for the study population and the correction is similar for native and immigrant households.

The analytic sample for the book will vary for different analyses. For analysis of net worth, total assets, and total debts, pooled samples from eighteen cross-sections of all the available panels are used. For analysis of asset and debt components, seven cross-sections of the 1996 and 2001 panels are used. Because the latter is a subset of the former, we describe the size of the former by panel-wave and nativity in table A.6. The total sample (370,140) indicates the number of households interviewed in the particular panel wave; the study sample (216,246) is what is used in the book's analysis. Six criteria are used to construct the study sample. First, 10,596 households are eliminated because they have no sampling weight (meaning that they do not belong to the sample). Second, 606 households whose head is not the primary respondent. Third, 1,518 households with total net worth at the top 0.5 percent of the sample distribution of total net worth. Fourth, 96,490 households whose heads are younger than twenty-five or older than sixty-four. Fifth, 2,105 households with missing race-ethnicity information. Sixth, 19,711 households with missing migration history information, which is due to the fact that wealth data were collected in waves different from the wave when the migration history questions were asked. The study sample in 1984 is particularly small because the migration history was in wave 8 when only three-quarters of the sample was interviewed and a larger attrition occurred in this late wave than earlier waves.

=== Notes ===

Chapter 2

1. Our own analysis shows that Cuba, Colombia, Haiti, Nicaragua, Ethiopia, Somalia, and Libya have minimal property right protection.
2. Under the Immigration and Nationality Act (1952) 10,000 investor visas per year are available, which is about 1 percent of all immigrants admitted annually. The SIPP does not identify investors.

Chapter 3

1. The definition of wealth here does not include expected Social Security benefits and employer pensions. In my view, studying them separately is more appropriate than combining them with wealth defined here because Social Security and pension, which are large components of wealth, exist conditional on a long stay in the United States and a participation in the mainstream economy. Thus, including Social Security and pension may affect a study of variations in wealth among those who do not meet these conditions.
2. A good source of consumption data is consumer expenditure (CE) but it has a small sample, few years, and little information on immigration.
3. There are many different definitions of liquid assets. For example, Haveman and Wolff (2004) consider either total net worth or financial assets excluding IRAs and pension assets.
4. About 800 Asian-origin households are headed by individuals older than fifty-five to sixty-four.

Chapter 4

1. The percentage for native white is not exactly the same as in table 3.1 because table 4.2 uses seven cross-sections of data from 1996 to 2003 and table 3.1 uses eighteen from 1984 to 2003.
2. Note that the majority of Dominican immigrants live in New York City, where real estate is very expensive.
3. Note that this threshold is set for liquid financial wealth, which is different

from the sufficient wealth holding status defined previously when the total wealth, including illiquid and quasi-liquid components such as the home and IRAs.

4. Because none of the sample Guatemalan immigrants has an IRA or Keogh account, the adjustment does not make any changes.

5. Some people own a business but do not necessarily operate it.

Chapter 5

1. Because of small sample sizes of households with second mortgages within each immigrant group, the negative home equity rates among households with second mortgages are not examined.

Chapter 7

1. We take the exponential of this coefficient and then subtract 1 from the resulting value,

$$100 \cdot (e^{-1.962} - 1)\% = 100 \cdot (0.141 - 1)\% = -85.9\%.$$

For small values (between -0.3 and 0.3) of the estimated coefficient, this is approximately $100\hat{\beta}\%$. For coefficients beyond this range, we use the precise formula.

2. In principle, model 3 can be applied to different classes, measured by different education groups. Going along with the attention to wealth gaps among racial-ethnic groups, the following analysis focuses on the separate analysis. for racial-ethnic groups.

3. To obtain this interpretation, I take the first derivative of log positive net worth with respect to age, set this derivative to 0 and solve for the age at which log net worth reaches the maximum:

$$age = \frac{-0.2245}{2(-0.0017)} = 66.$$

4. With a cross-section of data, one cannot identify each of the three variables in the linear combination of age = period – birth-year or the linear combination of age-at-arrival = period-at-arrival – birth-year.

5. We can take the log of only positive values.

Chapter 8

1. State unemployment rate data is from the Bureau of Labor Statistics (BLS) and covers the years from 1984 to 2003.

2. Take the black-white dissimilarity D_{wb} as an example, which is expressed as

$$D_{wb} = 100 \cdot \left(\frac{1}{2} \sum_{i}^{I} \left| \frac{w_i}{w} - \frac{b_i}{b} \right| \right),$$

where w and b denote the number of whites and blacks living in a MSA, respectively, i is the subscript for census tracts and I is the total number of census tracts in that MSA. The dissimilarity index addresses the evenness dimension of segregation. It ranges from 0 to 100, with 100 indicating the most uneven distribution. Usually the index is interpreted as the percentage of one of the two groups that would have to move in order to produce evenness. This interpretation does not preserve tract densities and is asymmetric, considering only one group's move. A more sensible interpretation is that the index is the sum of the minimal percentage of each group that has to move across census tracts in order to achieve evenness. To get the exact minimal percentage of whites pct_w and that of blacks pct_b, we need to decompose D_{wb} as:

$$D_{wb} = pct_w + pct_b = \frac{b}{b+w} \cdot D_{wb} + \frac{w}{b+w} \cdot D_{wb}.$$

3. This is calculated by

$$100 \cdot (e^{-.0376} - 1)\% = -3.7\%.$$

4. This is concluded from a likelihood ratio test (not presented here).
5. The potential multicollinearity threat of the four contextual variables was tested. It was found that no such threat exists.

Appendix

1. The same definition of household is used as that in CPS, that is, sub- and secondary families and secondary individuals are included in households. Note that the SCF uses primary economic unit, equivalent to the census primary families and individuals, excluding sub- and secondary families and individuals. Because the share of net worth held by sub- and secondary families and individuals is very small (0.44 percent), households are defined as the unit of analysis, which is consistent with most previous research on wealth.

═══ References ═══

Agarwal, Reena, and Andrew W. Horowitz. 2002. "Are International Remittances Altruism or Insurance? Evidence from Guyana Using Multiple-Migrant Households." *World Development* 30(11): 2033–44.

Alba, Richard D., Nancy Denton, Shu-Yin Leung, and John Logan. 1995. "Neighborhood Change Under Conditions of Mass Immigration: The New York City Region: 1970–1990." *International Migration Review*. 29: 625–56.

Alba, Richard D., and John Logan. 1991. "Variations on Two Themes: Racial and Ethnic Patterns in the Attainment of Suburban Residence." *Demography* 28(3): 431–53.

Alba, Richard D., and Victor Nee. 2003. *Remaking the American Mainstream: Assimilation and Contemporary Immigration*. Cambridge, Mass.: Harvard University Press.

Aldrich, Howard E., and Roger Waldinger. 1990. "Ethnicity and Entrepreneurship." *Annual Review of Sociology* 16: 111–35.

Altonji, Joseph G., and David Card. 1991. "The Effects of Immigration on the Labor Market Outcomes of Less-Skilled Natives." In *Immigration, Trade, and the Labor Market*, edited by John M. Abowd and Richard B. Freeman. Chicago, Ill.: University of Chicago Press.

Avery, Robert B., and Arthur B. Kennickell. 1989. "Measurement of Household Saving Obtained from First-Differencing Wealth Estimates." Paper presented at the Twenty-First General Conference of the International Association for Research in Income and Wealth. Lahnstein, West Germany (August 20–26, 1989).

Bean, Frank D., and Gillian Stevens. 2003. *America's Newcomers and the Dynamics of Diversity*. New York: Russell Sage Foundation.

Bean, Frank D., Jennifer V.W. Van Hook, and Mark A. Fossett. 1999. "Immigration, Spatial and Economic Change, and African American Employment." In *Immigration and Opportunity: Race, Ethnicity, and Employment in The United States*, edited by Frank D. Bean, Stephanie Bell-Rose. New York: Russell Sage Foundation.

Bean, Frank D., Jennifer V.W. Van Hook, and Jennifer E. Glick. 1997. "Country of Origin, Type of Public Assistance, and Patterns of Welfare Recipiency among U.S. Immigrants and Natives." *Social Science Quarterly* 78(2): 432–51.

Becker, Gary S. 1964. *Human Capital: A Theoretical and Empirical Analysis, with Special Reference to Education*. New York: National Bureau of Economic Research.

Becker, Gary S., and Nigel Tomes. 1979. "An Equilibrium Theory of the Distribution of Income and Intergenerational Mobility." *Journal of Political Economy* 87(6): 1153–189.

Bernhardt, Annette, Martina Morris, Mark S. Handcock, and Marc A. Scott. 2001. *Divergent Paths: Economic Mobility in the New American Labor Market*. New York: Russell Sage Foundation.

Borjas, George J. 1987. "Self-Selection and the Earning of Immigrants." *American Economic Review* 77(4): 531–53.

———. 1994. "The Economics of Immigration." *Journal of Economic Literature* 32(4): 1667–717.

———. 1999. *Heaven's Door: Immigration Policy and The American Economy*. Princeton, N.J.: Princeton University Press.

Borjas, George J., Richard B. Freeman, and Lawrence F. Katz. 1996. "Searching for the Effect of Immigration on the Labor Market." Working Paper 5454. Cambridge, Mass: National Bureau of Economic Research.

Borjas, George J., and Lynette Hilton. 1996. "Immigration and the Welfare State: Immigrant Participation in Means-Tested Entitlement Programs." *The Quarterly Journal of Economics* CVXI: 576–604.

Bound, John, and Harry J. Holzer. 1993. "Industrial Shifts, Skills Levels, and the Labor Market for White and Black Males." *The Review of Economics and Statistics* 75(3): 387–96.

Bradford, Calvin. 2002. *Risk or Race? Racial Disparities and the Subprime Refinance Market*. Washington: The Neighborhood Revitalization Project, Center for Community Change.

Carroll, Christopher D. 1997. "Buffer-stock Saving and the Life Cycle/Permanent Income Hypothesis." *Quarterly Journal of Economics* 112(1): 1–55.

Carroll, Christopher D., Byung-Kun Rhee, and Changyong Rhee. 2000. "Does Cultural Origin Affect Saving Behavior? Evidence from Immigrants." *Economic Development and Cultural Change* 48(1): 33–50.

Castro, Max J. 2002. "The New Cuban Immigration in Context." Paper 58. Coral Gables, Fla.: The Dante B. Fascell North-South Center, University of Miami.

Center for Housing Policy. 2006. "A Heavy Load: The Combined Housing and Transportation Burdens of Working Families." Washington, D.C.: The Center for Public Housing. http://www.nhc.org/index/chp-research-publications.

Chami, Ralph, Connel Fullenkamp, and Samir Jahjah. 2003. "Are Immigrant Remittance flows a Source of Capital for Development?" IMF Working Paper 03/189. Washington: International Monetary Fund.

Charles, Kerwin, and Erik Hurst. 2002. "The Transition to Home Ownership and the Black-White Wealth Gap." *The Review of Economics and Statistics* 84(2): 281–97.

Chiswick, Barry R. 1978. "The Effect of Americanization on the Earnings of Foreign-Born Men." *Journal of Political Economy* 86(5): 897–922.

Citro, Constance F., and Robert T. Michael. 1995. *Measuring Poverty: A New Approach*. Washington: National Academy Press.

Coleman, James S. 1988. "Social Capital in the Creation of Human Capital." *American Journal of Sociology*. 94(Supple.): S95–120.

Conley, Dalton. 1999. *Being Black, Living in the Red: Race, Wealth, and Social Policy in America*. Berkeley, Calif.: University of California Press.

Cummins, James P. 1981. "Age on Arrival and Immigrant Second Language Learning in Canada: A Reassessment." *Applied Linguistics* 2(2): 132–49.

Curtin, Philip. 1976. "The Atlantic Slave Trade, 1600–1800." In *History of West*

Africa, edited by Jacob Ajayi and Michael Crowder. New York: Columbia University Press.

Czajka, John L., Jonathan E. Jacobson, and Scott Cody. 2003. "Survey Estimates of Wealth: A Comparative Analysis and Review of the Survey of Income and Program Participation." Final Report submitted to Social Security Administration. Washington: Mathematica Policy Research.

Doeringer, Peter, and Michael Piore. 1971. *Internal Labor Markets and Manpower Analysis*. Lexington, Mass.: Lexington.

Durkin, Thomas A. 2000. "Credit Cards: Use and Consumer Attitudes, 1970–2000." *Federal Reserve Bulletin* September 2000: 623–34. http://www.federalreserve.gov/pubs/bulletin/2000/0900lead.pdf.

Durnev, Art, Kan Li, Randall Morck, and Bernard Yeung. 2004. "Capital Markets and Capital Location: Implications for Economies in Transition." *Economics of Transition* 12(4): 593–634.

Federal Reserve Statistical Release. 2000. "Consumer Credit." G-19, June 7, 2000. Washington: Federal Reserve Board. http://www.federalreserve.gov/releases/g19/20000607.

Fix, Michael, and Jeffery S. Passel. 1994. *Immigration and Immigrants: Setting the Record Straight*. Washington: Urban Institute Press.

Foner, Nancy. 1997. "What's New about Transnationalism? New York Immigrants Today and at the Turn of the Century." *Diaspora* 6(3): 355–75.

Fossett, Mark, and Warren Waren. 2005. "Overlooked Implications of Ethnic Preferences for Residential Segregation in Agent-based Models" *Urban Studies* 42(11): 1893–917.

Frey, William H., and Reynolds Farley. 1996. "Latino, Asian, and Black Segregation in U.S. Metropolitan Areas: Are Multi-ethnic Metros Different?" *Demography* 33(1): 35–50.

Gale, William G., and John Karl Scholz. 1994. "IRAs and Household Saving." *American Economic Review* 84(5): 1233–60.

Gallup Poll. 2007. "Gallup's Pulse of Democracy: Immigration" http://institution.gallup.com/documents/topics.aspx.

Glazer, Nathan, and Daniel P. Moynihan. 1963. *Beyond the Melting Pot: The Negroes, Puerto Ricans, Jews, Italians, and Irish of New York City*. Cambridge, Mass.: M.I.T. Press.

Goldscheider, Frances K., and Julie DaVanzo. 1989. "Pathways to Independent Living in Early Adulthood: Marriage, Semiautonomy, and Premarital Residential Independence." *Demography* 26(4): 597–614.

Goldscheider, Frances K., and Linda J. Waite. 1991. *New Families, No Families? The Transformation of the American Home*. Berkeley, Calif.: University of California Press.

Gordon, Milton M. 1964. *Assimilation in American Life: The Role of Race, Religion, and National Origins*. New York: Oxford University Press.

Grogger, Jeff, and Eric Eide. 1995. "Changes in College Skills and the Rise in the College Wage Premium." *The Journal of Human Resources*, 30(2): 280–310.

Hamermesh, Daniel, and Frank D. Bean. 1998. *Help or Hindrance?: The Economic Implications of Immigration from African Americans*. New York: Russell Sage Foundation.

Hao, Lingxin. 1996. "Family Structure, Private Transfers, and the Economic Well-Being of Families with Children." *Social Forces* 75(1): 269–92.

———. 2004. "Wealth of Immigrant and Native-Born Americans." *International Migration Review* 38(1): 518–46.

———. 2006. "The Complexity of Returns to Education: Race, Nativity, and Country and Field of Degree." Presented at the 2006 NSF Workshop on Human Resources. Arlington, Va. (October 20, 2006).

Hao, Lingxin, and Yukio Kawano. 2001. "Immigrants' Welfare Use and Opportunity for Coethnic Contact." *Demography* 38(3): 375–89.

Harrison, Lawrence. 1992. *Who Prospers?* New York: Basic Books.

Hart, Elva Treviño. 1999. *Barefoot Heart: Stories of a Migrant Child.* Tempe, Ariz.: Bilingual Press.

Haveman, Robert, and Edward N. Wolff. 2004. "The Concept and Measurement of Asset Poverty: Levels, Trends and Composition for the U.S., 1983–2001." *Journal of Economic Inequality* 2(2): 145–69.

Hu, W.Y. 1998. "Elderly Immigrants on Welfare." *Journal of Human Resources* 33(3): 711–41.

Huddle, Donald L., Arthur F. Corwin, and Gordon J. MacDonald. 1985. *Illegal Immigration: Job Displacement and Social Costs.* Alexandria, Va.: American Immigration Control Foundation.

Iceland, John. 2004. "Beyond Black and White—Metropolitan Residential Segregation in Multi-ethnic America." *Social Science Research* 33(2): 248–71.

Jasso, Guillermina, and Mark R. Rosenzweig. 1990. "Self-Selection and the Earning of Immigrants: Comment." *American Economic Review* 80(1): 298–304.

Jasso, Guillermina, Mark R. Rosenzweig, and James P. Smith. 2000. "The Changing Skills of New Immigrants to the United States: Recent Trends and Their Determinants." In *Issues in the Economics of Immigration*, edited by George Borjas. Chicago, Ill.: University of Chicago Press.

Johnson, James H., Jr., and Melvin Oliver. 1989. " Interethnic Minority Conflict in Urban America: The Effects of Economic and Social Dislocations." *Urban Geography* 10(5): 449–63.

Jones-Correa, Michael. 1998. *Between Two Nations: The Political Predicament of Latinos in New York City.* Ithaca, N.Y.: Cornell University Press.

Kao, Grace, and Martha Tienda. 1995. "Optimism and Achievement: The Educational Performance of Immigrant Youth." *Social Science Quarterly* 76(1): 1–19.

Keister, Lisa A. 2000. *Wealth in America.* Cambridge: Cambridge University Press.

Keister, Lisa A., and Stephanie Moller. 2000. "Wealth Inequality in the United States." *Annual Review of Sociology* 26: 63–81.

Kennickell, Arthur B. 2003. "A Rolling Tide: Changes in the Distribution of Wealth in the U.S., 1998–2001." Washington: Survey of Consumer Finances, Federal Research Board.

Kim, Pan S., and Gregory B. Lewis. 1994. "Asian-Americans in the Public-Service: Success, Diversity, and Discrimination." *Public Administration Review* 54(3): 285–90.

Krivo, Lauren J., and Robert L. Kaufman. 1999. "How Low Can It Go? Declining Black-White Segregation in a Multiethnic Context." *Demography* 36(1): 93–109.

La Porta, Rafael, Florencio De Silanes Lopez, Andrei Shleifer, and Robert W. Vishny. 1998. "Law and Finance." *Journal of Political Economy* 106(6): 1112–55.

Levine, Ross. 1997. "Financial Development and Economic Growth: Views and Agenda." *Journal of Economic Literature* 35(2): 688–726.

Lewis, Gordon. 1983. *Main Currents in Caribbean Thought: The Historical Evolution of Carib Society in its Ideological Aspects, 1492–1900.* Baltimore, Md.: Johns Hopkins University Press.

Lewis Mumford Center. 2002. "Metropolitan Racial and Ethnic Change—Census 2000." Albany, N.Y.: Lewis Mumford Center for Comparative Urban and Regional Research, the University at Albany, SUNY. http://mumford.albany.edu/census/data.html.

———. 2003. "Metropolitan Racial and Ethnic Change - Census 2000." Albany, N.Y.: Lewis Mumford Center for Comparative Urban and Regional Research, the University at Albany, SUNY. http://mumford.albany.edu/census/data.html.

Light, Ivan. 1972. *Ethnic Enterprise in America: Business and Welfare among Chinese, Japanese, and Blacks.* Berkeley, Calif.: University of California Press.

Light, Ivan, and Parminder Bhachu. 1993. "Introduction: California Immigrants in World Perspective." In *Immigration and Entrepreneurship: Culture, Capital, and Ethnic Networks,* edited by Ivan Light and Parminder Bhachu. New Brunswick, N.J.: Transaction Publishers.

Light, Ivan, and Edna Bonacich. 1988. *Immigrant Entrepreneurs: Koreans in Los Angeles, 1965–1982.* Berkeley, Calif.: University of California Press.

Logan, John R., Richard D. Alba, and Wenquan Zhang . 2002. "Immigrant Enclaves and Ethnic Communities in New York and Los Angeles." *American Sociological Review* 67(2): 299–322.

Lopez, David. 2001. "Los Angeles: Transnational City of Melange of Transnational Communities?" Paper presented at the annual meeting of the American Sociological Association. Anaheim, Calif. (August 18–21, 2001).

Lowell, B. Lindsay. 2002. "Remittance Projections: Mexico and Central America, 2002–2030." In *Billions in Motion: Latino Immigrants, Remittances and Banking,* by Robert Suro, Sergio Bendixen, Lindsay Lowell, and Dulce Benevides. Washington: Pew Hispanic Center.

Lucas, Robert E.B., and Oded Stark. 1985. "Motivations to Remit: Evidence from Botswana." *Journal of Political Economy* 93(5): 901–18.

Lundberg, Shelly, and Elaina Rose. 2003. "Investments in Sons and Daughters: Evidence from the Consumer Expenditure Survey." Prepared for the Joint Center for Poverty Research, September Research Institute conference, Family Investments in Children: Resources and Behaviors that Promote Success. Chicago, Ill. (September 19-20, 2002).

Lupton, Joseph P. and James P. Smith. 2003. "Marriage, Assets, and Savings." In *Marriage and the Economy: Theory and Evidence from Advanced Industrialized Societies,* edited by Shoshana Grossbard-Schecht. Cambridge: Cambridge University Press.

Lyman, Stanford M. 1974. *Chinese Americans.* New York: Random House.

Manning, Robert D. 2000. *Credit Card Nation: The Consequences of America's Addiction to Credit.* New York: Basic Books.

Martin, Philip L. 1986. *Illegal Immigration and the Colonization of the American Labor Market.* CIS Paper No. 1. Washington: Center for Immigration Studies.

Masnick, George S. 2001. "Home Ownership Trends and Racial Inequality in the United States in the 20th Century." Working Paper W01-4. Cambridge, Mass.: Joint Center for Housing Studies, Harvard University. http://www.jchs.harvard.edu/publications/homeownership/masnick_w01-4.pdf.

Mason, William M., and Stephen E. Fienberg. 1985. "Introduction: Beyond the identification problem." In *Cohort Analysis in Social Research: Beyond the identification problem*, edited by William Mason and Stephen Fienberg. New York: Springer-Verlag.

Massey, Douglas S., Joaquin Arango, Graeme Hugo, Ali Kouaouci, Adela Pellegrino, and J. Edward Taylor. 1993. "Theories of International Migration: Review and Appraisal." *Population and Development Review* 19(3): 431–66.

Massey, Douglas S., and Nancy A. Denton. 1993. *American Apartheid: Segregation and the Making of the Underclass*. Cambridge, Mass.: Harvard University Press.

Massey, Douglas S., Jorge Durand, and Nolan J. Malone. 2002. *Beyond Smoke and Mirrors: Mexican Immigration in an Era of Economic Integration*. New York: Russell Sage Foundation.

McCall, Leslie. 2000. "Explaining Levels of Within-Group Wage Inequality in U.S. Labor Markets." *Demography* 37(4): 415–30.

———. 2001. "Sources of Racial Wage Inequality in Metropolitan Labor Markets: Racial, Ethnic, and Gender Differences." *American Sociological Review* 66(4): 520–41.

McDonald, John F., and Robert A. Moffitt. 1980. "The Uses of Tobit Analysis." *The Review of Economics and Statistics* 62(2): 318–21

McDonnell, Patrick J. 1994. "As Change Again Overtakes Compton, So Do Tensions." *Los Angeles Times*, August 21, p. 1A.

Menjívar, Cecilia. 2000. *Fragmented Ties: Salvadoran Immigrant Networks in America*. Berkeley, Calif.: University of California Press.

Miers, Suzanne, and Igor Kopytoff. 1977. *Slavery in Africa: Historical and Anthropological Perspectives*. Madison, Wisc.: The University of Wisconsin Press.

Modigliani, Franco. 1986. "Life Cycle, Individual Thrift, and the Wealth of Nation." *American Economic Review* 76(3): 297–313.

Moore, Joan, and Raquel Pinderhughes. 1993. "Introduction." In *In the Barrios: Latinos and the Underclass Debate*, edited by Joan W. Moore and Raquel Pinderhughes. New York: Russell Sage Foundation.

Morales, Rebecca, and Frank Bonilla. 1993. *Latinos in a Changing U.S. Economy : Comparative Perspectives on Growing Inequality*. Newbury Park, Calif.: Sage Publications.

Morck, Randall, Bernard Yeung and Wayne Yu (2000). "The Information Content of Stock Markets: Why Do Emerging Markets Have Synchronous Stock Price Movements." *Journal of Financial Economics* 58(1): 215–60

Muller, Thomas, and Thomas J. Espenshade. 1985. *The Fourth Wave: California's Newest Immigrants*. Washington: The Urban Institute Press.

Myers, Dowell, and Seong W. Lee. 1996. "Immigration Cohorts and Residential Overcrowding in Southern California." *Demography* 33(1): 51–65.

Myers, Samuel L., Jr., and Tsze Chan. 1995. "Racial Discrimination in Housing Markets: Accounting for Credit Risk." *Social Science Quarterly* 76(3): 543–61.

National Predatory Lending Task Force. 2000. *Curbing Predatory Home Mortgage Lending: A Joint Report* (June). Washington: U.S. Department of Housing and Urban Development and U.S. Department of Treasury. http://www.hud.gov:80/pressrel/treasrpt.pdf.

Ogbu, John U. 1978. *Minority Education and Caste: The American System in Cross-Cultural Perspective*. New York: Academic Press.

Oliver, Melvin L., and Thomas Shapiro. 1995. *Black Wealth/White Wealth: A New Perspective on Racial Inequality.* New York: Routledge.

Orshansky, Mollie. 1965. "Counting the Poor: Another Look at the Poverty Profile", *Social Security Bulletin* 28(1, January): 3–29.

Otsuka, Misuzu. 2004. *Essays on Household Portfolio and Current Account Dynamics.* Ph.D. diss., Johns Hopkins University.

Park, Robert E. 1930. "Assimilation, Social." In *Encyclopedia of the Social Sciences,* edited by Edwin Seligman and Alvin Johnson. New York: Macmillan.

Pedraza, Silvia, and Ruben Rumbaut 1996. *Origins and Destinies: Immigration Race, and Ethnicity in America.* New York: Wadsworth Publishing.

Piore, Michael J. 1979. *Birds of Passage: Migrant Labor in Industrial Societies.* New York: Cambridge University Press.

Polachek, Solomon W. 1975. "Differences in Expected Post-School Investment as a Determinant of Market Wage Differentials." *International Economic Review* 16: 451–70.

Portes, Alejandro, and Robert L. Bach. 1985. *Latin Journey: Cuban and Mexican Immigrants in the United States.* Berkeley, Calif.: University of California Press.

Portes, Alejandro, Luis Eduardo Guarnizo, and William J. Haller. 2002. "Transnational Entrepreneurs: An Alternative Form of Immigrant Economic Adaptation." *American Sociological Review* 67(2): 278–98.

Portes, Alejandro, and Ruben G. Rumbaut. 1996. *Immigrant America: A Portrait,* 2nd ed. Berkeley: University of California Press.

Portes, Alejandro, and John Walton. 1981. *Labor, Class, and the International System.* New York: Academic Press.

Portes, Alejandro, and Min Zhou. 1993. "The New Second Generation: Segmented Assimilation and Its Variants." *The Annals of the American Academy of Political and Social Science* 530(1): 74–96.

———. 1996. "Self-Employment and the Earnings of Immigrants." *American Sociological Review* 61(2): 219–30.

Ranis, Gustav, and John C.H. Fei. 1961. "A Theory of Economic Development." *American Economic Review* 51(4): 533–65.

Reardon, Elaine. 1998. "Demand-Side Changes and the Relative Economic Progress of Black Men: 1940–90." *The Journal of Human Resources* 32(1): 69–97.

Rumbaut, Ruben G. 1994. "Origins and Destinations: Immigration to the United States Since World War II." *Sociological Forum* 9(4): 583–621.

Ryder, Norman B. 1964. "Notes on the Concept of a Population." *American Journal of Sociology* 69(5): 447–63.

Sanders, Jimy M., and Victor Nee. 1996. "Immigrant Self-Employment: The Family as Social Capital and the Value of Human Capital." *American Sociological Review* 61(2): 231–49.

Santiago, Anne M. 1991. "The Spatial Dimensions of Ethnic and Racial Stratification." Research Report 91-230. Ann Arbor, Mich.: Population Studies Center, The University of Michigan.

Sassen, Saskia. 1991. *The Global City: New York, London, Tokyo.* Princeton, N.J.: Princeton University Press.

Saxenian, AnnaLee. 2006. *The New Argonauts: Regional Advantage in a Global Economy.* Boston, Mass.: Harvard University Press.

Schill, Michael H., and Susan M. Wachter. 1994. "Borrower and Neighborhood

Racial and Income Characteristics and Financial Institution Mortgage Application Screening." *Journal of Real Estate Finance and Economics* 9(3): 223–39.

Schiller, Nina G., Linda Basch, and Cristina Blanc-Szanton. 1995. "From Immigrant to Transmigrant: Theorizing Transnational Migration." *Anthropological Quarterly* 68(1): 48–63.

Shapiro, Thomas M. 2004. *The Hidden Cost of Being African American: How Wealth Perpetuates Inequality.* New York: Oxford University Press.

Shleifer, Andrei. 1994. "Establishing Property Rights." World Bank, Proceedings of the Annual Conference on Development Economics. Washington (April 1994).

Smith, James P. 1995a. "Racial and Ethnic Differences in Wealth in the Health and Retirement Study." *Journal of Human Resources* 30(5): S159–83.

———. 1995b. "Marriage, Assets, and Savings." Working Paper Series 95-08. Santa Monica, Calif.: RAND Labor and Population Program.

Smith, James P., and Barry Edmonston. 1997. *The New Americans: Economic, Demographic, and Fiscal Effects of Immigration.* Washington: National Academy Press.

Smith, Kirby, and Hugo Llorens. 1998. "Renaissance and Decay: A Comparison of Socioeconomic Indicators in the pre-Castro and Current Day Cuba." In *Cuba in Transition, vol. 8. Papers and Proceedings of the 8th Annual Meeting of the Association for the Study of the Cuban Economy (ASCE).* Austin, Tex.: University of Texas at Austin. Latin American Network Information Center. http://lanic.utexas.edu/la/cb/cuba/asce/cuba8/30smith.pdf.

Smith, Robert. 1998. "Transnational Localities: Community, Technology, and the Politics of Membership within the Context of Mexico-U.S. Migration." In *Transnationalism from Below: Comparative Urban and Community Research*, Vol. 6, edited by Michael P. Smith and Luis Guarnizo. New Brunswick, N.J.: Rutgers University Press.

Spilerman, Seymour. 2000. "Wealth and Stratification Processes." *Annual Review of Sociology* 26: 497–524.

Stark, Oded, and David E. Bloom. 1985. "The New Economics of Labor Migration." *American Economic Review* 75(2): 173–78.

Sturges-Vera, Karen. 1990. "Historical Setting." In *Colombia: A Country Study*, edited by Dennis Hanratty and Sandra Meditz. Washington: Federal Research Division, Library of Congress.

Suro, Robert, Sergio Bendixen, Lindsay Lowell, and Dulce Benevides. 2003. *Billions in Motion: Latino Immigrants, Remittances, and Banking.* Washington: Pew Hispanic Center.

Todaro, Michael P., and Lydia Maruszko. 1987. "Illegal Migration and U.S. Immigration Reform: A Conceptual Framework." *Population and Development Review* 13(1): 101–14.

UNESCO Institute for Statistics. 2002. "Percentage Distribution of Population by Educational Attainment." Montreal, Quebec: UNESCO Institute for Statistics. http://www.uis.unesco.org.

———. 2005. "Cuba — Education System." IAU Online Databases. Montreal, Quebec: UNESCO Institute for Statistics, International Association of Universities. http://www.unesco.org/iau/onlinedatabases/systems_data/cu.rtf.

U.S. Bureau of Labor Statistics. 2007. Data extracted from regional resources. Washington: U.S. Department of Labor. http://www.bls.gov/lau.

U.S. Census Bureau. 2003. "The Foreign-Born Population: 2000." Washington: U.S. Government Printing Office. http:/www.census.gov./prod/2003pubs/c2kbr-34.pdf.

————. 2004. *Income, Poverty, and Health Insurance Coverage in the United States: 2003.* Current Population Reports P60-226. Washington: U.S. Government Printing Office.

U.S. Department of Housing and Urban Development. 2000. *Unequal Burden in Atlanta: Income and Racial Disparities in Subprime Lending.* Washington: U.S. Department of Housing and Urban Development.

U.S. General Accounting Office. 1993. *Tax Policy: Many Factors Contributed to the Growth in Home Equity Financing in the 1980s.* GAO/GGD-93-63. Washington: U.S. Government Printing Office.

Van Lehman, Dan, and Omar Eno. 2003. *The Somali Bantu: Their History and Culture.* Culture Profile No. 16. Washington, D.C.: The Cultural Orientation Resource Center, Center for Applied Linguistics

Waldinger, Roger. 1996. *Still the Promised City? African-Americans and New Immigrants in Postindustrial New York.* Cambridge, Mass.: Harvard University Press.

Warner, William L,. and Leo Scrole. 1945. *The Social Systems of American Ethnic Groups.* New Haven, Conn.: Yale University Press.

Warren, Elizabeth, and Amelia Warren Tyagi. 2003. *The Two-Income Trap: Why Middle-Class Mothers and Fathers Are Going Broke.* New York: Basic Books.

Waters, Mary C. 1999. *Black Identities: West Indian Immigrant Dreams and American Realities.* Cambridge, Mass.: Harvard University Press.

Western, Bruce. 2002. "The Impact of Incarceration on Wage Mobility and Inequality." *American Sociological Review* 67(4): 477–908.

Wilson, William J. 1987. *The Truly Disadvantaged: The Inner City, the Underclass, and Public Policy.* Chicago, Ill.: University of Chicago Press.

————. 1996. *When Work Disappears: The World of the New Urban Poor.* New. York: Alfred A. Knopf.

World Bank. 2005. "World Development Indicators 2005." Washington, D.C.: International Bank for Reconstruction and Development/The World Bank. http://www.worldbank.org/data, http://devdata.worldbank.org/wdi2005/index2.htm.

Zeng, Zhen, and Yu Xie. 2004. "The Earnings Disadvantage of Asian Americans Reexamined—the Role of Place of Education." *American Journal of Sociology* 109(5): 1075–108.

Zhou, Min, and Carl L. Bankston III. 1998. *Growing Up American: How Vietnamese Children Adapt to Life in the United States.* New York: Russell Sage Foundation.

Index

Tables and figures in **bold.**

labor market impact of, 253–6
positively and negatively selected, distinction between, 18
public opinion regarding, 5
racial-ethnicity-nativity stratification system and, 271–2 (*see also* racial-ethnicity-nativity stratification system)
self-selection of (*see* self-selection of immigrants)
social context and, 272–4 (*see also* contextual conditions of wealth attainment)
wealth as an indicator of economic prospects of, 52
Immigration Act of 1924, 134, 138, 142–4
Immigration Act of 1990, 83, 139, 143
Immigration and Nationality Act of 1952, 293*n*2
Amendments of 1965 (*see* Immigration and Naturalization Act of 1965)
Immigration and Naturalization Act of 1965, 134, 138, 142–5, 185, 225
immigration policies of the United States
Asian immigration and, 134
Chinese immigration and, 138–9
Cuban immigration and, 86
Filipino immigration and, 143
Guatemalan immigration and, 84
Haitian immigration and, 183
Indian immigration and, 144–5
Jamaican immigration and, 185
Japanese immigration and, 142
Mexican immigration and, 84–85
Salvadoran immigration and, 83
Immigration Reform and Control Act of 1986 (IRCA), 84
immigration theory. *See* international migration theories
India, 144–45. *See also* Asian immigrants
individual retirement accounts (IRAs), 117. *See also* retirement accounts
integrated framework for wealth ac-

cumulation. *See* racial-ethnicity-nativity stratification system
intergenerational transfers, 31, 44
international migration theories, 14
challenge to, 31–32
cumulative causation of migration theory, 19
as modifying wealth theory, 33–40
neoclassical economic theory of migration, 14–15
new economics of labor migration theory, 15–16
relative inequality theory of migration, 18–19
segmented labor market theory of migration, 16–18
world systems theory of migration, 16
IRCA. *See* Immigration Reform and Control Act of 1986

Jacobson, Jonathan, 283
Jahjah, Samir, 127
Jamaica, 185, 278. *See also* black immigrants
Japan, 141–2. *See also* Asian immigrants
Jasso, Guilermina, 18

Kennickell, Arthur, 287
Kenya, 187. *See also* black immigrants
Keogh plans, 117. *See also* retirement accounts
Kopytoff, Igor, 181
Korea, South. *See* South Korea
Korean War, 145–6

labor markets
immigration-induced competition in, 253–6
local conditions as context for wealth attainment, 247–8, 272–3
primary and secondary, distinction between, 16
Latino immigrants
Asian immigrants and, comparison of, 134